Diana Curroes

December 1st 1986

From Mary

SOMETHING UNDERSTOOD

Gerald Priestland

SOMETHING
UNDERSTOOD

AN AUTOBIOGRAPHY

ANDRE DEUTSCH

To Sylvia

First published 1986 by
André Deutsch Limited
105–106 Great Russell Street
London WC1

British Library Cataloguing in Publication Data

Priestland, Gerald
Something understood: an autobiography.
1. Priestland, Gerald   2. Broadcasters –
Great Britain – Biography
I. Title
791.44'092'4   PN1990.72.P7/

ISBN 0-233-97500-4

Photoset in Great Britain by
Rowland Phototypesetting Limited, Bury St Edmunds, Suffolk
and printed by St Edmundsbury Press Limited
Bury St Edmunds, Suffolk

Contents

Chapter One

ROOTS AND BRANCHES

The old lady looked indignantly at the book I had just autographed for her. 'But usen't you to be J. B. Priestley?' she demanded.

'That was a long time ago,' I said, 'I've been all sorts of things since then.'

In fact I have not been half the things I wanted to be: a musician (above all), a poet, a novelist, humorist, theologian . . . It took me thirty years to come to terms with the truth that I was, as I have always been, a journalist – a writer-to-order and to deadline, which I reckon now is nothing to be ashamed of and certainly nothing to regret. Within its generous boundaries I have been a sub-editor, obituarist, reporter, foreign correspondent, radio and television anchorman and commentator, popular moralist and speculator about God. 'Your husband's so *lucky* to have had such an interesting career!' cried a diplomatic wife at a Washington cocktail party. Sylvia, who gets rather outspoken after her second cocktail and hasn't much use for diplomatic wives anyway, retorted, 'It's not luck – it's jolly hard work.' And she spoke for herself as much as for me. I know all too well that successful careers are much less carefree than they appear to outsiders, and that the more singlemindedly they are achieved the more likely they are to have been at the expense of other people, especially one's nearest, dearest partner.

Women are so much more spontaneous than men. Years later, Rosemary Hartill, my colleague at the BBC, woke me up by saying, 'I think I've learnt more about God from the poems of George Herbert than from all the church sermons I've ever heard.'

Rosemary had just been appointed my assistant and I did not want her to discover my ignorance; so I nodded wisely to cover the fact that I had never read the poems of George Herbert. My schooling had bustled me through Chaucer, lingered interminably round Shakespeare and then vaulted over the seventeenth and eighteenth centuries into the romantics, whence I had been swept into the moderns via Yeats and Hopkins. Herbert sounded pious and frilly.

But as soon as Rose Hartill had stridden off on some assignment that I was too lazy to do myself – lugging with her the Priestland Collection of Plugs and Cables for All Occasions – I got out some Herbert and read. It *was* rather frilly. But then I came to a sonnet entitled 'Prayer' which dazzled, and still dazzles me with its shower of images each of which is a sermon in itself and seems to describe not only prayer but the whole universe of religious sensation: 'The soul in paraphrase . . . Reversed thunder . . . Heaven in ordinary, man well drest . . .' ending with four successive rocket-bursts of such majesty that they have reverberated in my mind ever since:

> Church-bells beyond the stars heard, the soul's blood,
> The land of spices; something understood.

Each phrase was not merely an image but a chord, a perfume, a whole landscape leading up to those final syllables *something understood*. I must have gazed at the lines for five minutes; they spoke directly to my condition. All my life I had heard those distant bells which had stirred by blood. I had gone as a traveller to the spice lands of the East. Surely now I understood something. But what? I know myself to be evasive and constrained in conversation. Sometimes I think I only exist on paper – that I write, therefore I am. So that if I wish to discover what, if anything, I have understood, meet it is I set it down.

Writing one's autobiography is a bit like writing one's will. It induces the same superstitious dread that one may be tidying up before leaving, and I do not wish to leave yet a while. I should like to watch how my wife and children go on developing their lives. Wistfully (though I am forbidden to nag about it) I dream of grandchildren. And I have a list of things I want to write or broadcast about stretching further into the future than I have any right to anticipate. Looking back, it has been a privilege to have lived such a life; a privilege that I hope has been earned, sometimes with agony, but if it were to be withdrawn tomorrow I should not complain. I have had good mileage out of my fifty-nine years.

There is not much to be said of my ancestors. We seem to have begun near Tarporley, in Cheshire, at what is now the Priestland Dog Boarding Kennels, under the name 'de Prestelond' circa 1369. Presumably there was some priest's land involved. There are several places with such a name, one in Kent (which when last heard of was a goat farm), one near Dumfries in Scotland, and one in County Antrim – an ill-favoured hamlet which, when I drove hastily through it a few years back, had the words NO POPE HERE painted across the road. Though commonplace the name is actually very rare as a family name; I only found one – an economist with a Finnish mother – in all the major telephone directories of the United States. Prestlands, Presslands and Preslands are widespread, and my paternal grandfather reached the conclusion that our form of the name was created as late as 1795 as the result of somebody's moving to Measham, which is just outside Ashby-de-la-Zouch, south of Derby and northwest of Leicester. I visited the place a few years ago and found two Priestlands still there: Albert and his son Selwyn, coal miners from at least four generations back, and as far as they knew 'the Priestlands *always* came from Measham'.

Relatives were emphatic that my great-grandfather did. What happened was that in 1842 the Archdeaconry of the Isle of Man fell vacant and was offered to the Vicar of Measham, Joseph Moore, who came of a renowned Manx family. Moore removed to the parish of Kirk Andreas in the northern tip of the island, taking with him his odd-job man John Priestland and his housekeeper, Elizabeth Stringer who, not surprisingly, obliged him by getting married. John was a carpenter and did the woodwork in the church which Moore erected at Andreas, while Elizabeth seems to have been more than a mere cook, being supplied by the Archdeacon with private quarters of her own and a nursemaid to take care of the little Priestlands, of whom there were seven, three dying in infancy. Two legends have been confided to me by elderly relatives: the first, that Elizabeth Stringer's mother was a gipsy ('That accounts for the supernatural in us,' I was told; though I am sure there is none in me). The second legend is that Elizabeth was an illegitimate daughter of the Earl of Derby – whose family were once hereditary Lords of Man – and that when Lady Derby complained about the obvious resemblance in the girl, she was handed over to Moore for removal to the uttermost parts of the earth – namely Kirk Andreas. Certainly, mildly aristocratic delusions persisted into my father's generation; though they may equally have been due to my grandfather's marrying a Gascoigne (a connection which once induced the present Duke of Norfolk to greet me as kin – on no good grounds that I know of).

Archdeacon Moore was something of a talent-spotter. Among those he helped was T. E. Brown, the Manx poet, author of 'A garden is a lovesome thing, God wot!'; and he followed this up by identifying his carpenter's eldest son Edward Priestland as grammar-school material. He sent him off to King William's College, in the far south of Man, where the headmaster was Dean Farrar, popular theologian, zealous supporter of Temperance and author of *Eric or Little by Little*. Science was virtually an unknown discipline in such a school, so Edward's education was along strictly classical lines, which seems to have suited him very well. He proved a formidable prize-winner in classics and theology before going on to accumulate scholarships to Cambridge to the value of £185, which was very good going for those days and should have made him self-supporting. At Cambridge he won the University Prize for Greek verse, and a silver cup which stands on my desk at this moment inscribed 'Edwardus Priestland Eloquentiae Praemium 1870', a prize for Latin declamation. In the preliminary classics examination, Edward got a First. But then, disaster. The health record of the Priestland clan had never been good and instead of the expected triumph, Edward was absent sick and was awarded an aegrotat degree. Not that this extinguished his career, for in 1874 we find him top in the Bishop of Lichfield's exams for ordination. Ordination itself followed two years later.

But Edward did not seem to have intended following the path of a parish priest. It was scholarship that appealed to him, and since his aegrotat ruled out a university post he turned his attention to school-mastering. Ordination was probably a consequence of this, since in those days one could not respectably aspire to the care and education of small boys without the Church's seal of approval. Almost certainly through Archdeacon Moore's contacts he found himself back in his parents' country as assistant master to the Reverend Thomas Gascoigne at Spondon House School at Spondon (which the family always called *Spoon-don*) just outside Derby. It was here that he also served his curacy and acquired a reputation for broad, tolerant church-manship and a lack of class-consciousness. In due course he prudently married a Gascoigne daughter and stepped into the headship of the school. There were five children of the marriage (Gascoigne had had thirteen), including Edward Andreas (named after the Manx connection), Alice Elizabeth (my revered Aunt Sal) and Francis Edwin, my father, who was born at Spondon in 1884.

Edward Priestland clearly thought of himself as a Manxman all his life and published a slim volume of verse, *Manx Memories*, to prove it. The link was maintained through regular summer holidays at Ramsey, where one younger brother was a bank manager and another, Arthur, ran a pharmacy which still bears the family name (though, when I last enquired, it actually belonged to a Mr Quark). Arthur was known as a bit of a lad and whooped it up in a pub round the corner every lunchtime.

Though the school flourished Edward evidently did not, for he retired from virtually everything at the age of fifty-seven. The village gave him an illuminated address and a purse of £150 in gold. All I know of his teaching style is that every morning, when he entered the classroom, the boys were expected to jump to their feet and chant 'We come to school to learn to think'. Apparently there was a great deal of such chanting in class: paradigms, declensions, mnemonics, exceptions, as well as moral precepts. I have been told that he was particularly admired as a preacher and that (immodest to say) he had a voice much like mine; in which case it must have been very like my two sons', for there is a Priestland face, voice, head, height and even foot which seem to go on from generation to generation.

Edward died in September 1914 and the school, having passed to one of the assistant masters, C. H. T. Hayman, removed to Brackley in Northamptonshire – a complication I would not bother to record but for the fact that the family school, in its new location, was to become part of my own destiny.

Naturally enough my father began his schooling at Spondon and then at a minor Midlands public school, Trent College, which at one period enjoyed an inexplicable popularity with members of the nobility of Siam. I do not gather that my father worked very hard but he scraped into Selwyn College, Cambridge and scraped out again with an undistinguished degree in the inevitable classics.

What to do now? Frank, as everyone called him, was a man of overwhelming charm and no ambitions. The obvious thing was to join Hayman as a teacher at Spondon House. This he did for a few years, but it was never a real vocation. The job was pettily paid, he longed to get away from the looming presence of his father, and at some point there was a scandal in the school involving 'mucking about with little boys' which poisoned the atmosphere. It was certainly not my father who did the mucking – the culprit had to leave the country – and in fact Frank was noted for his intense interest in the opposite sex. In the years between 1903 and 1923 he seems to have gone through a regiment of girls: I know of one ninety-year-old who still sighs at the memory of him and speaks of the 'fatal Priestland charm – that and the Priestland incompetence with money'. But part of the trouble was that Frank had neither the money nor the prospects on which to marry.

His elder sister Alice had married very successfully. She was a remarkable beauty to the end of her days and was snapped up by Sir Richard Cooper (Baronet), heir to a flourishing agricultural chemicals business with its headquarters at Berkhamsted in Hertfordshire. 'Cooper's' (which became Cooper, McDougall and Robertson, now absorbed into the Boroughs Wellcome Foundation) was noted all over the world for its sulphurous yellow sheep-dip and its cures for unpleasant parasites like dog-fleas, warble-fly and liver-fluke. Sir Richard – my Uncle Dick – was a good enough businessman and a shrewd judge of staff, but he had little interest in farming or chemistry. His hobby was Conservative Party politics and for a brief session he was Member of Parliament for Walsall. Quite how he came by Alice Priestland I do not know, but he was the sort of man who liked to build up a court around him and the outcome was that Frank was fitted up as a courtier or 'private secretary'. He was, in fact, an excellent messenger and diplomat (as well as diverting company) and for many years, whenever there was messy work to be done like a body to be identified, an erring husband to be tracked down or a widow to be consoled, Frank was deputed to do it. He did not, however, care much for the politics, having inherited his father's egalitarianism.

The turning point came, as it did for many thousands of bright young Edwardians, with the First World War. Frank volunteered promptly on September 2nd 1914 and was called to the colours straight from his father's funeral. At first they pitched him into the Royal Fusiliers, then the following year into the Sherwood Foresters as a Second Lieutenant, a year after that into the Loyal North Lancs and in 1918 into the Machine Gun Corps – a transfer for which he was grateful because it was the job of the big Vickers guns to stay back and give covering fire rather than to fix bayonets and go over the parapet.

Frank was thirty when the war broke out. The scrawled reports in his Officer's Record of Service remark that he was 'Keen, hardworking and reliable. A steadying influence on the younger men', but at a time when junior officers were dropping like flies it is strange that he had to wait two years for his promotion to Lieutenant, and he got only the most routine of decorations. Knowing him in later years I am quite certain he was a careful father to his platoon though, I suspect, rather lacking in dash – for which I don't blame him. He almost never spoke about the trenches. Perhaps what really saved his life was the fact that he got wounded in the left upper arm on the very first day of the Battle of Passchendaele, on July 31st 1917. More than fifty years later, as I was at my desk in Broadcasting House, the BBC receptionist rang me to say that 'Your father's batman is in the lobby'. And sure enough, he was; dressed in the uniform of a St John's First Aid man, up in town to line the route of some procession.

'I remember how your dad got hit,' he told me. 'There he was walking up and down in front of the platoon, giving us a pep-talk before we went into the trenches. Just carrying his ash-plant – never used anything else – and then bang! Down comes the first shell of the German counter-barrage and knocks us both into a crater – where we stayed for two days, with me looking after his arm. Only it struck me, when they took him away, I'd been a darn fool. Because I used my own field dressing on him instead of his; so I hadn't got one left for myself, do you see?'

With the end of the war, Frank went back to Cooper's, working sometimes at the Berkhamsted offices and sometimes at Sir Richard's London residence at Carlton Gardens. He seems to have met my mother somewhere in the dizzy whirl of dances and tennis parties that made up the Berkhamsted social scene in the early 1920s. He was an experienced forty, she was twenty-four and something of a flapper. I have a letter she wrote to her younger brother Alex, in South Africa, announcing her engagement. It is full of ripping tennis, a simply ripping play, Lady Cooper's awfully ripping house and her own 'booful' ring.

Nellie, or to be formal, Ellen Juliana Renny, said yes to my father on March 2nd 1924 and they were married in the lofty flint-faced church of St Peter's, Berkhamsted, with the benefit of a 'Marriage Benediction Hymn' written by Frank's father. 'Go ye in Peace', it began, but ended gloomily by wishing the happy couple peace in the hereafter at least. Nellie was dressed in white satin with a long train and carried an imposing faggot of lilies. Frank – six foot two, moustached, black hair parted down the middle – wore an uncomfortably high collar, cutaway coat and spats (an outfit which reappeared at family weddings for the next forty years, together with a top hat which could only be carried, giving my father the look of a rather dashing Edwardian undertaker).

The match must have been something of a comedown to Nellie's father, Colonel Alexander McWhirter Renny (Indian Army retired). The Rennys were Scottish mercenaries almost to a man, and when they married they married into the families of other soldiers. It was alleged that they were related to the Strathmores, and they were fussy about being spelled with a -y and not an -ie. A lost branch of the family was referred to as 'the Russian Rennys', who were said to have fought for the Czar against Napoleon and to have absconded with the family jewels.

My mother's branch had been for three or more generations in the pay of the East Indian Company, and her grandfather George Alexander Renny had won the Victoria Cross as lieutenant at the siege of Delhi in 1856, standing on the roof of the blazing magazine and hurling shells at the mutineers. Eventually the magazine blew up and my great-grandfather and his comrades escaped by the sort of providence which persuaded the Indians that these were supermen appointed by the gods to rule. The VC improbably came to light again only a few years ago, when it was abandoned by burglars on Ham Common before being restored to the senior branch. It gave me a certain *frisson* to view the scene of this heroism a century later, when the BBC posted me to Delhi myself, but there are no strings in my heart that vibrate in sympathy with either the Scottish or the military note.

My mother was born at the North Indian hill station of Mussoorie and was baptised in Christ Church there 'in the Diocese of Lucknow' by the regimental chaplain, her father being described as 'Lieutenant-Colonel, 7th Bengal Lancers'. I know this only from a baptismal certificate, for the original notice of her birth was entered in the regimental records, and goodness knows where they went after Partition. The lack of an official birth certificate gave my mother endless trouble later, and towards the end of her life I could only half convince her that she was in no risk of being deported back to Mussoorie as an illegal Asian immigrant. 'After all,' she would say, 'Father and Grandfather were born out there and if things got nasty I couldn't possibly prove that they were, well – like *us*.'

Nobody could have doubted that Nellie, with her square, school-girlish face, open forehead, auburn hair and dreamy hazel eyes was anything but Anglo-Scots. If they had, the colonel and his memsahib (herself the daughter of a general) would sternly have disabused them. They were, by all accounts, a terrifying example of the imperial mandate to rule; though my father quaked even more at the memory of the lady than of the colonel. 'It was,' he said, 'a bit like facing Queen Victoria after someone had failed to amuse her.' By the time Frank penetrated the Renny lines the colonel had almost burnt himself out, what with marching to Kandahar with Roberts in the Second Afghan War, sorting out the Afridi in the Khyber, retiring to Cheltenham and then returning to the colours to put the Indian contingent into France. He lived to see Nellie married but died before I was born; and so the only grandparent I ever knew – thanks to my father's late marriage – was the colonel's widow, the elderly Mrs Renny. She lived on into the Second World War, and I recall her being much addicted to clichés. 'No use crying over split milk,' she would croak, profoundly. 'What's done can't be undone. Least said, soonest mended.' To which my father would respond, 'Yes, as they used to say in Derbyshire when I was a boy: A clackin' day, a brackin' day.' This was entirely fictitious and made up on the spur of the moment, but it usually silenced the flow of clichés for a while.

A brother of the colonel's got promoted to Major-General and it was after his son Gerald that I was named, as a kind of post-war replacement; for Gerald, unlike my father, did not survive the great slaughter. I have one of his letters from the front and it is full of the dash and daring that was so typical of that generation but which we, more cynical, find it hard to credit today. This debonair spirit was Gerald's undoing. One April morning in Flanders he rode straight into a German trap and all that was ever found of him was his steel helmet with a bullet hole passing through it from side to side. 'He was such a cheery good fellow,' wrote one of his brother gunners, 'quite irresistible as a pal. It is hard that *he* had to go when so many rotters still live. I have always hated the Boche, but now I shall have a very deep personal score to pay back and – by God! – he shall get it every time I sit down to measure an angle!'

My mother was the middle of three Renny girls: Evie, Nellie and Rosie – plus the one boy Alex who emigrated to Natal to grow pyrethrum daisies. Despite the typing expected of them as a patriotic gesture during the War, and despite a fairly classy education at Malvern Abbey, none of them was expected to do anything except wait at home to get married, which they duly did. Evie, the most austere, married a man called Roland who designed railway engines. This I thought the pinnacle of romance, until my father brusquely informed me that Roland was a rotter and had run away. As usual my father was deputed to fetch him back, but got laughed at for his pains ('Poor Frank, always the errand-boy!' jeered the delinquent) and returned home empty-handed. Which was a shame, for Evie was left with two small girls and an even smaller boy to bring up, which she did with little money, great courage but, alas, little joy in her life.

Rosie, who looked like a smaller edition of my mother, was even more ripping and skittish and giggled a great deal. She had no children but enjoyed life in Iver married to a still more romantic engineer called

Jock Cockburn. For Uncle Jock was every boy's dream hero – he was an inventor.

And Jock really did invent things, though how he made it success-fully into the twentieth century I cannot understand; for his approach was half-way between those of Heath Robinson and Leonardo da Vinci. He would spend the morning in bed with his drawing pad and his slide rule, and the afternoon in his garage amidst a litter of wood, metal and hand-tools. He had been apprenticed as a boiler-maker on the Clyde where, I gathered, *real* craftsmen did things by eye. Nevertheless, Jock had the wit – by adapting Aunt Rosie's vacuum cleaner – to invent the first rotary lawn-mower, which kept him in royalties for the rest of his life. He went on to develop an automatic gearbox for tanks and a stabilised gun-sight which kept the gun pointing at the target no matter where the tank itself drove.

These early achievements made it unnecessary for my Uncle Jock to do much work thereafter, so he amused himself by sailing – which stimulated him to produce a self-reefing mainsail based on the roller blind – and by playing golf. For golfers he invented a wholly illegal tee, guaranteed to produce an enormous drive straight down the middle of the fairway from a gentle tap; and a training machine programmed to induce the perfect swing in the veriest duffer. As usual with Jock's inventions, the first was inspired by a kitchen clothes-peg and the second by an Anglepoise table-lamp.

There was an early form of electric storage-heater, and endless experiments with a marine propeller which was going to overcome the problem known as 'cavitation'. And there was the automatic hedge-clipper which ran on rails set into the hedge round the tennis lawn at Iver. This Jock proposed to develop into a system for picking all the tea in India, until I advised him that it would cause riots by ruining the unfortunate hand-pickers.

Most Leonardical of all were Uncle Jock's schemes for the flying bicycle. I still have photographs of a dozen models, some of them with Aunt Rosie or some neighbour's child pedalling desperately on them. As works of imagination they certainly deserved to succeed, but Jock's notes on the backs of the pictures tell a more prosaic story: 'July 1973: 36-inch disc. Tested with flapping gear. Very poor results with arm leading rotation. 2 blades removed & flapper gear scrapped. OK with arm trailing rotation. Altered to 30-inch dia. & good results obtained with auto-flap. 1500 rpm.' Quite literally the flying bicycle never got off the ground and the prizes that had been publicly offered for achieving manpowered flight went, in the end, to far more conventional designs using big old-fashioned propellers. The solution turned out to be in the use of ultra-lightweight materials; but Jock defeated himself with his conviction that it must lie in some weird, hitherto-undiscovered propeller design that would lift anything. To his Clydeside mind, propellers were everything. None of his flying machines had anything as dainty as wings.

Jock Cockburn was by far the most colourful of all my relatives and the only one who was not redolent of the Home Counties, for he looked Scots, sounded Scots and acted Scots to the end of his days. 'A worrrkman's wages is thirrrty shilling a week,' he would pronounce, 'thirrrty shilling a week. Put 'em up as high as ye like and they'll still be worrrth *thirrrty shilling.*' He was devoted to television which he always watched with the sound off, claiming that the words ruined every-thing. 'Saw ye on the television the other night,' he would tell me. 'What did you think of what I said?' I would ask. 'Och, I said I *saw* ye. I didna' *hear* ye. I dinna bother with that blether . . .' Rosie claimed that it was only the dancing girls he really watched.

Berkhamsted, my birthplace, has one shameful claim to a place in history: it was here that the Saxon nobles offered William the Con-queror the crown of England. For no very good reason the Normans chose to build a castle there; the ground was excessively swampy, which provided them with the water for a moat, but the site was overlooked by two nearby hills from which, from time to time, it was bombarded by mangonels and other engines of war. One such siege, led by the invading French, led to the fall of the castle shortly after the death of King John. For a time it was in the hands of its most famous lord, Edward the Black Prince (who bestowed upon one of his lieutenants the right to all the rubbish and manure from it) and later again Geoffrey Chaucer was clerk of the works there. But by 1500 the castle had mostly fallen down or been cannibalised by the town for building materials. Perhaps its most ennobling period since was during the Second World War when its remains became a concentra-tion camp for statues evacuated from London, and passengers on the LMS railway could look down with amazement upon a silent congress of the Burghers of Calais, prancing generals and gesticulating states-men.

Overhanging the town was the vast wilderness of Berkhamsted Common and the Ashridge estates, where the young Graham Greene used to sit playing Russian roulette with his father's revolver. Ashridge once claimed to include the common, and Lord Brownlow – the proprietor in the mid-nineteenth century – tried to assert his rights by casting an enormous iron fence round the common, which was seen as a direct challenge to the rights enjoyed by the townspeople. As luck would have it – bad luck for Brownlow – Berkhamsted had its village Hampden ready in the form of one Augustus Smith. One night in 1866 Smith brought a trainload of labourers up from Euston, equipped them with chisels and crowbars and tore the rails down. At daylight the populace swarmed in to picnic and pick up sticks, and when Brownlow counterattacked with a lawsuit, the courts upheld the people. The area today is patchily divided between Ashridge, the National Trust and a couple of golf courses; but Berkhamsted folk still assert their rights to fresh air and recreation upon it, as if in demonstration that the Battle of Berkhamsted Common (as it came to be called) remains morally won. Some time in the 1940s one of the golf clubs tried to set up pompous lists of bye-laws beside the main paths; but the ghost of Augustus Smith walked in the night and hurled them all into the gorse. I admit to lending him a hand.

Berkhamsted can hardly claim an unbroken record of civic pride. So long as royalty or royal favourites were at the castle the town got its charters and market days. But the mayor and corporation seem to have fallen asleep from apathy in the 1660s, never to be revived, and for ever after Berkhamsted came under the resented shadow of Hemel Hempstead, just down the road. For better or worse it was Hemel Hempstead that was chosen as the site of a flourishing New Town after the Second World War, and it was Hemel Hempstead that gave its name to the parliamentary constituency. Berkhamsted was not even a borough when I was born; it was merely an Urban District.

What really gave the place its meaning in life was the railway which arrived in the 1830s, swamping the town with lusty navvies who greatly enriched the local bloodstock. They would not have been called navvies had they not been preceded by the original 'navigators' who had earlier built Bridgwater's Grand Union Canal through the town; no small feat, since the climb over the Chilterns called for a liquid staircase of more than fifty locks. The canal brought timber, bricks and coal to Berkhamsted, and later the raw materials for Cooper's remedies. It also brought the narrow-boats with their brass-bound water cans and their cabins painted with roses and castles; and a slightly stagnant odour of canal water. The railway had its life and colour as well – all the smoke and thunder of steam on its way to Scotland – but above all, it brought people. By the eighteen-eighties you could get to Euston in forty minutes for half-a-crown and it began to occur to professional people that it was much pleasanter to keep the family in Berkhamsted and commute to town than crawl to and fro between the City and sooty Islington. In short, though there was work of a rustic nature to be had in and around Berkhamsted, it was as a dormitory for London that the town finally struck gold. By the time I arrived, in February 1927, it was doing very nicely in spite of the Depression.

My father was now 'something in home sales' and could afford to rent a small terraced house within two or three minutes' walk of the Cooper works. By that time, however, white-collared Cooper people were moving up the hill to greener pastures, and the terraces were going to the labouring class with sulphur on its boots. Word came down from on high – from Sir Richard himself, no less – that an address near the canal was no longer regarded as suitable for his brother-in-law. In any case, within a few months Nellie was pregnant. The baby, it was urged, would be better off up the hill, away from the chemical fumes and the damp.

Frank must have been in a quandary about this, for he still had no capital and neither had Nellie (until the colonel died and left her a few shares in Babcock and Wilcox Boilermakers, which she held onto for forty years). Probably not for the first time and certainly not for the last, Frank's sister, my Aunt Sal, came to the rescue. A word was spoken to the bank and up the hill went Frank and Nellie Priestland to Meadow Cottage, about the least that could be expected of a Cooper executive who was also a Cooper relative.

The symbolism was precise. Meadow Cottage was only just out of the town at the forking of two roads called Gravel Path and White Hill (the latter cut through the chalk, a spooky place by night). It was large for a cottage but small for a house, with sitting room, dining room and servants' kitchen downstairs and one large bedroom and three little ones up. There was also a verandah, an attic and, in the midst of the ground floor, a dark lobby from which the staircase rose; it also held what was referred to as 'the cigar cupboard', though it never had any cigars in it. Halfway up the stairs hung an engraving of King Cophetua and the Beggar Maid. It was the sort of house in which one might have found a rather faded literary lady and her companion.

The garden had its distinct compartments of herbaceous border, shrubbery, rockery and vegetables. There was an everlasting bonfire while, in a rotting shed, sat Rowe the gardener, drinking mahogany-coloured tea. From time to time he would emerge to indulge in one of his brief outbursts of forking, resentfully, at the flints of which the soil was mainly composed.

For the next rule of which my parents were made aware was that uphill Berkhamsted people did not prepare their own food, tend their own children or till their own gardens. They employed servants to do that for them – servants in the plural. They were cheap enough to hire, but before long Frank and Nellie found themselves saddled with a Scottish cook called Pearl, a Durham maid called Christine, Rowe the gardener and a living-out nursemaid on standby for the baby. Her name was Mary (though unaccountably I called her Neddn), but she had to wait for a while for her charge since my mother's first pregnancy miscarried. I was her second and final attempt, and I was born two and a half years after my parents' marriage. The stars made me a Piscean, to which I attach no importance whatever; but Aunt Sal, who was a firm believer in the occult (that gipsy blood, I suppose) had an elaborate horoscope drawn up which revealed that I would have much unhappiness from my friendships, would embark upon a period of 'splendid recognition of his talents' at the age of forty, and that the most appropriate occupations for me would be those of a piper or mercer. In fact my friendships have been rewarding without exception and my talents as either mercer or piper remain unrecognised. So much for the stars.

My earliest drama came before I could walk when I rolled off a deck-chair onto a sleeping dog below. The dog, not unnaturally, bit me, narrowly missing my left eye and leaving me with a couple of facial scars which I like to think Germans will put down to duelling. I remember nothing about it – the dog paid for it with his life – but my earliest memory is of a rather similar disaster a few months later, when I fell out of my high-sprung pram and slammed my face onto the clinker path outside the French windows. I can remember the scene exactly: my mother tinkering with the flowers in one bed, my father snipping at roses in another, me lying on my back gazing at the laburnum tree, and then suddenly the harsh blue clinkers rushing up to meet me and hitting me in the face. I was just a passive spectator looking out through my eye-windows: it was somebody else that climbed over the edge of the pram. The only other memories of infancy are those of taste: of noisy Ovaltine rusks; of gripe-water, vividly revived many years later by that of Kümmel; and of a tincture of myrrh, rubbed on my gums to relieve the pain of cutting my teeth. Later, when I was told the Three Kings had brought gifts of gold, frankincense and myrrh, it was perfectly obvious to me that the myrrh was to comfort the teething Jesus.

Early photographs show me to have had the standard baby appearance; at first all bibbed and balding, then gathering weight and hair, until by the time I could stand I looked like a petulant Charles Laughton scowling into the Box Brownie. At eighteen months I was taken off on my first seaside holiday, to Carbis Bay in Cornwall, and the following year to Bembridge, Isle of Wight. From then on the memories become more frequent, though far from continuous and (I must warn the reader) not necessarily very accurate. At one point I remember my mother asking me if I would like to have a brother or sister to play with. After thinking for a while, to see what the trap might be, I said I would rather not unless it was exactly my age; at which Nellie looked relieved, for she told me later that it would have been dangerous for her to try. In any event, I was stuck with the blessings and curses of Only Childhood, probably the most important factor in my life apart from the genes I was dealt at the moment of conception.

I was the sole only child of my acquaintance – or, so far as I could make out, in the whole of Berkhamsted. All my friends and relations seemed to come at least in twos, if not threes or fours. They thought me spoilt and no doubt I was reserved, not knowing how to cope with their puppyish romping and banter. But if spoilt meant getting too much attention from one's parents, I would have argued that I got far too little of it; they seemed to lean over backwards not to take me into their confidence, and, above all, not to allow opportunities for the cardinal sin of 'showing off'. My impression is of seldom seeing my father, because he left for the office before I was up and I was put to bed before he came home. Those were the days when small children – small middle-class children, at any rate – were constantly being rested and it was unthinkable for them to be up and about after six. As for contact with my mother, again I may have distorted the facts, but the memory I have is of being granted interviews with her morning and evening, in between which I was bathed and dressed and endlessly pushed or walked, first by Neddn and then by the housemaid Christine. Mothers, I was given to understand, were not to be pestered or disturbed. They appeared to suffer from a secret debility which called for a treatment known as 'having a nice lie down'. There was not much company to be had from the servants whom – a snob already – I soon learnt to despise. I made Christine's life a misery by mocking her Durham accent and by defiantly peeing through the leg-hole of my shorts instead of through the flies. Early on, it became clear to me that I would have to make my own world to live in, and populate it with my own subjects, chief among whom were a troupe of fluffy animals: the

inevitable Pooh and Piglet, Dismal Desmond, Pink Bun-bun and
Brown Monkey. Once I attempted to introduce a real boiled prawn to
the tribe, but it rotted in the toy cupboard and the whole lot had to be
laundered, which did none of them any good.

I seemed to spend endless hours lying in bed in my nursery,
watching the light patterns that filtered past the thick brown curtains
and listening for clues from the outside world – a gust of grownup
laughter from downstairs, the scrape of digging in the vegetable
garden, the giggling clatter of wagons being shunted down in
Berkhamsted goods-yard, and 'church bells beyond the stars heard'.
Every year, at Christmas, the bells would come to our very door: the
ringers of St Peter's would come crunching up the drive, stand in a
lamp-lit semicircle and play carols on their handbells. It was, I
suppose, a status symbol to have been selected for a performance;
though we paid for it with mince pies, toddy and a generous donation,
and my father would tell the ringers how, in his Spondon boyhood,
the guisers would come round performing the play of St George and
the Dragon, after which a boy would step forward and declare:

> I've got a little box under my arm,
> Some of your coppers would do it no harm.
> I've got a little box made of wood,
> Some of your silver would do it some good.

It is not that my parents did not care for me, in fact they doted on
me; but they were inhibited by the child-care fashions of the times, and
they could not help being caught in the uphill Berkhamsted style of
life, with its tennis and dinner parties and its running to keep up with
the Coopers. The Coopers occupied a succession of grand houses even
further up the hill, and as Sir Richard's sons grew up and married the
family colonised successively a chain of no fewer than six different
residences, reaching a triumphant climax at the top of the hill in a
mansion called Shenstone Court.

There were three Cooper boys: Bill, who inherited the title; Phil,
who sent everyone scurrying anxiously for the Table of Kindred and
Affinity when he married his mother's brother's widow, my aunt
Kitty; and Frank, the youngest, carelessly nicknamed Wanks. They
were all three, without exception, absolutely ripping and very generous towards me with their half-crowns. As cousins, they were more
like uncles, which was another consequence of my father's late
marriage. But with the exception of Frank, who became a qualified

Doctor of Science in the Cooper research laboratories, they had no very driving ambitions. Hunting they enjoyed, and there were winter meets with pink coats, a milling pack and a terrier in a bag with its head sticking out. Bill became Master of the West Herts and strolled up and down the corridors practising the strangled calls of the hunting horn. Among the trophies on his wall was the mask of a wombat, killed by hounds after escaping from Whipsnade Zoo.

Sir Richard, my Uncle Dick, acquired a graceful motor-yacht called the *Alice*, with a funnel and a bowsprit and a professional captain and crew. Later it was replaced with a somewhat more compact boat named *Aldick*, but my family album shows the Cooper court aboard the *Alice*, cruising off the Friesian Islands, with Frank and Nellie among them – she dreamy, he rather raffish.

Cooper opulence reached its fullest flower on Christmas Day, when relatives like the Priestlands were invited to a banquet. Already I would have opened a pile of expensive presents for which to say thank you, and the meal itself took one's breath away. There was a vast table that must have seated twenty, gleaming with silver, sparkling with crystal, rustling with crackers that sometimes contained Venetian glass animals. The Christmas pudding, somewhat too sodden with brandy for childish tastes, was stuffed with no mere threepenny bits but with florins and half-crowns. My father would play family jester and afterwards, if the weather was too bad for the short walk home, we would be driven back in the Rolls by the chauffeur, Partridge.

I am talking now of the Depression years of the early 'thirties, and perhaps it is hardly surprising I had no idea there was a Depression on. Once I saw hunger marchers passing through Berkhamsted, but assumed, because they had a band playing and banners flying, that they were soldiers on holiday. Beggars, of whom there were usually one or two about in Berkhamsted, always brought tears to my eyes. Having just been given half-a-crown by a godparent, I immediately dropped it into the hat of an old man who was singing a song about roses, but Christine snatched it out again and told me not to be silly. For days I had waking dreams of the old man starving to death in the gutter.

The tradesmen came to call at Meadow Cottage; not only Stupples the milkman and Crisp's the baker, who came daily, but twice a week Clarke's the grocer and Farmer's the butcher, to take orders. These were delivered by sluggish boys who had to push their heavy bikes up Gravel Path, romantic figures to me although I was not allowed to talk to them on the grounds that they were rough and 'don't speak properly'. At least once a week my mother would descend into the town to visit the shops in person and pay their books. This entailed calling at the bank, over whose counter I could not see for some years: what could be going on, that my mother had only to sign her name and collect as much as she wanted? I, on the other hand, had to *give* money to the bank. All the Cooper half-crowns went straight into a money-box designed like a leather-bound book, and when it was full the bank man unlocked it, counted the coins and took them away from me. On Saturdays, my father gave me a penny which I cannot remember ever spending. On the other hand, there were treats for free. The grocer usually gave me a barley sugar or an iced biscuit, and the shopping expedition ended with a bun and a glass of Horlicks at the Court Café or the Green Pantry (this was over Kaye's hat and dress shop, where my mother spent a good deal of time while I collected pins off the floor).

Very occasionally I would be taken to visit my father's office. By the time I was capable of being conscious of such things he had become publicity manager – what he called Propaganda – writing the advertising copy, working with the artists who did the lettering and pictures, and editing a magazine for the travelling salesmen. I realise now that he should really have been a country journalist, for he wrote a good businesslike article, got on well with all sorts and conditions of people and relished the small politics of everyday life. But he did well enough by Cooper's, commissioning a fashionable designer to do smart new labels for the products and discovering, on the firm's own experimental farm at Little Gaddesden, a photogenic rustic whom he named Old Shep and to whom was attributed whatever wisdom might lead farmers to the inevitable use of Cooper remedies. 'Old Shep says . . .' haunted the pages of the farming weeklies for many years, and my father used to parade the original round the agricultural shows, though his main function there was to pour as much free beer as possible down his fellow shepherds. Frank was happy to join in, and his embrace when he came home from one of the shows had an aroma of the tavern that I did not at first recognise but always rather enjoyed. My father, in fact, liked to drink in plebeian company and was always 'just popping in' to the British Legion Club, down a back alley in Berkhamsted, which was more of a sergeants' mess than for officers.

Of his staff in the publicity office I remember Miss Puddephat, Mr Radford and Mrs O'B. – Miss Puddephat solely for her remarkable name, which I used to recite as if it were a meal in itself. Mr Radford was a bright little Yorkshireman who drew pictures for me and tried, unsuccessfully, to teach me cricket; while Mrs O'B. – in fact, O'Brien – was a very attractive auburn-haired lady who must have given my mother a twinge or two of anxiety. Groundlessly, I am perfectly sure (in fact, I met Mrs O'B. in the street only a few months ago), but Nellie, having herself fallen prey to Frank's powers as a lady-killer, kept him on as short a leash as she could with a man who was sixteen years older than her. I remember, in 1936, when he wrote the words to a light ballad called 'On A Holiday', she became quite tetchy about his conferences with the composer, one Irene Gass.

Writing little verses was one of Frank's specialities. He published two or three in his salesmen's magazine, including one supposedly addressed by a shepherd to his sheep-dog:

> They can talk of Old Shep in the papers
> With photos and all sorts of fuss,
> But I'm thinking a really good sheep-dog
> Is worth half-a-dozen of us.

> Folks may say that dogs can't go to Heaven,
> No more than the foxes or stoats,
> But at Judgment I reckon they'll need you
> For shedding the sheep from the goats.

There is a harking back here to the Manx dialect verse of his father and T. E. Brown. But most of Frank's serious poems were meant only for my mother and would be far too embarrassing to print here. He had his greatest public success with comic monologues in the style of Stanley Holloway, which he delivered at works concert parties and Home Guard 'smokers'. There was one called 'On Strike' which began 'When I lays down me tools – I lays 'em down', and I have the manuscript of another about a Cooper's Dip salesman trying to get an order from Hitler; but the references are so parochial and esoteric that it would be meaningless to put down even a single stanza.

Amateur dramatics were all the rage in Berkhamsted. Usually it took the form of Gilbert and Sullivan or 'Miss Hook of Holland' or 'The Man from Blankley's', with my mother in the chorus and my father making a fool of himself in some knockabout role that did not involve singing. But in 1922 and 1931 there was a historical pageant in the castle ruins, and my mother was prettily type-cast as Joan, the Fair Maid of Kent. My father was not in the first edition, but in 1931 made an imposing Edward III, bearded and with a crown on his head. I was taken to see my parents perform and was introduced to His Majesty behind the scenes and fled from him, screaming. Of the action, the only things I can recall are a crowd of Ancient Britons running through the ruins in sheepskins, and a lady dancing on a hearthrug.

When I was five I was packed off to dame school to learn to read, write and tell my tables. It was a small private institution officially known as Hill Brow School, but universally called Benham Abbey. It was actually Miss Benham's not very spacious home in North Road, into which she packed eighteen or twenty small boys and crammed them for entrance to Berkhamsted or one of the prep schools, a job she did very effectively. Miss Benham was a wiry little woman with piercing blue eyes and grey hair gathered into a bun. She was as ferocious on the football pitch – which she ruled with a whistle of iron – as she was in the classroom, and she terrified me in either place. On the playing field I was always caught watching the trains go by; while in class I was so terrified of being laughed at by the others (for only children are not used to being laughed at) that I was struck dumb whenever she asked me a question. On my very first day at the Abbey, class began with a roll-call, to which everyone answered 'Present!'. Even I managed that; but after a week, had to ask my neighbour, 'When are we *getting* the present?' Laughter. Humiliation. But the torments had just begun.

I learnt to read quickly, and to write as well, though all forms of arithmetic seemed – and still seem to me – arbitrary and unreal. The only way, as with so much of my early education, was to give up hope of understanding why things were so and simply to memorise them. Meanwhile there was some relief to be had in the making of Christmas calendars, the cutting out of jigsaw puzzles and the weaving of small, lopsided baskets which we presented to our parents. My first effort was a *cheese* basket, which rather baffled them since they did not keep cheese in a basket and it had a hole in the bottom which unfitted it for holding anything much. Years later I found it at the back of a cupboard, unsullied by cheese or anything else.

I did at least make two good friends at Benham Abbey: a humorous boy called Ian Glendinning and a sporty one called Colin McDougall (whose father was the McDougall of Cooper, McDougall & Robertson – and the Robertson was one of my godfathers). Both boys had brothers and sisters and both lived in large houses with exciting gardens and shrubberies, opening up to me a social life of bonfires, wigwams and tree-climbing. Both of them also had extremely beautiful mothers who drove open touring cars with hair flowing in the breeze. Colin's father knew a director of the Lagonda car company, and once we were driven to Brooklands at a hundred miles an hour in a snarling monster with snakelike tubes coming out of the bonnet.

The Priestlands had no car – or not until I was about eight. My father flatly refused to learn to drive and my mother, who was not the boldest of spirits herself, had eventually to take the wheel of a sedate Austin Seven known as Bluebell. The fastest Bluebell ever went was 48 miles an hour, but she had a sunshine roof which enabled me to stand up in the front passenger seat and pretend I was the captain of a ship wallowing over the green oceans of Hertfordshire. It was not exactly keeping up with the Coopers but it served well enough for my mother's modest excursions. I cannot remember her taking it even as far as London. Alas, Bluebell served us only a few years; when the Second World War broke out, we did not qualify for a petrol ration and the car was sold to make room in the garage for rabbits.

I should have done better at Benham Abbey had I not been constantly ill. Like my father, I had the shallow Priestland chest and kept getting more or less serious forms of infection which, in those pre-antibiotic days, were usually treated by staying in bed and inhaling clouds of Friar's Balsam vapour. The more I stayed in bed, the faster I seemed to grow, and the faster I grew the more prone I was to infections. But personally, I seldom regretted another attack. It freed me from giving wrong answers and getting laughed at in class, and it gave me endless hours to get on with my passion for reading and writing. I read most of the children's classics like *Alice* and *Treasure Island* and Lear (who I still think was a great poet by any standard); I also read a great deal of sheer trash in the form of 'comics'; but most of all I adored accumulating useless information. My parents had given me the dozen or so volumes of *Arthur Mee's Children's Encyclopaedia*, and I read them as devotedly and systematically as if they had been the works of Dickens. By the age of eight I knew precisely how tea was grown and manufactured, what the name of every piece of mediaeval armour was, what Grace Darling did and the liveries of defunct Scottish railway lines. When I went away to boarding school, I used to take a volume with me every term for light reading; which maddened my mother, because it was always a volume she wanted to refer to while I was away.

The writing began very soon after the reading. In fact, I dictated my first 'story' to my mother before I could do either – a Beatrix Potter-inspired tale of some rats who lived in a barge on the canal, and stole crushed oats from the corn chandler's down near the railway station. Because she used to do occasional bits of typing for my father, my mother had a small Remington portable with a fan of type that rose up out of the body when you pulled a lever. It was a tough little instrument – I still use it as a spare today – and before long I was battering away at it myself, turning out a postcard-size 'newspaper' featuring the weather and the meals we ate. I had difficulty remembering to press the shift for capital letters ('The editor regrets there will be no capital letters in this paper so as to save time') and one edition was suppressed for intrusion into private grief ('The editor saw Christine crying after the milkman was nasty to her. The editor thinks it was rude of him to call her Goggles'). I managed to extract a ha'penny an issue from my parents, but efforts to extend the circulation to the boy next door met with resistance on all sides. The boy said everyone knew it had rained yesterday, and both his mother and mine felt self-conscious about the food news. I retired hurt and tried to write a play about a boy who was deeply misunderstood by his parents.

Just before I was eight, two profound upheavals took place: we moved house and I was sent off to boarding school. Quite why we left Meadow Cottage I do not know, but in terms of the social climb it was a great leap forward; for my parents purchased a plot of land which was not only at the top of the hill but well onto Berkhamsted Common in the village of Potten End, looking out onto mile after mile of gorse and bracken and beechwoods, where the air smelt like tweed and the skies were full of larks and nightjars. An architect was hired and a smart new house soon rose with four bedrooms, an Aga cooker in the kitchen and a garage for Bluebell attached. While it was being built we rented a lugubrious house in Berkhamsted called Midhill, which rather appealed to me because it was lit by gas (which you turned on and off with pneumatic switches) and had a dank little garden full of woodlice and snails. My mother was miserable in it and took to visiting the cemetery, where the colonel was buried under an enormous slab of granite with crossed lances on it. 'Was he a nice man?' I asked her once, as she changed the flowers. All she said was 'Ssh!' as if fearful he might hear.

The idea of sending me to boarding school was undoubtedly meant to make up for my being an only child. There would be lots of friends for me, and I would escape the perils (which I so much desired) of being spoilt by my mother. Besides, the family prep school – now transformed into Winchester House School, The Manor House, Brackley, Northants – awaited me inevitably, with C. H. T. Hayman (formerly of the Spondon establishment) licking his lips at the prospect. Equipped with an enormous trunk full of grey shirts, house shoes and Chilprufe underwear, and a wooden tuckbox containing pots of jam, a cake in a tin and some not-too-childish toys, I was put aboard the special train at Marylebone and sent into thirteen weeks' exile among strangers.

The Manor House was a fairly convincing fake of an Elizabethan mansion, with an elegant garden, upper and lower lodges and a stable quadrangle which included a large indoor hippodrome. It could take slightly more than a hundred boys and there were ample sports pitches for rugger and cricket. There was no question that, in Hayman's heyday (which this was), it enjoyed a very high reputation indeed. Hayman had called it 'Winchester' House to advertise the fact that the bullseye of his ambition was to secure regular scholarships in classics to Winchester public school – the toughest of nuts to crack – and this he regularly did. Failing Winchester, he was ready to settle for Rugby, Charterhouse or Lancing, or, at a pinch, Oundle, Uppingham or Stowe. Six, eight, even ten important scholarships were painted up on the honours board every year.

There is no doubt that, judged on these results, Hayman was a most successful teacher. His methods had been refined over thirty years. Public school headmasters could depend on the quality of the product they got from him, and he in turn could read the scholarship examiners like a mind-reader. 'Ah, Rugby,' he would say, 'they usually set a bit of Lucan. I wouldn't be surprised if they took *this* passage . . .' And they did. Classics, of course, ruled supreme and the basis of Hayman's classics teaching was the flawless memorisation of every possible tense and declension, Greek even more rigorously than Latin. The school hummed all day with the sound of incantation, like a Tibetan monastery, and when class was over the boys set to work memorising more for the next day. We took two or three grammars to bed with us for those precious moments before the light went out. We woke up early in the summer to memorise some more, until the bell went and we hurtled naked down the stairs to the cold plunge-bath. And at breakfast we were not merely permitted but encouraged to eat with our grammars propped open in front of us: *Aggo, ackso, eegaggon, eeka, eegmai, eechtheen – Hurray!*

We had to shout Hurray! as a reminder that the last word was spelt in Greek with a ch-th, which were Hayman's initials. Like most headmasters his nickname was Bags. Certainly the outstanding impression from the rear was of a pair of enormous brown trousers.

For those unfortunate enough to have been spotted as scholarship material the pressure did not ease even during the holidays. Bags would look up our homes on the map, find some place more or less equidistant between them where he would take rooms and require us to report for coaching sessions. I do not think I have ever worked so hard and so continuously as I did under Hayman between the ages of eleven and fourteen. Two or three boys who got far better scholarships than I did under his cramming simply burnt out when they reached puberty and fell to earth like spent rockets.

Unfortunately, Bags was a bully. A huge, Churchillian man with a bearish growl, he would lumber into class snarling and jeering, to pick on somebody who had just enjoyed one of life's rare upswings, and knock him down. Sometimes the blow was physical. The older boys would wedge their desks together in the back rows to keep him out. But nothing could ward off the bellows of 'Nah then! Nah then! Just because you're a birthday boy that doesn't mean you can slack with me!' or 'Nah then! Nah then! Scoring a try doesn't make up for not knowing the past tense of *didasko!*'

For a couple of years in the Lower School I escaped Hayman. But when I fell into the scholarship track he soon reduced me to a state of nervous collapse, so severe that my parents complained and I was subjected to the almost-as-awful ordeal of being apologised to by Bags in his study. "I'm just not *used* to being shouted at,' I choked. "You see, I haven't *got* any other enemies . . .' With a wounded howl he clutched me to his waistcoated bosom: 'An enemy! An enemy! That Frank's boy, of all people, should think of me as an enemy! Oh, forgive me my dear child, forgive me!' It was appalling, but thereafter he left me alone, apart from an occasional muffled snarl. As many an author has recorded, the atmosphere of those late Victorian prep schools did curious things to men: Bags's son was to become Sir Peter Hayman, of the Foreign Office, the Paedophile Information Exchange and other queer brotherhoods.

Sex, for most of us however, was to remain a closed book during our days at Brackley. Boys on the eve of leaving received a group lecture from Bags about the mysterious feelings which might come over us, and how the solution was to place a sponge soaked in cold water on the small of the back ('You'll see lots of boys doing it' – which I never did), but we simply did not wish to know about girls and were too young for the homosexual affairs which were to be a feature of our public schools. Or most of us were. Late in my career at Winchester House there arrived a boy whom I shall call Sellerman, far too mature for his thirteen years, who amazed us all with his massive genital equipment and profusion of pubic hair. Late at night in the dormitory, Sellerman goaded us into bogus confessions about girl-friends; and I, desperate not to be left out, confided that there was a girl called Eva at the stables on Berkhamsted Common, with whom I went out riding. 'Riding!' chortled Sellerman, 'you go *riding* with *Eva*! Do you hear that, you chaps, Priestland knows how to *ride*. Do you manage to stay on? Can you gallop?' 'No, mostly we trot,' I said. Sellerman was convulsed, and I dimly sensed that riding had more than one meaning. One day he confided to me that he had cornered one of the school maids in the laundry room, 'And she let me feel her milkers.' 'What were they like?' 'Absolutely wizard. What are Eva's like?' 'Oh, super!' I said, miserably, realising I could never go riding with Eva again. Farting and defecation were about the limits of our humour, though there was a certain ribald curiosity about the phe-nomenon of erection. Sellerman was the champion and could walk the length of the dormitory supporting a bath-towel on his.

My health was no better at Winchester House than it had been at home. I spent day after day in the school sanatorium, avidly reading *Boys' Own* annuals and writing poetry. The poetry came as an offshoot of the classical education; for one day, when I was set to translate a piece of Ovid about Orion and the dolphin, I found it came out quite easily as:

> O what land has not heard of –
> What ocean does not know –
> That famous man Orion
> Who lived so long ago?

Having written this, and two or three other gems from the classics, the obvious thing was to publish, and the surest way to do so was to launch my own magazine, mostly written by me. A few highly favoured friends were permitted to contribute minor items like jokes, my father had the result typed out with some carbon copies, and the first number of *The Woozle* was born. It ran to four numbers in all, before I left Winchester House, and the final one was set up in letter-press with a circulation of fifty copies, subsidised by the bene-volent Aunt Sal. Hayman called me a woozler and growled that woozling would never get me a scholarship. Nevertheless, it did.

The sheer inhumanity of separating small boys from their parents just when they should be gaining confidence in them is something foreigners can never understand about the British and neither, for the most part, can the boys. After a year or so one developed a protective shell, largely composed of conformity. What else could one do, apart from the futile gesture of running away to somewhere even more hostile, like Bicester or Banbury? Among the smaller boys, every term began with sobbing in the dorm, teddy-bears lynched and stuffed into chamber-pots, and 'accidents' in the night. These had to be reported tearfully to the dreaded Miss Ash, the matron, a tyrant in black bombazine whose interest in our bladders and bowels was like that of a conscientious confessor in his penitent. Every morning, junior boys had to present themselves at her sitting room, where she sat marking up her bowel-book:

'Please, 'Sash, I've been, 'Sash.'

'Lot or little?'

'Lot, 'Sash.'

'Hard or soft?'

'Hard, 'Sash, and – please – it hurt coming out.'

'Don't be dirty! Syrup of figs for you!'

Some little boys were so terrified of being irregular, they would lie sooner than confess to constipation. There was one dreadful disgrace when somebody farted in Mrs Hayman's sitting room where the new boys were being administered the comforts of a reading from *The Waterbabies*. Miss Ash was sent for with her bowel-book to track down the offender. When he finally cracked under interrogation, the boy was forced to humiliate himself with a public confession:

'Now say after me – I'm sorry I made a smell.'

'I'm (sob) sorry I made a smell.'

'And I'm sorry I lied to Miss Ash.'

'Sorry I lied to 'Sash – *boo-hoo*!'

'And I wanted to go to the lavatory . . .'

'And I wanted to go – *but I can't*!'

The rest of us sat round like seamen watching a shipmate being flogged. There, but for the grace of God, farted we . . . It confirmed us in our belief that women were heap big magic, to be feared and appeased at all costs, and placated with the opening and shutting of doors, the drawing out of chairs and the ruthless suppression of bodily functions. 'You know,' said one of my friends, ''Sash lives right next door to the lavatory *but she never uses it herself*.' We agreed it was probably because she was so incredibly old.

Fortunately my own guts fell in smoothly with the school time-table. My downfall, when it came, was of a spiritual nature. New boys were required to recite their prayers to Miss Ash before climbing into bed, and I – having repeated mine so often after the maid Christine – found myself concluding, 'And make me a good girl, Amen.' 'Girl!' woofed Miss Ash. 'Just listen to this everyone! Priestland thinks he's a girl! Oh, yes, you'd make a very good girl indeed, you wet!' With which she walked out, leaving me to be baited into tears by my fellows.

The food at Winchester House was wholesome but predictable. In relentless rotation there came slimy ham with compulsory fat, old roast sheep (hot and then cold), gristle pie, 'Twenty minutes off Dover' (which was scrambled egg with minced ham in it), smoked haddock-bones and long fat sausages (which were our favourite). There was always coarse brown bread and margarine, except on Fridays when the bread was white, and for puddings apple pie and custard and steamed roly-polies with blobs of suet which began transparent and went white as they cooled down. Constipation was probably inevitable, for fresh fruit was an extra, charged on the bill, and I sensed from the first that my parents were hard enough pressed as it was. I *could* have had a boiled egg for my tea, and I *could* have had an approved weekly paper like *Modern Boy* or *The Children's News-paper*, but to me they all spelt imminent bankruptcy, so I avoided them.

Hayman had two partners called Meikle and Davis – specialists in French and maths respectively – who helped to soften the blows, though they worked us almost as hard as he did. They also conducted the Sunday services in the chapel – allegedly the room where the barons drafted Magna Carta – where I was first indoctrinated with the Church of England's obsession with blood and guilt. For almost forty years after, I instinctively thought of the Trinity as Hayman, Meikle and Davis – with Bags as the wrathful Jehovah – and of Sin as being essentially the same as a black mark. Try as one might (and I tried very hard indeed) there was no avoiding the black marks of Sin, as we were constantly reminded by our weekly confession that there was 'no health in us'. 'Abide with me,' we wailed, 'Fast falls the eventide . . . Drop, drop, slow tears . . . See from his head, his hands, his feet, sorrow and love flow mingled down . . .' It was almost more than I could bear.

That I kept up my spirits at all was largely due to three of the younger masters, named Llewellyn, Mattinson and Hope-Gill, who not only taught well and humanely, but genuinely seemed to like boys. They had a certain gaiety about them, maintained by frequent visits to the pubs in Brackley high street, and we sensed that they were really closer to us than they were to Bags. There was laughter in their classes. Llewellyn sang excerpts from Gilbert and Sullivan in a lilting Welsh tenor, and instead of calling boys up by name gave each of us a signature tune, to which we responded when he sang. Mine, for some reason, was a cowboy tune called 'Old Faithful – we'll roam the range together . . .'

These three dragged me out of the slough of classical despond and made me realise that somebody did take my writing seriously, and that it could even bring me out top of the class. Once I wrote a description of a train going through a railway tunnel, and Hope-Gill read it out to the whole school. Wisely he did not identify the author – I would have paid dearly for that kind of 'showing off' – but I realised with a thrill that this was not just something I had written, it was *writing* and one day I might be a *writer*. Another time, Hope-Gill asked the class what it thought poetry was: I said it was something that had to be said, 'but it would sound silly if you said it in prose'. He gave a great cheer, 'Lord, let thy servant depart in peace – somebody understands!' He enriched my life from the *Dragon Book of English Verse*, and by lending me volumes like *The Bridge of San Luis Rey* and *The Story of San Michele* when I was in the sick-bay. Above all, through the productions he put on every summer in the Manor House gardens, he made me see Shakespeare as life and not just literature.

The school gardens were perfectly laid out for theatrical use, with a raised terrace at one end, lawns, walks and hedges. One year I was Flute the bellowsmender in the *Dream*, another year Sir Andrew Aguecheek in *Twelfth Night*, and always Hope-Gill managed to convince me that the few lines I was going to say were the most important words in the play, because they were the only words that could possibly keep it going at that moment.

Even more magical, though, was the discovery of music. I was 'put to the piano' as they say, but plodded joylessly through my lessons, never able to keep the two hands together, even though I had a good sense of rhythm and something like perfect pitch. It was not until Hope-Gill's production of the *Dream* that the sun rose for me over the world of orchestral sound. At first it was hardly an orchestra – only Miss Woods and Miss Joseph hacking their way through a violin and piano arrangement of the Mendelssohn overture in their bower under the mulberry tree – but as they repeated it, performance after performance, I began to understand what was going on and why. For my next birthday I demanded a gramophone record of it, and there was

'Fingal's Cave' on the other side. From then on I was hopelessly in love with music.

Games were never my strong point. By the time I was twelve I was six feet tall and it was said I had 'outgrown my strength'. Certainly I was constantly ill and when I did appear on the rugger or cricket field I was gangling and ill-co-ordinated, though by hurling myself unscientifically over the bar I once managed to win the school high jump. I suppose my height saved me from bullying, but for popularity I relied chiefly on two assets, a talent for clowning and my ability to tell stories.

My imagination was populated by a large cast of characters, chief among whom were a detective-and-boy-assistant duo known as Dennis and Martin, a rival team called Leonard and Lionel, and a talking koala bear. Sometimes their adventures were acted out in mime in the changing room, but mostly they were related out loud during school walks or after lights out in the dormitory. We were not supposed to be talking, and masters prowled the corridors to catch us at it; but as a dormitory captain I found the most effective way of keeping my charges in order was to use my story-telling as a kind of bribe, and in fact the masters knew this and tolerated it provided I shut up as they creaked past the door. Only Bags did not play the game. Once, at the climax of my dramatic narration I demanded, 'And what do you think happened to Dennis and Martin then?' 'They got a good walloping!' roared Bags, bursting in and grabbing a slipper.

Life, so far as I could see ahead, was to be an endless series of examinations, though the exams themselves arrived as something of a relief, moments of cool concentration for which the Hayman method prepared us very well. Every year we took the Common Examination for Entrance to Public Schools, and if we were in for a scholarship we would do old papers from the school we were in for as well. When the real paper came, there were few surprises and we knew how to pick our questions and allocate the time among them.

Bags toyed with the idea of Lancing for me (my parents, I think, had little choice), for Lancing had the reputation of being 'good for English' and my Greek was rather suspect and my maths even worse. Then he changed his mind – astutely as it turned out – and put no fewer than three of us down for Charterhouse whose headmaster, Robert Birley, was being talked of as a high flyer. The other two entrants were particular friends of mine, Anthony Ray and Oliver Popplewell, and the prospect of going on to a strange new school with at least two known companions comforted us greatly – but would it be possible?

Without a scholarship I was given to understand it would probably be Berkhamsted Grammar for me, and though I would have liked living at home once more, five years of the Hayman method made me see it as a devastating loss of face and waste of money. It seemed a bit unlikely that out of the twelve scholarships available, the Charter-house examiners would award three to the same prep school; but we crammed desperately and, in accordance with the method, were rewarded by being allowed to spend the weekend before the exams in bed, with choice food and not a schoolbook in sight.

A couple of weeks after the examination, Bags rose from his seat in the dining hall, waved a telegram and thundered, 'Three boys have been awarded scholarships to Charterhouse – Ray, Priestland and Popplewell! There will be a school half-holiday for each!' Pande-monium broke out. Anthony had done particularly well, coming second in the list, while I and Oliver had come respectively fifth and sixth. It was a golden year for Hayman, for he also got two scholar-ships to Winchester and four or five to other schools. I almost forgave him for the years of drudgery, though I could never bring myself to revisit Brackley and never saw him again after I left.

Llewellyn I did see, for he came to visit our trio at Charterhouse. Eventually he succeeded to the headmastership and, by all accounts, made it a school fit for boys to live in though never again to be used as the scholarship fodder we became.

That final year at Brackley transformed us all. Sitting in Bags's study one day we heard the broken voice of Chamberlain telling us our country was at war. Blackout shutters were fitted to the windows, the corridor outside the sixth form was converted into a gas-proof shelter with air-locks, and there were black marks for leaving your gas-mask in the dorm. One by one, Llewellyn and his companions went off to war, and to its horror the sixth found some of its classes being conducted by women, hitherto confined to the Lower School.

One day, in the early summer of 1940, trucks full of Canadian soldiers came rolling through the town and we lined the garden walls to cheer them on, bombarding them with chocolate bars from the school tuck-store. They were, Bags told us, on their way to throw the Germans out of France again: but within a couple of days they came rolling back. The sunlight on the garden hardened and grew cold.

Chapter Two

THE SOUL'S BLOOD

The war dropped the curtain on my age of innocence, when I was swung between being pampered by my parents during the holidays and slave-driven by Hayman during the terms. For despite my unforgiving resentment at being sent away to school, there were good times to be had during the intervals when I was at home. There were trips to London to see the Crazy Gang, Robertson Hare, the zoo, Madame Tussaud's – the capital seemed to me a glittering treasure-house of pleasures, with an Edwardian opulence that comes back to me whenever I hear Elgar's Cockaigne. There really were women selling sweet violets on the steps of Eros; there really were men in top hats and white silk scarves strolling down the Strand; and there certainly were treats for small boys about to be put on the train back to school. My father would stand me a slap-up lunch at 'The Troc' (where he drank gin-and-French, and Turkish coffee prepared by an elderly Sudanese in a fez), or at a small restaurant he favoured called de Hem's. The condemned boy, as he put it, ate a hearty meal, always starting with mixed hors d'oeuvres and proceeding through whitebait to a mixed grill, topped off with a sickening knickerbocker glory. Occasionally the effect was spoilt by a visit to a Harley Street dentist, rendered even more melancholy by the throbbing of a barrel organ in the street outside.

Summer holidays had their pattern, too. Always we spent three weeks in Cornwall, sometimes in the Penberth Valley near Porthcurnow and for three years running in the Isles of Scilly, staying each year on a different island. Chugging from one to another at the prow of a ferry-boat, imagining *Treasure Island* as we went, this seemed to me the way a boy ought to live; spinning for mackerel as the sun went down, pushing a net for prawns, rowing an old dinghy across St Mary harbour. Once, on Tresco, a shoal of pilchards – surely one of the last seen in those waters – came boiling in and the islanders cast a seine-net round it and drew it ashore. We gathered up baskets of quicksilver and I vowed that, when there were no more exams left to take, that was what I would do. The islands were covered with ancient tombs and rocky mazes, through which Dennis and Martin and I stalked German spies or smugglers disguised as tourists.

It never rained, of course – it never does in the age of innocence – and after long, warm bathes in the sea, so clear, you could see to pick cowrie shells off the bottom, my parents and I would lie on the sand reading aloud to each other: Richmal Crompton, Dornford Yates, Jerome K. Jerome and P. G. Wodehouse. For one whole summer I assumed the accents of *William*, muttering 'Golly! Crumbs! You'd think a chap could eat half-a-dozen rotten ole buns without their being missed!' My mother had to explain to people who I was. William had an insatiable appetite for sixpenny cream teas with island blackberry pie; and once a pair of holidaying medical students took me off behind a rock and made me tipsy on bottled cider.

Occasionally my parents would take along my cousin Margaret as company for me, seeing we were so much of an age. We should have got on well together, in spite of William's well-known contempt for girls, but what worried me was the thought that one day I should have to marry her if I wasn't careful. Everybody got married, it appeared, and the only girls I knew well enough or seemed likely to know were my cousins; but since they either giggled or looked down their noses at me, the prospect was intolerable. I am afraid a good deal of our time together was devoted to my demonstrating that the match with Margaret would not do.

Potten End was strictly a paradise for one. Its delights lay not so much in the new house, which my parents named Bryher after a favourite Scilly isle, but in the great wilderness of Berkhamsted Common which captured my imagination – an amalgam of the Garden of Eden, Macbeth's blasted heath, Tolkien's Mordor, Hardy's Egdon Heath and the Old Gold Common of A. A. Milne. It stretched for miles, through Ashridge and Northchurch out to Ivinghoe Beacon and the Dunstable Downs. The Brownlows had criss-crossed it with bridlepaths along which I could bicycle for hours. Remembering my mother's tales of tent-pegging in India, I carried a bamboo cane borrowed from the potting-shed and speared up scraps of paper as I rode, or hopelessly pursued an occasional deer escaped from Ashridge. Towards the end of a dry summer, fires would break out among the gorse and a siren would sound down in Berkhamsted to call out the volunteer fire brigade. I would spend hours up a pine tree,

THE SOUL'S BLOOD

fire-spotting, so that I could leap on my bike and help beat out the flames. The rumour was they were started by gipsies, for there were two or three dells where their caravans sometimes rested.

When I was small (insofar as I ever was) the fun of the common lay in its forests of gorse and bracken, which closed over my head as I burrowed into them. I made nests and hideouts, igloos of plaited bracken, and stocked them with emergency rations of dog-biscuits, bought from the village post office. Along with these were stored armouries of fighting sticks: long ones for use as lances on the bicycle and short ones for hand-to-hand combat, though there was nobody to fight with. Years later, these adventures were revived when, as a visiting member of the Potten End Home Guard, I used to wriggle through the undergrowth with an old American Remington rifle, trying to outwit the forces of Little Gaddesden on night ops. My earlier prey consisted of golfers. I used to lurk near the holes to see where they lost their balls, and then sell them back to the professional at the club house.

By the time I was thirteen, puberty was throbbing through my loins and my brain, though I had no idea it was the same chemistry affecting them both and that the stickiness in the night and the yearning in the daytime were signs of the same season. What bothered me most of all was that, at a time when the conscious levels of my mind were becoming increasingly fascinated with logical systems of ideas there were volcanic depths beneath them which kept heaving up great lava-flows of emotion which I could neither understand nor control, though I struggled desperately to do so. It was the common that was my battlefield, where I went out daily to wrestle with my inner fires. It gave me room to be alone, and if anything confirmed me in my character as an inward-looker and a contemplative it was that common, especially in winter when the bracken died down into a fox-coloured mantle, the trees gesticulated gauntly against the sky and the sun crept sullenly along the horizon.

Under a northeast wind it became a bitter place. The snow fell deep upon it, drifting into the golf bunkers, and ice would freeze over the puddles in the horse rides, splintering crisply as I rode over them. As I fought the vain battle to subdue my emotions to what I considered the rule of pure reason, the rigour of the landscape seemed to me a personal ordeal in the wilderness, a punishment I deserved, almost a biblical experience. And yet I was now an atheist. The hymn-book Christianity of the prep-school chapel fell off me and blew away like a handful of ashes, for it was rooted in no experience whatever. Perhaps one day, I told myself, I would believe in something; but for the time being, exhausted, there was nothing to do but sweep out the rubbish.

Somewhat under the influence of W. B. Yeats, I wrote:

> A winter hanging in the wind,
> And then, when the skull is bare,
> New bees may swarm into the mind
> And comb their honey there.

But there was also a mood of wild defiance, brought on by the autumn gales:

> Yes, I am mad, I am mad!
> A red leaf rent from its branches
> Pirouetting away in the arms
> Of the frenzied, fanatical wind.
> Sane in my madness and mad in my sanity –
> Vanity! Vanity!
> You who have bees in your bonnets, rejoice!
> For I have a bee in my soul.

The last thing I would have dared to do was to show any of my verse to my parents. My father, in any case, was usually working down at Cooper's, though he was fascinated by the common himself. He loved walking it and knew every footpath for miles. He also knew the gipsies who camped in Cherry Bounce (where there had once been a cherry orchard) or beside the Horseshoe Pond, and he had a sympathy with them because of the family legend that his father's mother had romany blood. 'That's why we can feel things other people can't,' he would tell me, 'and that is why we love the heath.' Unlike me, my father was an optimist. Once we found a chequebook some golfer had dropped on the fairway. 'We'll hand it in and perhaps there'll be a reward,' my father said. 'What shall we get?' I asked eagerly. Father paused. 'They might,' he guessed, 'give us a blank cheque to fill in for any amount we like.' In fact they said thank you very much, and no more. But for days after I combed the common for chequebooks.

My father remained a Micawber to the end of his life, though he never earned as much as eight hundred pounds a year. 'If he wanted a bottle of whisky, he just went out and bought one,' one of his friends told me after his death, 'however red his bank balance.' When he retired and found himself with the usual lump sum on his hands, he spent his way happily through it and had to be rescued by the Cooper family, which had a special fund for such disasters. It generously took care of my mother after Frank died.

The outbreak of war brought upheavals of every kind to add to the woes of puberty. Old Mrs Renny had been living at Sutton with my Aunt Evie and her children Vivien, Margaret (my unintended), and little Charles. But Sutton was deemed dangerous because of its proximity to Croydon aerodrome; so the five of them came to stay with us in 'Bryher', first as guests but soon as permanent refugees who were rather less than welcome. My father found Evie shrill and domineering, I resented being outnumbered in my own home by my cousins, and the colonel's widow – now bedridden – lay peevishly upstairs spying on my activities through the window. In fact it must have been a humiliating experience for them all, crammed into two small bedrooms and sharing our kitchen; but it alienated me from the house and made me happier than I would otherwise have been to go back to boarding school.

There was much digging. My father got permission to use an empty building-plot next door in which he and some hired men dug a Z-shaped trench as an air-raid shelter. It resembled something from Flanders, but when it was roofed with corrugated iron and covered with earth, the roof fell in and the labour was wasted. Aunt Sal then came to the rescue by financing the construction of a beautiful brick-lined shelter with electric light in the shrubbery where the nightingales sang. It drove out the nightingales, filled up with water and threatened to electrocute anyone who set foot in it. In any case, Potten End was never troubled with air-raids.

There was further digging next door on behalf of the Dig for Victory campaign, and this time more rewarding. Peas and beans, cabbages and celery sprang up, and a forest of Jerusalem artichokes. Potatoes, for some reason, were never a success, perhaps because the heavy clay was too unyielding. My father, who always woke early, became a dedicated dawn digger and my mother – who had never been any kind of a housewife down in Berkhamsted – took to the country crafts of jamming, bottling and pickling with unsuspected flair. She cured hams and salted beans, while her preserves were so perfect in looks as well as taste that they carried off prize after prize at the Women's Institute, of which she became a devoted member.

Self-sufficiency went further still. Ducks and hens were recruited for the next-door plot (sometimes they caught the pest and had to be dosed with Venetian Red and locked in the potting shed). Bluebell the

Austin Seven, denied a petrol ration, was sold off so that the garage could be lined with tiers of rabbit hutches. At times there were up to forty of them in residence, breeding does with their litters and youngsters being fattened for the milkman to come and ring their necks; while out on the lawn hopped a Flemish buck named Paul who was exempt from the death threat. The rabbits were not only excellent eating (my mother made a cold jellied pie which would have graced a royal banquet), but their pelts were cured and made into fur gloves – another rustic accomplishment. My part in this industry, when I was at home, was to prowl the hedgerows with a sack gathering hogweed, groundsel, vetches and clover such as rabbits love to eat.

The declaration of war was, at the time, something of an anticlimax: no air raids, no gas attacks, no naval battles in the North Sea after the style of Dover Patrol – the board game we all played at Winchester House. Instead, trainloads of evacuees appeared at Berkhamsted station, name tags in their buttonholes, gas-mask boxes round their necks *and* (it was reported) nits in their hair. My mother gathered up a busload and was told to billet them on the remote hamlet of St Margaret's, which reacted by bolting its doors and hiding in the attics. The evacuees themselves, mothers with children, were no more enthusiastic. Where was the fish and chips, they demanded, where was the cinema and where was the Rabbi? My mother offered them the Vicar of Great Gaddesden, at which one indignant mother said she would rather go back to 'Ackney an' 'Itler than stick 'ere at the mercy of a bloody vicar. Eventually a mobile fish and chips van was actually dispatched to St Margaret's and the mutinous evacuees bedded down in the parish hall; but by the end of the week all but a handful had gone back where they came from.

My father's retort to Germany was to climb up to the attic and bring down his armoury from the previous encounter: a still-unsharpened infantry officer's sword, a massive British revolver and a businesslike Luger automatic with two clips of ammunition. At first there seemed no call for civilian resistance, so Frank joined the Special Constabulary which equipped him with a heavy oak truncheon and an armband and told him to keep an eye on the Potten End water-tower, a hundred yards from our house, in case of saboteurs. A few months later, in a panic at the German invasion of the Low Countries, the government announced a force of LDVs, or Local Defence Volunteers, who became the Home Guard of Dad's Army fame, and there were mass defections of the middle-aged from the Specials and the Air-Raid Wardens.

Potten End quickly paraded on the village green a platoon which could only be described as motley. The local gentry all claimed officer status and most, like my father, could produce illegally kept revolvers to support it. Loitering outside the common herd, they eyed one another for signs of dominance, a position eventually achieved by my Uncle Duncan (in fact, a godfather) who was the Robertson of Cooper, McDougall and Robertson and had briefly held the rank of acting captain in the previous war. In addition to its revolvers the officer corps was distinguished by superior overcoats hung with optional extras like binoculars, map-cases and water-bottles. The working classes, less gloriously arrayed, knew their place and shuffled into line with anything from a crowbar to a poaching gun. Providence produced a sergeant who was duly instructed to 'carry on', and within half an hour Potten End was devoted to the warlike business of sloping its arms and dressing by the right. In the village hall its womenfolk settled down to the supporting role of buttering buns and brewing up tea.

After a few weeks the administrative bumph began to flow and my father was dispatched to the other end of the county where a veteran of the Spanish Civil War was conducting a course in hand-to-hand street fighting for LDVs. 'Very interesting, really,' Father reported. 'What you do is to find a shop and dig a hole into the basement just inside the display window. Then you put some ladies' underwear (that's what Germans like, apparently) on display there, and wait in the basement with an axe. The old Boche comes along, sees the underwear, jumps through the window, down the hole into the basement, where you hit him with the axe.' 'But there aren't any shop-windows in Potten End.' 'That's just what I thought. I shall have to pass it on to the chaps in Berkhamsted High Street.'

It must have been the same school of warfare that came up with our *pièce de resistance*, the Northover Projector. This was little more than a drainpipe on a tripod, supposed to propel a bottle of petrol against the side of a German tank, and since it was both very inaccurate and slow-firing there was little enthusiasm to man it. Eventually a permanent emplacement was built for it at a spot where Germans were least likely to pass, and for all I know it is still there, overgrown with brambles. Had the Germans chosen to invade West Hertfordshire it seemed to us they would land gliders and parachutists on Berkhamsted Common where the best thing we could do would be to harass them, exploiting our knowledge of the terrain. Potten End platoon training therefore consisted mainly of map-reading and footpath walks, very popular with the village poachers who brought their snares along. The Germans, fortunately, never showed up, but on one occasion the platoon got inspected by General de Gaulle, the Free French leader, who had a weekend residence near by and looked icily disapproving of the *Anglais* who had been designated his last line of defence.

Falstaffian though it was, the Home Guard was probably the best blow ever struck for democracy in that part of the world. Parading on Sunday mornings prior to falling out into the Red Lion, gentry and labourers got to know each other in a way they would not otherwise have done. All kinds of trade and dealing went on, favours exchanged, things slipped under the counter, and when the war was over the annual reunion dinners continued well into the 1950s. It had a good deal to do with my father's entry into local politics on the Labour side, for it gave him a deep affection for the country working man and an understanding of the hardships the labourer was up against. My father's other great insight into the community was the Potten End bus, a red-and-cream vehicle that lumbered up and down between the village and Berkhamsted with its load of shoppers and commuters. It was licensed to carry thirty but no one was ever left behind, so that at peak hours up to fifty passengers were crammed aboard. Being over six feet tall Frank was physically incapable of standing in the aisle and was permitted by the driver to perch on the bottom step, acting as unpaid conductor and packer-in, calling out the stops for those too hemmed in to see where they were. When the war ended and private motoring resumed, Frank was rewarded with a month's free travel.

But Potten End was my home for less than half the year. In September 1940 I packed my trunk and my tuckbox for Charterhouse, which meant heading south to Godalming instead of north to Brackley. This was an unfashionable direction at a time when the threat of invasion or at least air raids was persuading many middle-class parents to send their children to schools in the Lake District or even to North America. That may have been one reason why Charterhouse was reduced in numbers at that time; but I suspect it meant that the parents who selected it did so because they valued it for academic reasons and not because it was conveniently close to London. At any rate, it was a very serious school under Birley and one was little aware of the importance either of games or money.

The war was always present. Food became increasingly spartan (chunks of turnip baked in batter were a regular feature), and soon after I arrived the upper floor dormitories were cleared of beds and the lower rooms were braced with baulks of raw elm, which exuded a smell of public urinals.

It was that first term that Charterhouse experienced its only bombing – a stick of petroleum bombs which just missed the central block and the founder's statue, to spatter harmlessly across the playing fields. These were punctuated with heavy posts to stop gliders landing, and in the valley below a number of flooded ditches described as tank traps had been dug. Even the lake where the school boat-club went sailing had been snagged with tree trunks to discourage seaplanes. And once a week, in chapel, the names of old boys who had fallen for their country were read aloud.

The school had been founded in London by an Elizabethan racketeer named Thomas Sutton, to save his soul. The old monastic Charterhouse still stands, and I was part of the labour gang sent up from Godalming when the war ended to remove the sandbags from Sutton's tomb. The cloisters were being used by the Ministry of Food to hoard tinned pineapple, and we took the opportunity of looting a couple of cases.

The old Charterhouse had educated men like Joseph Addison, John Wesley, William Thackeray and Robert Baden-Powell, but in 1871 the school was removed to the greener pastures of Godalming, to a cluster of malevolent gothic buildings on a hill overlooking the town, later expanded by eight large Edwardian boarding houses and a lofty chapel by Sir Giles Gilbert Scott known as the Zeppelin Shed. Or that was the school of my day; for since then the Edwardian hostels have been replaced by a complex of boarding houses in the modern style, and there are up-to-date centres for science, music and the arts. Money has clearly flowed into Charterhouse in quantities which my parents and my friends' parents could never have found. The war must have muted any tendency to ostentation, but among my contemporaries there was an air of money hard come by.

The scholarship trio from Winchester House was broken up, to the extent that the freckled Oliver Popplewell was assigned to a house known as Robinites while Anthony Ray and I were put in nearby Daviesites, where our housemaster was Walter Sellar. Together with a chum called Yeatman, Sellar had scored a hit some ten years earlier by writing the immortal *1066 and All That* and, indeed, two or three more farcical classics; but by the time I fell under his care, it was hard to tell where the comedy came from. Dour was the word for him, and there was a theory among the boys that Sellar had actually set out to write a perfectly serious book which Yeatman had subverted. I should be more charitable, for 'Salt' Sellar took great pains with me and it may even have been that those pains exacerbated the gastric ulcers that distressed and ultimately destroyed him. My parents, I know, respected him, but I stayed for too long in that childish frame of mind which refuses to believe that teachers are human beings, too, and insists that there is a great gulf fixed between them and us. Some of them, I fear, found it convenient to encourage the prejudice.

There was a wide enough gulf between us newcomers and the older boys in Daviesites. The Charterhouse of 1940 was no longer a jungle of bullies and buggers (though there were a few of those about), but the social philosophy was that the boys should govern themselves on the basis of seniority. Each year you were allowed a little more in the way of walking here, talking there or leaving some button undone, but until you had served your time you had to obey the orders of your seniors, no matter how unreasonable. Thus, if you were a 'newbug' and a monitor summoned you to take a message to another house, you had to take it no matter how desperate you were to get your work finished for the first period in school. The theory was – and it may even have been true – that it gave everyone a chance of eventual leadership while inuring them to life's unfairnesses. But I was in no mood for unquestioning obedience. It seemed to me particularly nonsensical that one could not speak to a senior without first asking his permission to speak to him, and outrageous that a senior could make personal remarks about you to his cronies about which you were forbidden to 'answer back'.

In Daviesites, at least, there was little beating (Salt detested it and rarely granted permission), but there were plenty of punishments in the form of writing lines or cleaning cadet corps equipment. It seemed to me that people should polish their own equipment instead of inventing offences to get it done for them, and that the writing of lines was, if anything, worse because so useless. I was not a popular fag, finding it impossible to show respect for boys whom I considered stupider than I was. It was all part of the cult of reason which I had embraced, and no doubt it made me intolerably priggish as well as subversive. The trouble was, from the seniors' point of view, I was both too big (at over six feet) and had too much subtlety of tongue to be put down for simple 'festivity' as cheekiness was called. So I agitated among the proletariat, wrote bitter poems about 'the seven severe chief sheep' who sat at the top table of our Long Room, and argued passionately about justice with a head monitor who was intelligent enough to see that beating me would do no good. He was a dark, handsome young man named Derek Lester, whom I much admired; and I grieved when he was killed later as a Guard's officer. One of his right-hand monitors, and one of the few mathematicians in the house, was Robert Neild who rose to become a distinguished economist.

Since I had won my scholarship in classics, into the classical stream I was thrust. There was no provision for doing anything else until one had taken the school certificate, which was roughly the equivalent of O Levels and was sometimes called matric. English, whether literature or language, was a pushover. I could write like a bird could fly. French and Latin I found simple enough, especially when the task was to translate them into English. Science I could just scrape by in by concentrating on the biology questions and turning them into English essays, but the real nightmares were mathematics and Greek.

If maths meant geometry I could just about see what was going on; but when it came to arithmetic and algebra there was no connection with reality at all, just an unreasonable insistence that one must accept the axioms. Why *should* one and one make two? One *what* and one *what*, for one of them might be bigger than the other. I was always being told you couldn't add apples and pears, though why shouldn't that make two *fruit*? As for negative numbers, when you reached nothing what was the point of saying how much less than nothing you had? And contrivances like quadratic equations were pure fantasies. Nobody I knew actually used quadratic equations in real life. Percentages, yes, but never quadratic equations or the differential calculus. I became quite unpopular with the class for keeping it in while I challenged their validity.

Classicists, however, were not expected to take their maths too seriously. They *were* expected to get on with their Greek. But this had always been a torment to me under Hayman and it became more and more so at Charterhouse as the texts became harder and we were required to undertake the writing of verse in classical Greek. This, I felt, was going too far; it was totally useless and unreasonable; so I staged the equally useless and unreasonable protest of sitting at the back of the class studying Robert Morton Nance's *Cornish for All*. If we were going to study a dead language, let it be really dead. As part of my dream career as a poet I had just discovered the Celtic Twilight and Foyle's bookshop: my locker was stuffed with Yeats and Lady Gregory, with Hunt and Bottrell's Cornish fairy-tales, with a Bible in Welsh and a translation of *Ivanhoe* in Irish. I wept over the dooms of

Cuchulainn and the sons of Usnach. The sheer romance of it all had me by the throat.

In the end, thanks to Salt, the authorities gave way. There was no question of my taking Cornish for school certificate, but instead of Greek I could cram myself for history, which I gratefully did and won a credit in it. I got distinctions in English, French and Latin, another credit in general science and just scraped by in maths. I was now free to stop worrying about the rest and specialise in the history which really appealed to me, not because I was a natural historian (Birley soon perceived that when I came to work under him) but because it provided the opportunities for hours of reading and writing.

Once again, poor health came to my aid. Because I was growing too fast and had a poorly shaped chest I caught every respiratory infection that was going on that draughty hilltop. Dr Latham, the school medical officer, would apply his stethoscope, listen for a moment or two and pronounce 'Three weeks!'; whereupon I was packed off to serve my sentence in the school sanatorium and subjected to a course of a pre-antibiotic drug known as M&B 693. This produced pleasingly romantic hallucinations whose subjects I was able to dictate for myself, so that I could lie in bed witnessing Irish legends or sailing through the Isles of Scilly, which could then be turned into poetry or short stories.

There was also the chance of interesting company in the neighbouring beds. During one bout of illness I fell under the influence of one of the school intellectuals called Romanes. Besides showing me his poems which included such impressive lines as 'Hark! The tympanic harmonies of the thelassic broads!', he convinced me of the all-illuminating truth that *Nature was the origin of Evil*, a theory which I expanded into a manuscript filling a whole exercise book and greatly perplexing Salt Sellar. Because of my health I was often excused games (which I disliked anyway, being too cumbersome to be much good at them) so instead I was set to write essays and poems for him. I think he preferred the latter and was pleased when I had one, in the fragile style of Walter De La Mare, published in the stiff, stuffy pages of *The Carthusian*. It was twee as well as technically flawed, but it charmed the school ladies who read it, especially the Daviesite house matron who confided to me that her father had been a poet – really quite a good poet, by the name of Edward Thomas, who had been killed in the First World War. I bought a selection of his poems and was enthralled. But it depressed me to learn how many poets of his generation had died in war: was it to happen again? Would it happen to me if *I* became a poet?

Another of Salt's problems was a boy called Omar Shakespeare Pound, son of Ezra Pound the American poet who at that time was broadcasting anti-semitic propaganda from Italy on behalf of Mussolini. Young Omar had been placed under the guardianship of T. S. Eliot who sent him off to Charterhouse where Birley, Sellar and the rest of the staff agreed that the sins of his father should in no way be visited on the son. The boys, however – as boys will – adopted a far more prejudiced attitude. Pound, in short, was bullied and jeered at; though it must be admitted he was a bumptious and irritating boy in any case. Perhaps we were two of a kind, for Salt asked me to befriend him, which I did, and as a result on the rare occasions when Eliot came to visit his ward I was granted an audience of the great man.

Once he came to see me while I was serving one of my three weeks in the sanatorium and using it to struggle through *The Waste Land*. Eliot sat on the end of my bed and looked solemnly through my scribblings, picking out two or three good lines and advising me to throw the rest away. 'That is the saddest thing about being a poet,' he observed, fixing me with eyes like weak tea, 'most of it has to go into the wastepaper basket.' I plucked up the courage to ask him why *The Waste Land* had to have notes at the back, like one of my classical texts. 'Well,' he said, 'there used to be a lot more of it, but most of it had to go and then the publisher said it was too short to make a book. So I put in the notes to make it longer again. Do you think it looks too clever?' I said it did, rather. 'Try reading it out loud,' he advised. 'A lot of it is people talking.'

Stephen Spender came down once, in his fireman's uniform, to give readings to a small literary society known as the Lit and Pol. I can remember nothing of what he said, but the Lit and Pol itself was of enormous importance to me. It was the personal coterie of Harry Iredale, a white-haired master of homosexual flavour who held court in his private sitting room in a guest-house known as Oak Braes, where he dispensed hot cocoa, Mozart and Anglo-Catholicism and encouraged his protégés to read 'papers' on artistic and intellectual subjects. He fished for talent in the classroom, inviting boys to 'come and see me *afterwards*', and spent long hours in the afternoons pretending to cultivate the flowerbeds beside a busy route to the playing-fields where he could chat up passers-by.

Since he had neither boarding house nor family to care for, Harry was available for consultations at all hours. There was a steady stream of boys in and out of Oak Braes, much to the resentment of house-masters who did not seem able to find the time or whose wives did not fancy the boys coming through to the private side of their houses whenever they felt like it. That Harry's politics were mildly pink did not help. That he made special pets of boys who were good-looking as well as intelligent roused even darker suspicions, though I doubt if he was ever foolish enough to commit indecencies with them. Teasingly, he would egg them on to think for themselves, steering them towards this poet or that painter but never refusing to listen to their own discoveries. In my case he sat patiently through hours of Louis MacNeice and Sibelius, wincing only slightly when I dismissed Mozart as 'mere beauty'. Some boys were even banned by their housemasters from calling on Harry and an attempt was made to crush the Lit and Pol by launching a grander rival to it. But few of his friends would desert the gentle Harry and most of them attended both groups. I, for one, remain profoundly grateful to him.

As I do to another extra-curricular influence, George Draper. George had been invalided out of the band of the Grenadier Guards, where he played the clarinet, and found a billet at Charterhouse as 'wind instrument instructor' (which meant that he was not ranked with the gentlemen of the senior commonroom). In this capacity he taught everything from the bugle to the bassoon, and having reached the conclusion that I could never get both hands together on the piano I flew to him for an alternative. The school oboe was unemployed, so I tried that for a term or two; but when it fell apart in my hands, I took to the French horn – an instrument of great nobility which I never mastered but enjoyed blowing for several years. Proficiency did not really matter, anyway; the important thing was to be swept along by the orchestra in the act of music-making and to listen to George's treasury of tales about the life of the professional musician. Wind instrument players, in my experience, are the best company and the best raconteurs in the world. George would relate how he had played in the gutter at Piccadilly Circus one night in order to raise the cab fare to get back to barracks in time; how he had marched onto the stage at Covent Garden as a soldier in *Faust* and got his halberd stuck in the portcullis; and how his commanding officer had caught him moonlighting in a dance band ('Only luckily I knew the lady he was with wasn't his wife').

George Draper smuggled me into a number of his outside musical engagements, into orchestral rehearsals, recordings and BBC studios. And I had a standing invitation to drop into his home in Peperharrow Road, at the foot of Charterhouse hill, where his radiogram and his collection of classical records were at my disposal and his pretty

Australian wife brought in tea and cake. George was an enthusiast for Debussy and Ravel, but it was he who introduced me to the austere majesty of Sibelius. Why this composer has always spoken direct to my soul it is hard to say, for I know there are others greater. Partly it is that I can follow his method of argument, of gradually assembling disconnected fragments into a whole; partly that he so often recalls the wind-tossed woodland landscapes like Berkhamsted Common and the grounds of Charterhouse where I walked and dreamed with my head full of music and poetry.

As I worked my way through the Sibelius symphonies, it seized me that I, too, had to be a composer – that words were the merest prattle. Out went the Celtic Twilight and in came Ebenezer Prout on counterpoint, Forsyth on orchestration and Adrian Boult on conducting. The ambition was doomed from the start, for I had not the slightest natural talent for music; but George listened helpfully as I outlined schemes for symphonies and took hours hammering out the opening bars of a piano concerto which I could not possibly play. I scored page after page of rhapsodical rubbish in a shorthand that only I could make sense of, and not always then. The best I ever managed was a brass fanfare whose first and last performance collapsed in a heap at a school concert, and a set of discordant part-songs. It took me about two years to acknowledge that I was not and never would be a musician; though I still worship the art and (with a great deal of help from my friends) like to concoct signature tunes for my radio series.

I had to content myself with playing in the orchestra (which had been much neglected and which George Draper had to rebuild from scratch) and with singing bass in the choir. Charterhouse chapel had been designed in the monastic *cantor et decanus* style with the seats facing inwards across a central aisle, so that each side could see the other and it was easy to keep together, pushed along as we were by a monstrously powerful organ which was rumoured to have been rejected as too big for Guildford Cathedral. The choir, which occupied two opposed centre blocks, was trained by the bluff T. P. Fielden (or 'Tippy' as he was known), assisted by the more sensitive John Wilson, now probably Britain's leading hymnologist. Between them they taught us how to sing long passages unaccompanied and unconducted, without losing pitch. Most public school old boys feel a moistening of the eyes when they recall those favourite hymns, those 'golden evenings brightening the West', and for all the resentment I felt at the time, I am no exception. It was not only the tunes but a special, husky timbre which you do not get in cathedral choirs, for most of our trebles were within a year of their voices breaking while the tenors and basses had not long broken theirs and knew none of the tricks of the trade. The handful of altos were superannuated trebles, backed up in exposed passages by the basses singing falsetto behind their psalters.

Inevitably we did *Messiah*, but in the Mozart orchestration which includes horns, so I opted for the orchestra. This had to be reinforced for the occasion by a dozen students from the Royal College of Music, including a first horn. The demotion suited me well enough, for I was shaky on the high notes and was glad to leave it to my colleague to give me the cues.

It was a pity the reinforcements had not included a trumpet; for when the vital obbligato to 'The Trumpet Shall Sound' arrived, our school trumpeter died the death. Quick as a flash, first horn clapped his instrument to his lips and took over, transposing the trumpet part into his own and making it sound as if the entire number was part of a horn concerto. When the performance was over and the school trumpeter was creeping away to hang himself, I asked our hero to remind me of his name. Which was Edward Downes, since famed as a conductor. 'I've played horn with Downes,' I boast deceptively.

Not all my experiences in chapel were so exciting. As the school atheist it was important to emphasise the meaninglessness and boredom of divine worship, which I did by refusing to bow my head during the Creed and by annotating my hymn book with scornful comments during the sermon. Tippy had included some of his own compositions in the book, which I considered particularly tedious and labelled, 'Just the thing for God's funeral', 'Slow and soppy Tippy' or 'Wake me when it's over'. Unfortunately, when I left Charterhouse the book somehow fell into Tippy's hands and he roared off to Birley demanding some kind of proceedings be taken. It was Wilson who dissuaded him and, to my continuing unease, preserved the book of which I am not proud.

The school chaplains, Anderson and Snow, did their best to entice me into their prayer meetings and confirmation classes but after a few encounters during which I lectured them on my Nature is Evil theory, they gave up. In fact I remain suspicious of piety in the young – eleven to twenty-one is probably a decade which is better left spiritually alone – and certainly there was little sign of piety among my contemporaries. They were content, however, to be models of Anglican conformity and tended to disapprove of my explicit godlessness, which ranked as 'bolshy'. I maintained my outward defiance to the end, immune to the arguments of C. S. Lewis and *Who Moved the Stone?*, but inwardly I despaired. Either there was no God for anybody, in which case life was just a shuffle to the cemetery, or He had withdrawn Himself from me personally as a punishment. The sin-sodden liturgy of the Church of England did not help. There was 'no health in us', and as I looked up at the figure hanging on the Cross it seemed to say, '*You did this to Me.*'

In fact the first waves of Depression were beginning to wash over me. There were times, as I sat over my preparation in Daviesites contemplating my future, when the only thing clear was that there was *no* future: I could see a narrow path beside a river leading into a dark wood which I knew was the end of everything, a wood in which lay a deep pit of nothingness. In another daydream I found myself standing at the stern of a ferry watching the bitter waves unroll behind it. Pretentiously I wrote:

> Me, dead, return to my infinity;
> Resolve my body, salt to salt.
> And let oblivion remember my bones once more,
> That were put forth as froth upon the shore.

Trudging gloomily about the school I could not make up my mind whether I was Hamlet or Macbeth. For days I would abstain from conversation or give up all but a mouthful of my rations to eager neighbours.

But there was one activity that snapped me out of my gloom. With groundsmen away at the war the odd jobs on the school estate were carried out by a labour squad known as the Pioneers, and pioneering was accepted as a substitute for the compulsory games I hated. We built paths through the woods, dug compost pits for the vegetable gardens and felled trees and cut them into logs to heat the boarding houses. Tree felling I found especially satisfying. There were plenty of tottering veterans about the grounds and I found a natural skill in working out where to cut them so that they fell cleanly and in the right direction. Afterwards we sawed them into 'cheeses' and split them up into logs with long-handled axes. Again there was a skill in knowing where to drop the blade so that they yielded to the minimum effort. Holly and ash were easy and oak, too, if you hit it along the tiny crack that always lies across the centre. Elm was invariably a bastard and had to be lopped off from the outside inwards. Even then you generally ended up in a fury, bashing in wedges with a sledge hammer. And each sort of wood had its distinctive smell: oak like vinegar, wet elm pissy and holly bitter.

Pioneering was organised by Jasper Holmes, housemaster of Veritas, who resembled a jolly friar dressed in corduroy shorts. He worshipped manual labour and well-kept tools, believed that boys should run themselves democratically and had no use for petty privileges or hallowed school traditions. He also had three very pretty daughters and an attractive wife who – almost alone among the sparse female population of Charterhouse – fraternised with the boys as fellow human beings. Jasper was always organising harvest camps and extra tree-felling drives in the school holidays, which, to my parents' sorrow, I much preferred to going home where I now knew almost nobody my own age. It was at these labour camps that I met and fell madly in love with one of Jasper's daughters. Since she was at school at nearby Frensham Heights we were able to continue our assignations, by bicycle, through one long glorious summer. Snuggled against her bosom in the long grass, I felt that at last the interior struggle was over, that the dark wood had burst into leaf and there was a future, no bottomless pit at my feet.

I think it is a cruel and unnatural punishment (as well as a social handicap) to bring up boys as we were brought up. It had never dawned on me till that first love that a large part of my turmoil was due, quite simply, to sex – or the lack of it. We nudged each other lasciviously when a particularly rosy-cheeked new boy came into bloom in the front row of the trebles, and housemasters kept an anxious eye open for signs of buggery in the shrubbery or the early symptoms of older boys buying younger boys raspberryade at 'Crown', the school tuck shop. But apart from packing the timetables with mental and physical activity there seemed nothing anybody could do to restore the balance of nature. It says much for the benefits of self-abuse that we were not far more depraved than we were.

There was a girls' school called Priorsfield not far from Charterhouse, so I persuaded Salt to invite some of the girls over for a House concert one evening. We would sing them a madrigal or two, perform a humorous sketch, and a boy named Seaman would play solos on the tuba. But when the time came a saboteur threw the main switch blacking out the lights and the party dissolved in a confusion of farts and giggles. At least one boy, a friend of mine called Dennis Brewster, benefited; for in the darkness he struck up a friendship with a Priorsfield girl which soon transformed him from a surly trouble-maker into a contented member of society. Salt could hardly believe the change and I did not like to tell him the cause of it, covering up Dennis's tracks during his romantic outings.

My own resurrection through love was too good to last. The competition for Jasper's daughter was intense and before long she found somebody more mature. To do her justice, being wooed by me must have been like having one's leg assaulted by an over-affectionate puppy-dog. Paradise was lost, however, and I sank back into bleak despair. It seemed inevitable that within a couple of years I should be called up and killed like Derek Lester and Edward Thomas.

It was not that I really lacked good friends. The two or three years following my own scholarship produced an intellectual mafia which achieved some distinction, managed to stay in touch with one another and even married wives who came to like each other. Anthony Ray, the oldest of my chums, followed Birley on to Eton and became one of his housemasters, besides being an excellent bassoonist and con-noisseur of ceramics, evidence of good taste also reflected in his marriage to a ceramicist, the graceful Veronica. For some reason the law recruited many of my peers. Oliver Popplewell became a judge; and, unwittingly, the inspiration for the naming of my second son Oliver. George Engle, the top scholar of our year, got knighted as Chief Parliamentary Counsel, the man who actually drafts the laws that Parliament is asked to pass. Witty and abrasive Conrad Dehn, my chief rival among the history specialists, is now one of the most brilliant QCs at the Bar. And there were legal careers for others like Clive Wigram (who became president of the Oxford Union, married the daughter of an attorney general and shocked us all by dying in his early twenties), for the wrily humorous Patten Bridge and for James Lemkin. Almost all of these went on to win scholarships to Oxford, for Cambridge (for no obvious reason) was scarcely considered by Carthusians. Cambridge was for scientists.

Also of our year was David Raeburn, classicist of warm heart and deep passion who became the school Gielgud. I sometimes played opposite him in minor parts such as Radius the Robot in Capek's *R.U.R.* – my one theatrical triumph, for I succeeded in frightening the bursar's wife out of the hall with a simulated display of hatred for David. The Raeburns were a large and artistic family presided over by Walter, the Labour lawyer, and his beautiful wife Dora. Fascinated by large families, I used to be invited to stay with them in the holidays and made my mark by *writing backwards* in their visitors' book, a feat which is easy enough for anyone naturally left-handed who has been made to switch to the right. David went on to Christ Church and ultimately combined classics and theatre by getting English public school boys to perform Greek drama in the original; first at Bradfield and then at Whitgift, of which he is now headmaster.

The natural leader of our group was undoubtedly George Engle, a large Buddha-like figure possessed of both real learning and an irrepressible sense of life's absurdities. As a constitutional draftsman he was, at one time, a specialist in giving independence to former British colonies and helping them to sort out their tangles afterwards. In this capacity he got lent to the government of Nigeria, though there was nothing he could have done to prevent it almost falling apart in the Biafran Civil War which started while he was on leave. Not long after, he was rewarded with an office on Whitehall overlooking the Household Cavalry's dung heap.

George and I remain the closest of friends (or did until that disclosure). So do our wives, Irene and Sylvia, who have resigned themselves to becoming associates of the Old Carthusian mafia. For more than forty years I and George have pursued each other round the globe with flippant postcards and dubious limericks. 'Dear Gerry,' reads one of George's notes, which I date to about 1944, 'It may be of interest to you to know that a duodenal mezzotint of the Bishop of Bath and Wells taking the waters by Johnny Walker has been discovered by Father Herbert Snood-Drugget in the Baptistry of the Grand College of Jesuits at Rondebosch. Apart from a slight fading of the left ear the likeness is in good condition and Professor Foster-Carrot has vouched for its authenticity.'

There is no record of how I responded to this parody of Beach-comber. But when George got his KCB I comforted him with an Official Knight's Kit containing a packet of night-lights, some Knight's Castile soap, a copy of *Night Thoughts*, some bath salts, Bath Olivers and a bathmat. Apart from anything else, the man is worth knowing for his massive library of pointless literature. Among the works he has loaned me to read during various illnesses have been:

The Tablet of Memory: a kind of eighteenth-century *Guinness Book of Records*, containing such information as 'Bawdy-house: a famous one, erected at Rome by Pope Sixtus IV, and the Roman prostitutes paid His Holiness a weekly tax – 1471.'

Lessons for Children (1818): 'Englishmen love roast beef and plum pudding. The Frenchman loves soup and salad. The Italian loves macaroni. The German loves ham and pompernickle. Turks sit cross-legged upon carpets. Negroes are black; it will not wash off. Greenlanders drink train-oil.'

The Windowdresser's Handbook (1912): an American work which suggests, for example, enhancing a display of black hosiery with 'a couple of Piccaninny babies in a tub'.

The Handbook of Taxidermy (1825): which includes not only how to stuff an elephant but how *not* to try stuffing a human being: 'The trials which have been made have only produced misshapen, hideous objects'.

Home Life with Herbert Spencer: by TWO (actually two maiden ladies who kept house for the Victorian sage). Spencer was a prude, hypochondriac and all-round champion eccentric who always travelled by train slung in a hammock, keeping his current manuscript in a brown paper parcel attached to his waist by string. He had no use for any opinions that differed from his own, excluding them with a pair of ear-stoppers like American children's ear-muffs. My favourite gleaning from this work describes the philosopher contemplating a picture of the galaxies: '"Thirty millions of suns!" he exclaimed. "What does it all mean?" And then, without a pause but only a change of voice: "The fluff still comes out of that cushion, you know," as, with a wave of his small, thin hand towards it, he passed rapidly out of the room, leaving us bewildered at the quickness with which his mind worked.'

It is gifts like these that make one's schoolboy friendships worth preserving.

These were my immediate friends and contemporaries. Somewhere in the offing was a future politician named James Prior, though I am ashamed to say I was not much aware of him at the time. Nor do I remember much about P. B. H. May, already making a name for himself as a cricketer. With the exception of Oliver Popplewell, who kept wicket, our year was notably non-sporting. On the whole we disapproved of keenness on the playing field, as we did of excessive zeal on the parade ground. Conrad Dehn's house, Saunderites, made a monopoly of the school drill competition, so the rest of us left it spitting, polishing and yelling orders to itself. There was, in fact, a great deal of cadet corps activity, with the object of seeing that Carthusians, when called up, rapidly became officers rather than common soldiers. To my surprise, I turned out to be an excellent (left-handed) shot. But Anthony Ray and I persuaded one another that the Navy was more romantic and we further persuaded Tippy Fielden, who happened to be a keen sailor, to form a naval section of the cadet corps, where about a dozen of us studied the *Manual of Seamanship*, spliced rope and insisted on marching to the cry of 'Port,

Port, Port, Starboard, Port!'. The Navy was so flattered by our devotion that after a perfunctory exam several of us were promoted to Cadet Petty Officer.

There remain two other figures, a year or two junior to myself, that I can hardly overlook. The first was William Rees-Mogg. William, now I look back on it, seems always to have been destined to become what he became: editor of *The Times*, chairman of the Arts Council, grey eminence of the Board of Governors of the BBC. William was never young and his appearance has scarcely changed since the age of fourteen. He arrived at Charterhouse with a scholarship and a pile of blank-verse epics and was soon strolling up and down on the masters' lawn, hands behind back, engaging members of the teaching staff in adult conversation. As a Roman Catholic he declined to attend chapel and, whether on grounds of physical delicacy or because the very notion was absurd, never disported himself on the games field – though he was a constant observer of cricket matches on whose boundaries he would find yet more mature company.

The rest of us, I am sorry to say, mocked William and often treated him badly; which was a mistake, for he was a dangerous enemy. Once, in a careless prank, I wrote a note promising the finder a reward of one pound, signing it with William's name and house and putting it in a bottle which I tossed into the river. It was retrieved in Godalming by two of the town lads who trudged up the hill to claim their prize. William, however, recognised my writing and told them that Mr Priestland of Daviesites would doubtless honour his promise, which I had to. Later, as drama critic for the school magazine, Rees-Mogg gave me a stinking review for a part that hardly deserved notice at all.

I say that he was never young; but what I really mean is that he played old when he played at all. Once he came upon me in the school woodlands damming streams, and joined in. After a while I realised that I was getting no water at all because William had gone upstream of me and diverted all the tributaries into a system of his own. When I protested he replied that he was ready to negotiate but it was bound to cost something. As a first offer, perhaps a shilling for ten minutes' supply . . . Years later I called on him in the antiquarian bookshop he acquired in Pall Mall, and he was late for the appointment. I browsed through his stock and found it excessively dry. 'William,' I said, when he came in, 'you do have some very boring books here.' 'Fortunately,' replied William with his characteristic watery lisp, 'books do not have to be interesting to be very, very expensive.' By that time he bore me no malice, I think, and friends who worked under him on *The Times* reported him to be a good editor in that he indulged only a few innocent fads of his own (for example, a yearning to restore the Gold Standard), saw to it that there was a fair balance of views in the middle pages, and went home early most evenings, leaving the working journalists to get on with the job. By this reader, at least, he is sorely missed.

Far more closely than by me, William and the others were being watched by yet another observer – one Simon Raven. Brilliant when he could be bothered, handsomely copper-headed but with a world-weary slouch and drawl, Simon moved through Charterhouse trailing an odour of brimstone. Simultaneously attracted and repelled, Harry Iredale wondered if he might not already have done his deal with Mephistopheles. Most of the scandals about Simon – sexual, financial and alcoholic – turned out to be true. He parted in disgrace with his school, his college and his regiment, to be rescued at last by a publisher who set him to work in a hotel in Deal turning out a sequence of popular novels under the pretentious title *Alms for Oblivion*.

To me, Simon's novels have always seemed rather nasty but very readable – just the thing for the flight across the Atlantic. But what makes them privately fascinating is that so many of the characters are drawn from our contemporaries at Charterhouse. I seem to have escaped mention myself, which is just as well, but there is no mistaking the fictionalised William Rees-Mogg whom Simon has embellished with some very curious sexual tastes indeed. The last time I met Simon, at dinner with the Engles, he looked the most ravaged of the lot of us; but he charmed my wife with the elegance of his conversation, even though she dislikes his books.

One evening in the summer of 1944 there was a rattling noise in the sky and one of the first of the German flying bombs came diving over the Charterhouse rooftops, like a motorbike with a broken silencer, to drop into the valley near Farncombe. During the next few weeks we were to see or hear many more cut out and explode, but the first was the nearest. Back at Berkhamsted another one crashed into a field just as my cousin Margaret was jogging past on a cross-country run, throwing her to the ground and depositing a wicked steel shard just a few feet from her head.

My own life must have been charmed, for in the end the war never really happened to me. I was accepted for a midshipman's training programme called the Y Scheme, designed (it was said) to produce teenage officers who would steer a landing-craft onto a beach and not necessarily come back. It meant putting in some time during the holidays on a pair of wooden hulks in Portsmouth Harbour known as the *Foudroyant* and the *Implacable*. They were moored to windward of a floating coal bunker which showered them with grime and made the trio a highly combustible target for German incendiary raids. But these seemed the least of our perils. The Napoleonic latrines, or heads, aboard the hulks discharged straight into the water, in which we were required to swim every day. Not surprisingly we all contracted diarrhoea, thus maintaining a steady flow of recycled sewage into and out of the harbour. By night we were slung from the bulkheads shoulder to shoulder in canvas hammocks, incapable of making the dash to the heads without setting the whole row groaning and swaying. Not that much sleep was possible anyway, since we shared our prison with a course of Visual Signals Ratings who set themselves the task of educating us in the entire repertoire of naval dirty songs:

> So she went to town an' became an 'ore (they chorussed)
> An' 'ung a notice on 'er door –
> From sweet sixteen to sixty-two
> They all 'ad a bash at 'er ringarangaroo!

After which it was usually:

> Roll me over in the clover,
> Roll me over, lay me down and do it again!

The dormitories of Charterhouse had nothing to compare with it. If there were officers responsible for us, they must have decided to abandon ship and leave us to the fire bombs. Rowing was one of the few useful skills we acquired, and a certain amount of primitive sailing, though we did it in the heavy wooden whalers and cutters that had been standard ships' boats for almost a century.

By the time I was of age to report for full-time service the war had ended and I was told by the Navy to come back when I had finished my education. Being six or eight months older than I, most of my peer-group won their university scholarships before I did and were then obliged to go off and serve in the forces first.

I had a lonely last year at Charterhouse. My first two efforts at Oxford failed. I did not get into Christ Church nor did I get the scholarship I especially fancied to Maurice Bowra's Wadham. But in the autumn of 1944 I was elected to the top open scholarship in history at New College and went up to swear a solemn oath in Latin which, I was then informed, made me a temporary deacon of the Church of England and thus required to wear a white surplice in chapel.

About this time Hugh Trevor-Roper (Lord Dacre, to be) became my mentor. An Old Carthusian himself, he would appear mysteriously about the school, dropping hints of missions to the Resistance, and delivering exciting lectures about the Reformation which combined the eloquence and the anti-clericalism of Gibbon. Two years running he set and corrected our external examinations and fortunately he approved of my rather creative approach to the facts of history and of my style of writing. There was, however, a temporary fall from grace when Trevor-Roper set, as our general essay, the subject of mumbo-jumbo. He had expected an intellectual polemic against religious orthodoxy; but I, having just read rather too much Sacheverell Sitwell, produced an overripe description of a cannibal orgy instead. It was not well received, but I took the hint and abandoned the style in my New College papers.

Birley was delighted with the result. 'Such a good scholarship,' he wrote to my parents. "He is a very able boy. I do not know that he is a natural historian, but he has not only imagination and good taste but some real creative literary power. I read an essay he had written in his final examination which seemed to me quite outstanding. And it is always very satisfactory when a boy with such a thoroughly independent mind and such academic interests is ready to play a full part in the ordinary life of the school . . .' To my surprise it emerged that he was even impressed by my Pioneering activities.

My father and mother glowed, though in the muted fashion of English middle-class parents who think it is dangerous to praise children to their faces in case they get swollen heads. I was never sure whether I really had done well or only what was expected of me. Aunt Sal, who had footed so much of the bill, was less inhibited. Receiving me at the Cooper palace of Shenstone Court, where she presided like a dowager queen, upright, white-haired, ivory-skinned, she confided that I was my grandfather born again and must accept the freedom of the house, the gardens, her private library, and an annual subsidy for books of my own at Oxford. To the disappointment, once more, of my mother I spent long hours of my vacations across the common at Shenstone Court wallowing in the books, the luxury, the agreeable aroma of whisky and lilies of the valley.

My New College award also entitled me to a second scholarship given by Charterhouse to talented leavers. As for the 'ordinary life of the school' to which Birley referred, now I had my college place and the money to pay for it I could devote most of my energies to tree-felling, music, poetry, school societies (of which I collected and neglected several secretaryships) and the running of Daviesites, for Salt had made me head monitor. In this role I tried to remember what had so much oppressed me as an underling. I cut down the fagging duties, abolished petty privileges and trivial crimes, trusting that boys would behave reasonably if treated reasonably; and they did. It may seem hardly worth recording (and not a little self-regarding) today, and yet I can tell from letters of mine kept by my father that I was passionately concerned about it. I knew that there were murmurs that I lacked dignity, fraternising with the lower orders and working alongside them instead of giving orders from the rear, and that the lack of old-fashioned discipline made the house too easy-going and un-ambitious to win competitions. But what I wanted above all was to avoid any boy suffering the misery that I had suffered.

A whole term went by without my having to summon a house 'court' to award punishments. Seniors had to polish their own corps equipment. Sellar was puzzled, then impressed, writing, 'The house is well-behaved and happy in his care and I can always rely on him for good judgment of character. When he has aimed at reform he has always tempered his aim with discretion and not strained after the impossible. He leaves here with many honours.'

Some, however, eluded me. Every summer there was the inter-house choral competition, usually won by David Raeburn and his Pageites. I determined that Daviesites would present, in the spirit of the times, a rousing song about the glories of our Soviet ally – 'so dear to every worker' as the lyric put it. The words were outrageous enough to the instinctively conservative ears of the bourgeoisie, but to make matters worse I conducted them with my coat off, my sleeves rolled up and a patch of sweat under each armpit – how else should a workers' anthem be conducted? Daviesites came bottom and Birley remembered the ruction for the rest of his life, though he was far from being a reactionary himself. I believe he was known at Eton as Red Robert, though it is said this was because the Etonians mistook his portrait of Johannes Brahms for that of Karl Marx.

I wish that I had managed to get closer to Birley and absorbed more from him, for he was undoubtedly a remarkable and enlightened man, as his contributions to liberal education in postwar Germany and South Africa were to show. But to me he seemed icy and aloof. I suspected him, too, of favouring Saunderite boys, whose housemaster he also was in a measure of wartime economy which I think was mistaken. I ought to have heard plenty from him as a member of his history Sixth, but his duties as head meant that he often had to cancel his classes. When he did commission an essay he was better than most of my teachers at detecting the lack of real knowledge behind my theories. 'But what does this actually *mean*?' he wrote in tiny red letters beside one long woolly sentence about Luther. Nothing, alas, and he knew it. His own favourite figure of speech was to identify 'the most portentous' this that or the other. Some general had been rowed across a river in a six-oared boat: 'the most portentous six-oared boat in history' it became, and when Alfred burnt the cakes (which Birley demonstrated to be a hard historical fact) they were 'the most portentous cakes in history'.

What I learnt from him most lastingly was how to read a miniature orchestral score and a taste for Gerard Manley Hopkins, T. S. Eliot, Richard Hooker and the Jacobean dramatist John Webster. The fact was, I believe, that for all his stature he was an immensely shy man, lonely as most headmasters seem forced to be and subject at certain periods of his life to a form of dizzy depression which came over him in chapel – a visitation which he and I were to have in common. I repeat that I am sorry not to have been closer to him, for he wrote to me with great enthusiasm about my work towards the end of his life and we were able to talk as equals at a dinner which our little mafia gave for him in his retirement.

For me the end of Charterhouse came in July 1945 and I have rarely and reluctantly been back. The war in Europe was over, the war in Asia would soon be so in a way none of us guessed, and to everyone's stupefaction Labour won the British general election despite Churchill's warning that a Socialist gestapo would be inevitable. Suddenly one realised that even he was only a politician now. Taking my cue from my father, I had written up to Transport House and become a one-boy clandestine branch of the Labour Party. Upon the shelves of Shenstone Court (of all unlikely places) I had discovered writers like Douglas Reed, Shaw and Strachey who convinced me that Britain had been betrayed by the Toryism of the pre-war years, and I was horrified by the evidence of where that had led in the films and photographs of the concentration camps.

Socialism seemed to me the inevitable conclusion of reason and justice – though I would have been mystified if anyone had pointed *me* out as an example of class privilege. I felt it a punishment rather than a privilege to have been worked so hard, and I was all for the abolition of the public schools or at least the admission of large numbers of working-class boys. Birley himself was not averse to the idea and invited a group of Labour MPs down to inspect his school. I was chosen to serve as escort to one of them, but found to my horror that instead of wanting to tear the place down or nationalise it he was utterly enchanted by it. He had visited Eton, too, he told me, and chortled happily at the way members of Pop had worn dabs of sealing-wax on their top hats. 'Real tradition!' he cried. Later he invited me to come round his Limehouse constituency, or what was left of it. Climbing over the piles of rubble, it was the first inkling I ever had of how the East Enders had suffered while I slept snugly at Charterhouse or Potten End.

Beside myself the only other Labour sympathisers in the school were Harry Iredale and the romantic Dennis Brewster – romantic in more ways than one, for he was an excellent pianist with locks of dark hair that tossed across his brow as he played, anything from Rachmaninov to my own tormented piano concerto. Dennis's leftishness was probably due to the fact that his father was really a working man, though a skilled one, and combined being a licensed reader in a Hampshire church with the manufacture of secret components for aircraft, which he made in the garage at the back of his house.

William Rees-Mogg denounced me and Dennis as subversives, prophesying the end of British democracy as we knew it and (quite rightly, as it turned out) refuting our claims that a Socialist government would surely get on better with the Russians than a Tory one could. 'Mark my words,' said William, 'if Stalin comes to dine at Downing Street, *he'll never leave.* Not that he would choose to dine with *Major* Attlee.'

But bliss was it in that dawn to be alive – and likely to stay alive – while to be eighteen and on the way to Oxford was very Heaven. On the last day of term Dennis and I marched down the long hill to Godalming station singing proudly:

Arise ye workers from your slumbers!
Arise ye prisoners of want!
For Reason in revolt now thunders
And at last ends the age of Cant!

Frank Priestland as a lieutenant
in the Machine Gun Corps, *c.* 1918.

Nellie Renny, *c.* 1920, before
her marriage to Frank Priestland.

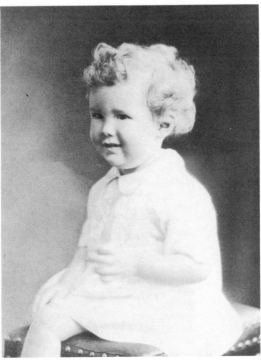

The author, aged about two.

Sylvia Rhodes, Oxford 1948
(*photo: Ramsey & Muspratt*).

Sylvia and the author on their wedding day, St John's Wood, London, May 1949
(*photo: London & County Press*).

Chapter Three

WHO IS SYLVIA?

Dear Mother and Father,

First, thank you for the ration book which I forgot. I have the knives.

I had thought, when I left Charterhouse, that I would have to start at the bottom again and only be treated as an adult in my final year. But there is nothing of the despised days of the new boy about a freshman's life at Oxford. Every day I feel more and more sure that I came to the right university and the right college. I am so excited that I can only express it in fragments.

Reading in the Bodleian Library: it is like some great cathedral where you bow devoutly over the sacred texts. Only, you can't help yourself to the books; you fill in the name and number of the work you want and an assistant like a waiter brings it to your place. I have never seen so many books and libraries – all the wisdom of the ages on the menu. If your tutors have good connections they write you notes introducing you to the more exclusive libraries like the Codrington in All Souls, which looks like something in a Dutch painting with desks miles apart staring at each other across acres of tiled floor. Then there is Pusey House (rather pious) for philosophy, and Barnett House and Nuffield for politics and economics. New College has a pleasant library of its own, but the books I want seem usually to be out and I use it mostly for novels and poetry.

Lectures are sometimes interesting, sometimes very dull indeed. Roy Harrod is about the only economist I can understand. But that is all right: one simply goes to the interesting lectures and cuts the others. You are not obliged to attend any at all. On the other hand you can go to any lecture on any subject, whether you are supposed to be studying it or not; so I go to hear David Cecil and C. S. Lewis if I can get in. My economics tutor does not seem to mind, saying there is more value in half-an-hour's reading than in an hour's lecture. In fact I reckon to go to one lecture a day and two tutorials a week – one with Ronald Hope, my economics man and one with Dr Falk with whom I do moral philosophy (the theory of right and wrong, which is thrilling) – and I do five or six hours' reading every day.

In the orchestra we are preparing to accompany the Bach Choir in Brahms's Requiem. It is very exciting to rehearse in a really big orchestra under Thomas Armstrong, though I am not really good enough and try to play my horn rather quietly. Still, there is another band got up by one of the music students where we just go thrashing along, come what may (*Mastersingers* and the *Unfinished Symphony*) and actually have more fun. I think I shall sneak away from the other orchestra before we get onto something that really shows me up.

Last night I went to Ibsen's *Wild Duck* at the Playhouse Theatre. There are two theatres here, as well as two cinemas.

In the afternoon at about 3.45 I stop reading and go off to the Ashmolean Museum where Sylvia Rhodes, a sister of Paul Rhodes who was at Daviesites, is studying at the Ruskin School of Art. She knocks off at 4 and we have tea together, either in my room where we toast crumpets in front of my gas fire, or in the town.

The chapel and choir at New College are magnificent and only sing the finest Elizabethan music. It is more like a church, with an altar that reaches right up the east end, crowded with tier upon tier of saints and martyrs. At the west end of the aisle the organ stands on an arch that acts as a screen as well. The seats face inwards across the aisle and at the evening services it feels like Christmas with the shaded lights and echoing harmonies.

Every Sunday, Oxford is full of the clamour of bells from every church and college. New College has cloisters like a monastery, and a bell tower that stands on its own and chimes the quarter hours in a rather melancholy way. And at 9 p.m. the Big Tom bell over Christ Church gate strikes a hundred-and-one like the end of the world. Had you realised that a bell gives off several notes at once when it is struck?

The food, so far, is rather good compared with Charterhouse. A lot of fish, but well cooked. Quite hotel standard.

Most people here live in sets of rooms with two bedrooms opening off one shared sitting room; but I got put into a single bed-sitting room when I arrived. They said it would be temporary until someone turned up for me to share with. But it suits me, so I am staying as I am. My 'scout' – the male servant for the staircase –

mysteriously whisks away all my dirty teacups and returns them spotlessly clean. The rules say we are forbidden to tip scouts, but I doubt if that is a good idea.

I founded my account with the National Provincial. The manager welcomed me like an uncle, said he knew Mr Thomas of the Berkhamsted bank well, and bade me look upon his branch as what he called my 'financial club'. I nearly asked for some sherry but felt the cheque might not impress him that much. The blank cheque you gave me for the New College bursary was filled in for 26 pounds. Scholars do not have to pay caution money, which is flattering.

So far my expenses have been mostly subscriptions: to two series of concerts, to the Film Society and to the Union which is the students' club of universal value. It offers meals, a creaky old library and the only bar in Oxford one is officially allowed to go to (though you can get a glass of port or sherry at the college buttery. There is a huge fuss over the port, as if it were the college gold reserves). The Union is also an accommodation address, an employment bureau and, of course, a famous debating forum where I suppose I might speak if I get up courage to. Once a member, you can also use the corresponding facilities at all the English universities, Dublin, Paris and (should I ever get there) Bordeaux. I found it saved money to pay 11 pounds down for life membership.

The commoner's gown is a silly rag that hangs down the back of your neck, so after much detective work I managed to procure a scholar's gown which looks more dignified. As I arrived here a bit late they had all vanished from the outfitters but I tracked one down to a man in Balliol who had just got his degree.

Well, more than anyone else I must thank you two for all this, for I don't think I would have dared to try if you had not put the possibility before me and kept up your faith in me when I did not at first succeed. However I come out of here, even to have *been* to Oxford is a tremendous honour. It will also be a great preparation for life, but that is not all. I do not want to go through life thinking tomorrow never comes. Today was once tomorrow, and there is an absolute value in the present which will not last – it is something on its own, apart from its value as preparation. The future is an immortal today, and though it still means hard work it is real and it is thrilling.

Yours ever,
GERRY.

That is how I wrote to my parents a week or so after going up to New College; and in addition to feeling ashamed of the rather vacuous sentiments at the end ('What does that actually mean?' Birley might have demanded) I was surprised when I unearthed the letter at its wide-eyed enthusiasm for everything. I do not now remember it as having been quite so intoxicating, for there was as much to alarm as to delight me.

Somewhere along the line I had taken the decision to abandon history and take a mixed course in philosophy, politics and economics usually known as PPE or modern greats. I am sure this was for the best, for I had no real interest in deciphering ancient charters, while the P, the P and the E turned out to be useful foundations for the journalism I was eventually to practise. New College did not seem to care and I do not think that David Ogg, the senior historian who had given me my scholarship, even realised that I had deserted him. In the event, the history I had done turned out to cover a good deal of the politics course; but I had read no serious philosophy and the economics led me back into the nightmare world of mathematics.

I made a bad start by catching a late train from Berkhamsted, changing at Bletchley onto the old LMS line that ran across country and arriving after dark at its terminus opposite Frank Cooper's Oxford Marmalade factory. It was a clammy October night and I peered with growing panic at the succession of lamp-lit halts that plodded slowly by: Winslow, Marsh Gibbon, Bicester . . . was Oxford really there? It was, but it had no welcome for me, as it seldom has for anyone. Cambridge is an open city, displaying its charms to any passer-by; but Oxford is a secret society, turning its back on hoi-polloi. I got my bicycle out of the guard's van, hoisted my bags onto the cross-bar and trudged off in the direction of shadowy spires. Useful instructions on how to find New College were apparently too complicated for anyone to give, and I had to follow vague waves of the hand for half an hour before I found it – or rather the furtive lane and wicket-gate that serve as a disguise for its inner glories. And that is how I ended up, supperless, in my permanent temporary bed-sitting room.

New College has two splendid quadrangles of some antiquity, one of them opening into a pensive garden constructed in a corner of the old city walls; but it also has a range of sinister Victorian buildings, ornamented with gargoyles and battlements, along one side of Holywell Street, and it was to one of these that I was assigned. The staircase was dark and rather dreary but it was secluded, enjoyed the luxury of its own bathroom (whereas most people had to resort to a monastic bath-house over a hundred yards away) and was heated by gas fires instead of rationed coal. This coal was stored in a large dump just outside my staircase, and late at night one could hear the rattle of coal-poachers who had exhausted their daily scuttle. The dump was patrolled, sporadically, by the college porters. A friend of mine, an ex-commando who had taken the trouble to dress in black and blacken his face and hands for the operation, once had to spend half an hour flat on his face in the dump while a porter prowled round the bottom of it.

One possible drawback of the staircase was that the Dean, Alan Bullock, had rooms at the foot of it. Fortunately he did not live there. More fortunately still, or so I thought, the rooms commanded a side-door opening into Holywell, so that provided one could rouse a confederate inside the college and get him to open this door from the inside, it was possible to overcome the midnight curfew. The trouble was, living just over the door, I became everybody's confederate and could hardly get to sleep for the patter of pebbles against my window. Eventually I told one caller to bugger off and climb in the hard way, behind the library. 'Well, thank you for the advice, but this is the Dean,' came the reply. As I let him in he said this would have to stop, wouldn't it? and I confessed that frankly I would be very grateful if in future he could find some way of locking the door from both sides. Regular curfew-breakers regarded it as too soft an option, anyway.

My immediate next-door neighbour was the philosopher Isaiah Berlin, then at the height of his intellectual and vocal powers, for he thought faster than he could speak and spoke faster than most people could think, leaping across whole stages of his argument in an effort to keep up with himself. In Isaiah's early days H. A. L. Fisher was Warden, and although the great historian had been virtually paralysed by a stroke it is said that his last words were provoked by one of Isaiah's outbursts. As Isaiah paused for a quick breath it was noticed that the Warden was making one of his rare efforts to speak. The Fellows gathered round attentively to hear the two words 'Conversazione – Berlin!'

Berlin's *conversaziones* were far beyond me. I was offered philosophy tutorials with him and actually shared two with a fellow undergraduate named Geoffrey Warnock; but it soon became clear that while Geoffrey could just about keep up, I never would. So we parted company with no hard feelings and I took my Introduction to the Theory of Knowledge from Herbert Hart. Geoffrey, a lovably owlish fellow, actually became a philosopher himself; indeed, Principal of Hertford; indeed, Vice-Chancellor of Oxford, besides husband to Dame Mary Warnock who soon became a Baroness – enabling 'varsity wags to say they supposed this promoted Geoffrey from Principal Boy to playing the Baron.

My efforts to keep up with Isaiah were not helped by the distractions he introduced, presumably because trying to teach me occupied only a corner of his mind. In one of his rooms he kept a hand-made gramophone with an enormous papier-maché horn on which he played classical music while I read my essay, or he would let loose clockwork penguins on the hearthrug. Students who came to him early in the day were quite likely to find Isaiah in bed recovering from a hangover; and one of my contemporaries – sitting at the bedside quietly expounding the Categorical Imperative – was badly shaken by the irruption of Isaiah's Russian mother who threw the philosopher on the floor and the undergraduate down the stairs. The hangovers must have been bad ones since, judging by the empties left for the scout to dispose of, they were based on Kümmel, a sort of highly alcoholic gripe-water, which Isaiah and David Cecil used to quaff together in the room next to mine. In the small hours of the morning I would wake to hear them hooting and fluting their farewells to one another, up and down the staircase: 'Good night, dear boy, good night!'

Doing three subjects together, each divided into various branches, meant that over the three years one had a variety of tutors. Herbert Hart stood me in good stead until he switched to jurisprudence, when I was passed on to Stuart Hampshire at All Souls. The influence of A. J. Ayer and logical positivism hung heavy over Oxford in those days; and probably no bad thing, for a great deal of metaphysical nonsense was being talked when they came on the scene. One had to be careful about mentioning one living Oxford philosopher in the presence of another (the cattiness was sometimes due to matrimonial as much as professional rivalry) but I do not doubt that the rather surgical approach was good for me and taught me to use the language with greater care.

My chief tutor in politics was James Joll of New College, who was appropriately jolly. In fact the subject, as I chose to read it, was largely British and Commonwealth history. I joined the university Labour Club and scrimmaged with the Tory hooligans when Aneurin Bevan came to speak, but hardly a thought of true Marxism crossed my mind inside the tutorial room or out of it. The stars of the Oxford Socialist scene were Peter Parker, Anthony Wedgwood-Benn, Shirley Catlin (later to be Williams) and William Rodgers; but by far the most popular of the political clubs was the Liberals, because they were known to have the prettiest girls and to organise the best punt-parties.

Economics were a grimmer affair. Ronnie Hope taught me the basics, which meant Marshall, Benham and a little Keynes; but he went off after a while to work for the Missions to Seamen. I then passed to E. H. Phelps-Brown and to Michael Fogarty of Nuffield and Kenneth Knowles of the Institute of Statistics. Kenneth, who was writing a book on strikes (which he traced back to the Valley of the Kings and the refusal of the Israelites to make bricks without straw) introduced me to the realities of economics – what actually happened, instead of what was supposed to. He also introduced me to his wife and their children and to his numerous extra-curricular activities which included designing stained-glass windows, rebuilding antique pianos and constructing elaborate chinoiseries out of painted card-board – it seemed to me he was the complete renaissance man, for he had in fact been educated as a classicist. He and Eunice lived off the Banbury Road in the unforgettably named Squitchy Lane, and their house became for me the kind of cultural sanctuary that I had found with Harry Iredale and the Raeburns. Kenneth, more than any other Oxford figure, was my hero; he seemed to me happy, brilliant, a good husband and father, everything that a man should be. Alas, if he charmed me – as he still does whenever I meet him – he charmed the opposite sex to distraction. I did not at that age realise how public success and private disaster can run together, the one visible, the other invisible. Now I keep in touch with Eunice and the children, especially with Jeremy who is a distinguished biochemist at Harvard and with Angela who has had a blood-curdling career as a forensic pathologist; but I find it hard to approach my former idol Kenneth for fear of forgetting which marriage he is on. I should, I suppose, remember my own imperfections (though they are different ones) and judge not that I be not judged. The last I saw of him, he was featured in one of the Sunday colour-supplements, happily engraving glass.

The Squitchy Lane household welcomed not only me but the Sylvia to whom I coyly confessed in my letter. Paul Rhodes had been a couple of years behind me at Daviesites, a small, freckled boy whom convention would have forbidden my befriending but for the fact that he, like Dennis Brewster and myself, was 'musical' and we got together for music-making. By Charterhouse standards Paul was close to a genius. He could improvise in any form, key and tempo you demanded and he could play the gigantic chapel organ while barely able to reach the pedals with his feet. He is still an able choirmaster and composer of popular oratorios, but perhaps his musicality was too casual, as if he hardly wanted it but could not help it. His real passion was for gadgetry, for taking things apart or putting them together with his hands. Even the organ was seen as a vast musical gadget. For a time he worked for one of the great organ-builders and tinkered with plans for an instrument based on recording the notes on tape; until he left to manufacture plastic sinks in Dorset, and then to run a garage in Lincolnshire, and finally (to the great relief of his anxious family) to work for the Church Commissioners looking after bishops' palaces. A chequered career and maybe not the wildest of successes by the worldly standards of the Carthusian mafia; but thanks to a remarkably astute choice of wife in Maggs, the Paulines (as they are known to my own children) turned out to be one of the most attractive families we know, capable of everything from house-building and home-brewing to providing a highish Anglican service complete with organist and small choir.

I owe a great debt of gratitude to Paul. As I was about to leave Charterhouse he remarked, meaningfully, that one of his elder sisters, Sylvia, was going to Oxford to paint at the Ruskin School. A few weeks later he sent me the address of her digs. Since the affair of Jasper Holmes's daughter had already made it clear to me that life was empty without a girlfriend, and since there was a desperate shortage of them in male-dominated Oxford, I wasted no time in finding Sylvia's lodgings and inviting her to the aforementioned *Wild Duck*. Paul had mentioned that she played the flute, so in a gesture meant to impress (actually it baffled) I presented her with an antique military fife which I had bought in a junk-shop for five shillings.

Sylvia was tall and slender with pretty round breasts, an oval face, fine chestnut hair and freckled complexion. She would have made a pre-Raphaelite swoon. Having completed three years as a day student at Hornsey School of Art, she wanted to get away from home for a change and thought of the Ruskin. Its artistic standards, under Albert Rutherstone, were frankly not high; but the standards of beauty set by its girls were dazzling. The more dedicated undergraduate art-lovers, like myself, even signed up for part-time life classes to be near them; while at coffee- and tea-times we loitered among the plaster casts in the Ashmolean Museum for the students to emerge from their annexe. Then it was off down the Cornmarket to the Cadena Café where a string quartet played relatively highbrow light music (even Purcell by request) or to the British Restaurant in the Town Hall where young men gallantly sacrificed their tuppenny puddings to their young ladies. These establishments, of which there were three or four in the town, were a kind of citizens' canteen where it was possible to get a cheap, stodgy meal 'off the ration'. The colleges and their dining halls being full to bursting, it was necessary for a proportion of the undergraduates to eat out in the 'BRs'.

As a scholar I was allowed to live in New College for my entire three years. But the Ruskin had no residential accommodation at all, and all its students had to live in digs. As suspect bohemians they went to the bottom of the market. Sylvia went through a series of shady places, beginning along the Iffley Road in what turned out to be theatrical lodgings, occupied for much of the year by the cast of the perpetual pantomime running at the New Theatre. She had not been warned of this when she first arrived and was taken aback to be greeted on the stairs by a midget. A conjurer and both ends of the horse were also in residence, for these digs were below star level. Sylvia insisted that I take her to the New to watch them in action. The conjurer carried the midget onto the stage in a suitcase – which grew legs and ran away from him and was pursued by the horse. It was funnier than Ibsen, but Syliva felt a little self-conscious at the breakfast table next morning, for there had been some rude business with the midget chasing the horse about with a bucket and shovel. Another fellow-resident turned out to be the female model at the Ruskin; did one, or didn't one, try to separate the nude from the clothed?

The Iffley Road digs nearly extinguished Sylvia altogether, gassing her with the geyser in the bathroom as she was washing her hair. A passing actor heard her moan as she fell, and broke down the door. But the police came round to make sure it was not attempted suicide and bullied her as she lay on her bed gasping for breath, head splitting, stomach heaving. The landlady, Mrs Davies, sent for me to assure the detective that Sylvia was in good spirits and had everything to live for – me, for example. He seemed more impressed by the argument that people don't try to kill themselves standing up with shampoo in their hair.

The Oxford winters were depressing enough without such reminders of mortality. A damp and unhealthy place at the best of times, the city was afflicted in those immediately post-war years with a series of fogs, smogs and freeze-ups, power-cuts, fuel shortages and belt-tightenings that seemed like a punishment for any undeserved pride in our victory. From the moment the Japanese capitulated, rations got shorter and shorter and those of us who had voted Labour comforted ourselves with the reminder that this was how the oppressed working classes had always lived. Now there was to be a fair share of misery for all. Not only meat, fats, sugar and everything tinned but bread, biscuits and even potatoes went under controls. A popular restaurant in the High was closed down for cooking its food in something described as horse oil, and a neighbouring Chinese restaurant had no rice but barley with the chop suey. The New College cuisine lowered its standards so far as to serve whale meat, in various forms, twice a week.

At least this gave the determined wooer some new approaches. Flowers and chocolates were out, but iron rations were as good as gold. The Iffley Road digs were heated, if at all, by open grates; and Sylvia's was fired by offerings purloined from the New College coal dump. My technique was to spot a particularly large lump at the foot of the heap, drop a raincoat over it, carry it up to my rooms and wrap it in brown paper, and then portage it by foot and bus to my lady's chamber. 'I've brought this for you, my darling, as a token of the warmth of my heart . . .'

Even better received were the fruits of many hours' queueing outside the Summertown cake factory. There was no scope for dinner parties in the Oxford of the 1940s, but afternoon tea was highly competitive. The problem was, how to find the goodies? Marks & Spencer's crumpets were off the ration but demanded butter, and I developed a delicacy of my own by scooping out the insides of oranges and setting them in their own skins with gelatine. Oliver & Girdon's cake factory at Summertown on the Banbury Road was allowed to sell a certain proportion of its output, theoretically damaged goods, off the ration; and every morning there was a long line of undergraduates on the pavement outside to buy them. It was as good a place as anywhere to read philosophy (logical positivism will always mean cakes to me) and since Sylvia's presence was required in the life class I had the advantage of her. Shortcake tarts filled with dates and topped with chocolate were the basis of my courtship, and proved irresistible. I pressed my suit with buns and coal and clothing coupons (of which I had an extra allocation because of my height), and wheedled peppermint patties and nylon stockings out of the American GI scholars in my college. The greatest luxury of the week was to be invited by one of these to take Sunday brunch at the American canteen in the Haymarket – bacon, eggs and pancakes with maple syrup, washed down with Coca-Cola. The effect was queasy but reassuring; perhaps we had won after all.

The Americans that I recall were a good deal older than I, but then so was most of the University. The majority of men had come back from the war to finish their degrees in a hurry and get on with their lives, and there was nothing of the rowdiness or frivolity that clings to fictional Oxbridge. Those few of us who had come straight from our public schools at the age of eighteen found ourselves trying to keep up with a generation of sober, wiser sloggers who had no time for putting chamber-pots on the martyrs' memorial or pushing corporation buses into the Isis. There were very few figures around who dared to strike any but the most conventional poses – one striking exception being Kenneth Tynan, the future drama critic, who paraded Oxford in a purple suit, arrived at the Union wearing a green carnation, and put on a production of *Hamlet* that was dominated by the presence on stage of two enormous wolfhounds. The demob generation took no notice and went on swatting over its books. It was amazing that men who had just liberated Europe were prepared to put up with the under-graduate curfew and the proctorial rules forbidding entry to the town pubs, but they did. Perhaps there was neither the money nor the liquor for drunkenness, for I can hardly remember any.

Phelps-Brown was my moral, as well as my economics, tutor; which is to say he supervised my conduct and my curriculum too. He was a soldierly and somewhat intimidating man who obviously approved of the new Oxford earnestness. When I told him I hoped to go into university journalism he sternly commanded me to keep out of it and mind my studies. In this I am sure he meant well – ultimately I got what I wanted – but it was a pity. Soon after I got to Oxford I heard that the *Isis* magazine was looking for staff, so I called at its office and was given a routine story or two to cover, like the launching of OXFAM (then the Oxford Committee for Famine Relief) at a meeting in the town hall. These I managed reasonably well; and then, by a stroke of good fortune, came up with a story of my own. I ran across Hugh Trevor-Roper who was working at Christ Church on his classic *The Last Days of Hitler*. Surrounded by documents and interrogation transcripts, including Hitler's appointments book, he told me the whole story and expressed his doubts – never entirely cleared up – as to whether Martin Bormann had survived his Führer or not. It was a scoop for *Isis* and the incoming editor, Gerard Slessenger, proposed to make me chief reporter on the strength of it. To my humiliation, Phelps-Brown vetoed the idea: 'You will find that sort of thing very small beer when you go down,' he observed. I am still sorry that I missed the opportunity, never since made good, of learning more about print journalism. Years later, in the BBC, I found myself working to Gerard Slessenger once again and hoped I made up for letting him down.

So my literary life remained genteel. I wrote more and more poetry, two or three first chapters of novels that got no further (they were so choked with tragedy), and a dozen tiny short stories that were really no more than observed episodes. It was Sylvia who made me realise that as a would-be serious writer, I was building on sand. I charged through the non-fiction shelves of the Berkhamsted Boots' Lending Library like a combine harvester, and gobbled up Aunt Sal's popular history and biography, but I had not read the master novelists at any level above John Buchan and R. L. Stevenson. Sylvia was appalled. She set me to work on Thomas Hardy (who moved me to tears with his suffering women), on D. H. Lawrence, Dostoievsky and Thomas Mann, and I proceeded next through Trollope and Galsworthy, Dickens and the Brontës to become obsessed with the now under-estimated Joyce Cary (who was then still to be seen bouncing along the pavements near Keble College – though I never plucked up the courage to thank him for his work).

If I had a mentor in prose it was Naomi Mitchison, who descended on Oxford from time to time like some gipsy matriarch to visit members of her tribe. Her daughters Lois and Valentine I used to meet in the cake factory queue, while her son Avrion was a fellow scholar at New College and a particular friend of mine even though he was a scientist. Av Mitchison would, I suppose, have been a hated target for the animal liberationists, for he spent most of his time doing experiments on mice, of which he had bred a specially cancer-prone variety. Not that he tortured them in any way. Av was one of the gentlest and most humane people I have known, and still is. His work consisted of giving the mice injections – half of them distilled water, as a control group – but as each injection counted as one 'experiment' the raw figures made him look like a mass vivisectionist. His devotion to the mice was such that he eventually took to living in the laboratory, cooking kippers over Bunsen burners, drinking coffee out of beakers and sleeping under the benches. There was something of a panic every morning to get the signs of housekeeping out of the way before the professor arrived; but it was hardly a reclusive way of life, for there were jolly parties in the lab, too, with strange distillations served from pipettes and titbits shared with the mice. *That*, however, was frowned upon, for it upset their regime and on one occasion a troupe of rodents destined to die of carcinoma enjoyed a premature release from over-eating. It was generous but unscientific, said Av.

Naomi pored over my gemlike short stories and liked a phrase here, a transition there, but put an unerring finger on the influences they showed. 'You've been reading too much Saki and De La Mare,' she said. 'Makes it look like a shelf of Edwardian knick-knacks. If only you knew what you really wanted to write about, *having* to write would bring the style with it. That's what journalism does, of course.' I began to realise she was right, but the forbidding shadow of Phelps-Brown stood between me and the opportunities.

There was still poetry, though. One of my companions at Ronnie Hope's tutorials was Richard Donovan, a tin-legged Anglo-Irish Old Rugbeian flute-player. I only mention the tin leg because, having lost one limb at school following the maltreatment of a football injury, Richard was to lose the other a few years later in a traffic accident. He allowed neither disaster to make the slightest difference to his charm or his mobility and to this day is farming the family estate in County Wexford, very largely by his own physical exertions. This is not to say he leads a carefree existence – very far from it – but for the kind of courage which does not oppress the beholder I know few to touch him.

Richard introduced me to a fellow Old Rugbeian, an Ulsterman named Charlie Brett, who had followed him to New College; and Charlie was a poetry addict. It was not so much that he composed it, but he had compiled a manuscript anthology of his own which he illustrated – you could almost say illuminated – with tiny marginal pictures. From this he gave readings to a group which gathered in his room at the top of the Victorian gate-tower, a group of New College poetasters and their girlfriends, mostly drawn from St Hilda's. Charlie also knew the poet and critic Patric Dickinson who graced us occasionally with his presence and commented, quite robustly, on our efforts. I tried him with a rather depressed piece I had written contrasting my own inner turmoils with the calmness of an oak tree I had seen on one of the backwaters:

> Alone by idle waters, the oak tree does not despair,
> Knowing (although) that these tenacious leaves must fall.
> And though the wolf winds leap at the oak's throat,
> Crack frost like a whip over the wan banks,
> Though the leaves drop to the water and do not shift,
> Then blacken, sink, the oak devises buds.
> Being one in itself; having purpose, faith and law.

Dickinson dismissed it as a crude example of the pathetic fallacy. 'An oak's got to do what an oak's got to do,' he remarked. 'Why envy it?' There were other, better poems in the style of Auden and MacNeice and inevitably there were the sort of love poems that one would as soon see in print as one's love letters. One, however, did get published in the University Poetry Society's broadsheet:

> Will the moon come down heads or tails,
> Hovering in mid night, tomorrow's toss?
> Shall we hear ravens or nightingales
> In tomorrow's evening thickets? Cross
> The gipsy's palm with silver –
> The stars are not deceivers, ever.
>
> But the moon's a double-headed penny
> That's never yet come down at all.
> And as for us, there is not any
> Star whose bluff we dare not call.
> Crossing the Rubicon with Sylvia
> The stars' reflections shatter in the river.

The implication was that Sylvia and I had already 'crossed the Rubicon', which created quite a stir among our friends; but in fact our relationship, though passionate, was unbelievably chaste. On my side it was an acute attack of the puppy syndrome: I persecuted her with affection, I would not leave her a spare moment to herself for fear some other man would attract her attention, and I waited on her with a servility bred of my curious upbringing – that women were a different race, superior yet suffering from mysterious handicaps which called for every possible service and sacrifice by attendant men. At the same time any criticism they made of what you did for them showed such a rejection of your efforts to be perfect that the only possible reaction was one of rage – which nevertheless had to be suppressed. At times it must have been suffocating for Sylvia, and reduced her to a resentful sulk. But every time she tried to throw me out I would respond with a more spectacular gesture than ever. One morning, during vacations, she rang me up at Potten End to tell me it was all over. Within half an hour I was on my way by bus to Oxford with a suitcase full of books which I sold to Blackwells; used the proceeds to buy an antique cameo brooch, which I knew she admired, from a shop in St Giles; and by tea-time was on her doorstep in London to sweep her back into my arms. At least, after three years of such an intense relationship, no one could accuse us of not really knowing one another.

Sylvia's family, the Rhodeses, were at first sight one of the last relics of Victorian England, comprising seven children (three boys and four girls) brought up in one of the lofty houses in Belsize Park, Hampstead, with maids and cooks in attendance.

The Rhodeses were of Norman crusader lineage going back flawlessly to Liulphus del Rodes, Jordanus de Rodas and a succession of Simons, Hugos and Gregorys. Sylvia's father, Hugh Rhodes, had been a senior civil servant who died on the eve of the Second World War soon after moving his family to an even grander house and garden in Turner's Wood, Hampstead Garden Suburb. I regret not having known him, for he was evidently a man of humour and culture, a cat-lover, a violinist, and an admirer of the old Germany. His music and intelligence brought him many German Jewish acquaintances – he prided himself on *looking* Jewish (it was the prominent Norman nose) – and when the Nazi persecutions began he kept open house for Jewish refugees, some of whose descendants remain family friends.

Hugh Rhodes married a Patricia Scrymgour from Colchester – Helen Edith Laurie Patricia, to give her the full grandeur of her baptism – one of the daughters of an architect who made his fortune designing the early blocks of flats in St John's Wood, near Lord's cricket ground. On Hugh's premature death the money became a godsend for bringing up the seven young Rhodeses. No fewer than three became doctors, one a solicitor, and all the rest went to college of some sort. Pat would dearly have liked to be an architect herself but was born a generation too soon. She was determined that her daughters should be as well qualified as her sons, and they all were. The Scrymgours (*without* an 'e' after the 'g', they insisted) were related to the hereditary Royal Champion, the knight who used to ride into the coronation banquet and offer to fight anyone who dared contest the sovereign's right. My mother-in-law, frail though she looked, threw down the gauntlet to fate and licked it in single combat. She was, besides, an English Presbyterian and it seemed to give her both a strong sense of duty and the inner strength to carry it out. As if bringing up her family was not enough, she was constantly dashing off to do good works among the poor of Kilburn on behalf of the Church. Oddly enough, although incorrigibly romantic about the young, she was ruthlessly realistic about the elderly: 'That decrepit old thing would be *much* better off dead,' she would declare of some unfortunate who was probably ten years younger than herself.

Patricia Rhodes was a practical, everyday saint – one of those in whose presence it is quite simply easier to be good. Like most saints she could produce a smile of pure bliss. But she was hardly the still centre of her family, for she was in perpetual motion, whizzing up and down the stairs, in and out of the house, as if trying to fulfil her declared ambition to drop dead while running for a bus. She dressed like one of her Kilburn poor, hair awry, face tense with concentration. The family kept to its rooms (of which there were many) for if one emerged one was liable to be seized upon instantly for some job. A succession of ill-tempered housekeepers provided a rather basic diet, but their services were not deemed to include clearing the enormous dining table or washing up. Born members of the family, knowing this, would rise and vanish at the crucial moment, leaving the luckless guest and whichever Rhodes had invited him or her to deal with the lot. I once complained at the unfairness of this, and was told that since visitors were usually courting one of the Rhodeses the couple was assumed to be only too glad to be left on its own.

The ordeal by dinner-table was certainly daunting. Any remark one dared to make was promptly set upon by six or more Rhodeses – brother Stephen, the lawyer, being particularly rigorous. Many a suitor never came back for a second helping. I, however, was impervious in the armour of my intellectual pride. Businesslike though she was, Mrs Rhodes loved young lovers and beamed happily as her daughter's young man lectured her on philosophy, politics and economics. For I soon discovered that if I concentrated on the mother it scarcely mattered what the rest of the clan thought. They were a close team but in the end it was she who decided what goals to let through.

It helped if one worked one's passage. I cleared the table and washed up diligently. I helped to feed the gaggle of despondent and illegal hens who lived under the bushes in the garden (one changed sex, started crowing and had to be gagged every morning). I helped to carry out chairs and tables whenever it stopped raining and tea in the garden was decreed. Most memorably, I helped to 'go coking'.

In those days of fuel shortage it was possible to supplement the household's ration by presenting oneself at the Hendon gasworks on Saturday mornings to buy twenty-eight pounds of coke 'off the ration'. Even this was supposed to be limited to one share per family, which would barely satisfy an old-fashioned boiler for a day. But eight shares, two hundredweights, was enough for a whole week. Accordingly, every Saturday, all available Rhodeses plus their girlfriends, boyfriends and assorted camp-followers were called on parade at

Turner's Wood, issued with a sack apiece and instructed to proceed independently to the gasworks. Here they were to mingle with the queue *and pretend not to know one another*. Having purchased their twenty-eight pounds they were to stagger off round the corner where a car would be waiting towing a trailer 'borrowed' from the Parachute Regiment (I forget which ally of the Rhodeses supplied this, but there were two or three possibilities). Into the trailer went the coke, the sacks were returned, the casual labour discharged, and the family made its way home to unload the treasure into the bunker behind the kitchen. Almost anyone who knew them got drawn into this furtive operation, and to me it seemed a logical extension of the courtship by coal which I had invented at Oxford.

Before long I brought Sylvia home to Potten End to meet my parents. My father's charm came easily, but my mother felt ill-at-ease with the girl who was so clearly replacing her in her only son's affections, and for Sylvia the contrast between her own extended family in London and my very narrow range in the country was just as uncomfortable. Aunt Sal took to her immediately and the liking was returned, but Berkhamsted had nothing to compare with the plays and concerts and galleries, the intellectual stimulus of London. Frankly, after you had walked the common for a day or two and made a few brass rubbings in the flinty churches, it was boring. So I spent more and more time during the vacations either staying at Turner's Wood or bicycling up there for the day along the Watford bypass – a trip that took me little more than an hour.

Knowing Sylvia meant knowing her group of friends, most of them made at Hornsey Art School. The central trio, which has stood the test of time, consisted of Sylvia, Ann Gould and Gerda Fox – three very attractive girls whose impact on the Carthusian mafia, when it met them, was devastating. Sylvia was the only one to marry into the mafia, but the others met most of it and the memories (I fancy) cling.

Ann was perhaps the most *fatale* of these *jeunes femmes*; certainly the hardest to partner successfully, as various men were to discover in course of time. Her fragile, innocent prettiness was deceptive. Numerous wolves approached this lambkin licking their lips, only to find themselves winded by her intelligence and outwitted by her singlemindedness. She was also the untidiest person I have ever known, neatly turned out in person, but spreading waves of chaos around her wherever she settled. Forty years after I first met her she had two daughters but no husband, two houses but no home, and was calmly enquiring about the possibility of buying an abandoned

Methodist chapel near Land's End. Her particular craft was etching, but by that time she was running the photographic library for *The Sunday Times*.

Gerda was a potter and had a voluptuousness of figure that would have set Renoir reaching for his flesh tones. She had fled from Germany with her father (a Jewish furrier), her mother and her equally alluring sister Renate. She had raven hair, wide eyes and walked with a sway which made men turn their heads and bump into lamp-posts. She was always entranced by the oddities of people, and entranced others as she described them with only the faintest of continental accents: 'That man with feet like mice – yes? – like little scurrying mice . . .' Gerda and a friend of hers called Fay knocked Oxford off its hinges by setting up a workshop between the Woodstock and Banbury roads called the Isis Pottery, where they made and sold mugs and vases of a remarkably fine quality. No brew of cocoa, from Keble to Christ Church, could respect itself without an Isis mug around it. How many proposals of marriage the potters turned down I have never dared enquire, but in the end Gerda shrewdly selected a Slav-American named Warren Rovetch and went to live happily ever after in Boulder, Colorado. I saw her the other day, more voluptuously turned than ever, and full of forgotten memories of eccentric behaviour, her accent quite unaffected by more than thirty years in the United States.

Sylvia added two further friends to my repertory company, one male and one female. The latter was Annelie, the girl next door in Turner's Wood, daughter of a distinguished refugee lawyer named Kurt Sluzewski whose passion was to organise string quartet concerts in his own home. Many a Sunday evening a dozen or so of us would crowd into his music room to hear Haydn, Mozart, the early Beethoven, with Slu himself playing first violin a trifle harshly, though his violist and cellist were as good as professional. It was the kind of home culture the composers must have had in mind when they wrote their music, and – alas – no recording, however flawless, can substitute for it.

Annelie, an outgoing, affable girl of sturdy build, seemed the ideal companion when Sylvia and I determined to spend our first summer vacation from Oxford in a youth hostelling tour of the western Highlands. Gerda wanted to come too, and by good fortune she had then in tow a music student called Bobby who not only composed in the style of Sibelius but had access to a couple of cottages which might come in handy. We consulted maps, bought ourselves boots and rucksacks, and planned a route from Mallaig to the Cuillins, Glenelg, Shieldaig and other romantic sounding places.

The romance went sour. Quite early on, Bobby and Gerda quarrelled and Bobby withdrew to the island of Mull, leaving me to face a three weeks' hike with three extremely nubile girls following hungrily in my footsteps. The hunger struck at every level, for if England was short of food, the Scottish highlands were even shorter and what shops there were – more like trading posts in the outback – had little to offer except sawdust bread a week out from Glasgow and packets of powdered potato. We had arranged for parents to dispatch us food parcels at intervals, and fell upon these like famine victims when they arrived; but in between we had to coax eggs out of resentful crofters, pollock and coley from reluctant fishermen. I had brought Froissart's *Chronicles* with me to read and sympathised gloomily with the accounts of how Edward III's invading army had had to carry all its food with it into Scotland 'so barren was that countrie . . .'

It rained incessantly and we scarcely saw the Cuillins through the mist. Attempts to find short cuts led us through bog after bog, and our sturdy boots became waterlogged boats: I posted mine home and wore gymshoes which at least dried quickly. The men's dormitories were full of incomprehensible Scots, so I sought company in the forbidden territory reserved for women; at Dornie I was caught there by the warden. 'I'm most fearfully sorry,' I gasped, leaping to my feet. The kilted clansman fixed me with a knowing eye: 'But ye're *no* sorry!' he declared. I spent the next morning clearing the latrines.

The girls did their best for me, each one knitting a section of a vast green pullover which, when assembled, was clearly in three different styles. They roused much hostility among the Scottish hostellers, most of whom subsisted on porridge or baked beans, by taking over the cooking stoves to prepare me (supplies permitting) elaborate three-course meals. Gerda's jam omelettes were like caviar to the general, and my reputation went ahead of me as 'yon Sassenach wi' the harem.'

So what am I complaining about? That it was not a hike but a sexual tightrope walk. Honour kept me loyal to Sylvia, but I could have fancied any of them – were t'other dear charmers away – and they knew it. Every glance, every phrase, every hand held out crossing a stile was evaluated like a love letter. The fragile foursome would have flown apart had it not been for the fact that we were stranded in hostile territory and had to cling to one another for sheer survival. Around Loch Torridon the midges descended in swarms, causing so much misery to each of us that it became impossible to think of love. We crawled back to London ready to grant total independence to Scotland.

The following summer we courted disaster in another clime. The continent of Europe was opening up again and France was the obvious objective. 'It's one of the great days of your life,' said Ronnie Hope, 'the day you realise that you, too, smell of garlic.' So Sylvia and I, Sylvia's younger sister Diana, Richard Donovan and Charlie Brett collected our first passports and took the train for Paris – Sylvia cluttered with the authentic artist's kit of oils box, canvases and folding easel. We stayed in the rue Bonaparte and loitered in the Café de Flore, trying to spot existentialists. We did the Grand Palais, the Petit Palais, the Louvre, the Luxembourg and the Jeu de Paumes. We scaled Montmartre and tramped round Montparnasse, and when we realised the money was going faster than it should we went down to the Gare de Lyons and picked a destination at random: La Tour du Pin, a little town in the Dauphine.

There we spent the Quatorze Juillet, all fireworks and dancing in the streets to the band of the *sapeurs pompiers*, and my left-handed prowess at the shooting galleries won us several bottles of inferior wine. The inn we stayed at had genuine mediaeval sanitation – a sheer drop under the bum in a closet – but we ate well and sang sea shanties for the benefit of locals who did not want to hear them. We knew, however, that on the continent students were expected to sing. After a few days we rambled on through Saint-Genix-sur-Guiers and somewhere I forget the name of on the Rhône, and at Annecy, on a bus, I lost most of our money. I had rashly appointed myself banker, instead of leaving it distributed among the party, and the wallet containing the francs to pay our hotel bill fell out of my pocket. The others sent me to Coventry and we scraped our way back to London with our tails between our legs. But at least we had developed a taste for 'abroad'.

The male friend Sylvia added to my collection was Gerard Hoffnung, without doubt the most unforgettable character I shall ever meet. He had been at Hornsey with Sylvia, Gerda and Ann, but was thrown out (to his great surprise) for refusing to follow the syllabus and caricaturing the models, drawing butterflies on their bottoms and infesting his still life with creepy-crawlies. He was exiled by the Ministry of Labour to an Express Dairies bottling plant, where he created havoc by pulling the wrong levers, and was finally set up as an air-raid warden with a little hut in Hampstead Garden Suburb until the end of the war.

Gerard had begun to draw as a child in his native Berlin. The influence of Wilhelm Busch, of Bosch and Brueghel are inescapable in his work which I first noticed, appropriately, in the magazine *Lilliput*. By the time I met him in person he was out of his air-raid hut and working freelance from his home in Thornton Way. A short, square figure in country-squire tweeds, always behaving a good thirty years older than he really was, he seemed more like an eccentric uncle than a contemporary. 'Aaaah!' he would cry, '*my* Gerry – and *my* Sylvia!' and there would be much chortling and digging in the ribs before we were led upstairs to his sanctum – a weird amalgam of housemaster's study, bachelor's den and alchemist's laboratory; bedroom, workroom and smoking room all in one. There were pipes, ocarinas, paint brushes, books, gramophone records, framed drawings, beer mugs, at first a small saxophone and later a family of tubas in a twilit clutter from floor to ceiling. One usually had to sit on the bed.

As Sylvia predicted, our first bond was music. Gerard specialised in high-frequency whistling, while I preferred to hum or sing. But we shared the same favourites and between us we could sketch in the main parts of a score. This went on all over London, in the tube, on buses, sometimes over the telephone. With a few cuts, we could manage *The Rite of Spring* on the 28 bus between Golder's Green and Kensington Church Street, on the way to the Albert Hall for a Prom. The recitals continued for some years, until Gerard's music became more professional and he actually took lessons on the tuba. Since the instrument only really began with Berlioz (and has flourished ever since) Gerard's taste became more contemporary while mine was going steadily backwards into the Tudor period. It was not that I minded sitting through albums of Alban Berg – I positively enjoyed being conscripted into the audience for *Wozzeck*, in spite of the dig in the ribs at every tuba entry; and I was quite as ravished as Gerard at our discovery of Ravel's *L'Enfant et les Sortilèges*. But my efforts to persuade him that Tallis's motet in forty parts was as magnificent as the Walton First Symphony were a failure: there was no tuba in Tallis.

There were numerous other links between us. Almost any friend of yours was bound to get at least an audition as a friend of Gerard's. The Hoffnung network included not only artists, writers and musicians but almost anyone who could talk entertainingly, put up with Gerard's monstrous sulks whenever the limelight slipped away from him, and, of course, provide an admiring audience. His strongest dislike was of untidy, *dirty* people. There was one perfectly nice girl he deliberately avoided because he swore she never brushed her hair or scrubbed her fingernails. He said she put him off his food; and food was very important to him. It was Gerard who first took me to Wheeler's and introduced me to oysters. Sylvia, who shuddered at the very thought of them, was so provoked by the spectacle of our enjoyment that she forced herself to like them too.

Michael Flanders (who lived in the Garden Suburb) and his musical partner Donald Swann were members of the Hoffnung circle. I suppose we were some of the first to hear their songs as they tried them out at suburb soirées before launching them onto the stage in *Penny Plain, Tuppence Coloured* and their own *Drop of a Hat* revues. In their way they were oddly like Gilbert and Sullivan; Michael glad to be the witty entertainer, but Donald always straining after something more artistic, more spiritual that was actually never as good as the comedy. Without the teasing that Michael supplied, the twist of lemon in the lyrics, there was always a danger that Donald would slide into something mawkish, as he tended to do after Flanders's death. But then Donald, like me, had the black bird of depression hovering over his shoulder and practised gaiety to keep it away. It is not an act that can be maintained for ever, nor, in my experience, can Christian faith provide the cure, though Donald turned to that too. Meeting him in later years I find it tragic that a man who gave so much happiness to others should himself be so sad. But perhaps it is the Russian in him.

Gerard came to visit us at Oxford, some ten years before his classic performance of 'the Bricklayer's Tale' at a Union debate. I cannot remember much about the visit, except that half way across the great quadrangle of Christ Church he stopped a venerable academic and enquired whether he were a professor. He was, it transpired, of pastoral theology, or Christian apologetics or hermaneutics or some such. 'Splendid!' said Gerard, shaking him warmly by the hand. 'Well done! Keep it up!' And we left the professor looking more encouraged than he had felt for years.

The Oxford system of leaving all one's exams to the very end was calculated to produce a growing sense of panic in the final term. The politics would be all right, the philosophy was touch and go, the economics promised to be a disaster; so I crammed like mad on Keynes and Boulding. Whether or not I got my degree, the next fate awaiting me would be my national service with the Navy. The prospect of being separated from Sylvia was almost unbearable; so, being twenty-one years of age, I determined that we should get engaged – and would have married her on the prospects of an ordinary seaman's pay if my parents had not descended upon Oxford and gently dissuaded us.

The engagement, however, was allowed to stand and we decided to announce it at a party on the river on Sylvia's birthday in May 1948. The morning of the party I ran up the narrow stairs to Charlie Brett's tower room, found him out, ran down again, and was walking down Long Wall Street in the direction of Magdalen Bridge when the world turned bright yellow and I found I could scarcely breathe. I sank down on a doorstep and rang the bell over my head. It turned out to be the residence of a New College don, who dragged me in and sent for the ambulance. Arrived at the Radcliffe Hospital it turned out that I had had a spontaneous pneumothorax – in short, I had burst a lung, weakened by a succession of chest infections and finally ruptured by my scamper up Charlie's stairs. It was, they said, rare, interesting and dramatic, but not threatening to life. All I really had to do was lie perfectly still for some weeks while the lung healed itself naturally and medical students queued up to clink coins together on my chest and listen to the echo.

Poor Sylvia must have thought she was about to be prematurely widowed, but our friends very sensibly staged the party to cheer her up and then came round to the hospital to cheer me up as well. At Avrion Mitchison's suggestion they bought me a potted plant, an enormous green phallus which swelled and swelled at the end of my bed until the nurses could hardly look at it without blushing, and which finally ejaculated a huge scarlet lily. We gave the nurses a difficult time in our ward, for the man in the bed on one side of me had two wives who had to be kept from meeting one another, while the man on the other side was a haemophiliac who delighted in sharpening razor-blades in the palm of his hand. 'You get sick of being molly-coddled all the time,' he explained. 'This is the only thrill I get.'

At least I got the satisfaction of hearing that the Royal Navy never wanted to see me again and that Oxford University would allow me an extra term to take my finals, which I rather think I needed. Provided I moved gently there was no reason why I should not spend the summer abroad reading in the sun, and a friend of the Rhodeses got me a post in eastern France teaching English to the *préfet* (or chief administrator) of the Haute Marne, at Chaumont.

Still in his early twenties, he was a former classics professor and resistance hero named Edgard Pisani. The family must originally have come from Pisa and on the strength of some years in Malta his father claimed to have been British for a time; but they had settled in Tunis and Edgard had the bearded good looks of a Barbary pirate. His resistance heroism had included escaping from the Germans by provoking an abscess in a tooth and then giving his escort the slip at the dentist's; after which he managed to infiltrate the Paris police headquarters and led the uprising on the Ile de la Cité. He certainly radiated authority, even in a grade-three *département* like the Haute Marne, where I once saw him dissolve a communist demonstration with a balcony-speech that would have done credit to de Gaulle. As the years passed I saw him rise through senator, minister, EEC commissioner to – at last notice – proconsul in the disgruntled colony of New Caledonia. I was sure he would eventually make it to President of the Republic, but I fancy he lacked the grass roots for that.

I can't claim I taught him English very well – when I met him in Washington twenty years later we rapidly turned to French – but Edgard did me a favour by letting me sit in on his cabinet meetings, learning, in particular, about the highly methodical system (in fact bequeathed by the German occupation) under which the state controlled everybody's wages. Chaumont itself was an extremely boring town. Funerals – at which good Republican men walked in procession but scornfully declined to enter the church – were about the most exciting things that ever happened. But I stuffed my memory with details of French industrial relations and when I got back to Oxford was able to brighten up my economics answers with first-hand examples which the examiners could hardly challenge. I think it probably saved my degree. At any rate, I got a good second.

There remained the little matter of a job, although in those days there was never any doubt that a university graduate would be able to find one. 'What are *you* going to do?' I asked one of my most agreeable contemporaries who was sure of a first in philosophy. 'Join the family firm, I'm afraid,' he said gloomily. 'That being . . . ?' '. . . whaling.' And he prodded his New College rissole.

My family firm would have been Cooper's, and I am sure Aunt Sal would have fitted me up, if I had asked, as she had done my father. But it was now unimaginable that I should do anything but write, and Naomi Mitchison had pointed the way; so I applied to the University Appointments Board for something in journalism. The openings were few and very stuffy. There was little newsprint to print news on, ex-servicemen were claiming their old jobs back, and my illness had made me a late starter in the field for that year. The appointments people sent me invitations to become a sub-editor on the *Encyclopaedia Britannica*, a précis-writer for Keesing's *Contemporary Archives*, or a research economist with the National Coal Board.

The last thing I wanted to be was an economist. But coal, newly nationalised, had a popular socialist ring about it, so I applied. At the interview I got carried away by my souvenirs of the French economy and the next thing I knew there was a contract to come and work at Hobart House. Do that for a couple of years, I thought, and I might get a job as an industrial correspondent. Still, my pen hovered reluctantly over the dotted line.

Saved in the nick of time. The appointments board wrote to say that the BBC had decided to recruit six graduate trainees in the news division – the first time it had taken on such creatures, though in course of time they were to become the most sought-after of media élite. I applied, mentioning how desperate the Coal Board was for my services, and got an almost immediate interview at which I did my French economy act once more. While I was about it, they said, I might as well go and see the talks department, too. At that time the BBC regarded itself as the royal priesthood of the English tongue and even had an official known as the Director of the Spoken Word. I do not think I was considered important enough to see him; instead I was interrogated by one of the retired naval officers who tended to administer the Corporation. 'Do you like beer?' he asked. In fact I didn't, but replied evasively that it all depended on the kind of beer. 'Ah, Priestland,' said the sailor wearily, 'I fear you are *un jeune homme sérieux* . . .'

Talks did not want me, but to my joy news did (even though beer turned out to be just as important to them, if not more). I was engaged as a trainee sub-editor, tore up the Coal Board's contract, and gratefully signed one under which, for £440 a year, I promised the BBC all my efforts, energies and imaginations, waking or sleeping, on duty or off duty, indeed the very breath in my body to do with as it would. I showed the document to one of the Old Carthusian mafia and he pronounced it to be unenforceable, an instrument of terror rather than a legal contract.

Some 33 years later, as I was signing off from the BBC and the chief personnel officer was stripping me of my security pass, car-park ticket, stop-watch and other badges of rank, he froze as he came to one item on his checklist. 'My God!' he exclaimed. 'You never signed the Official Secrets Act. Not only that, but you were never even *apprised* of the Official Secrets Act. News people are meant to, you know. You're not even supposed to reveal what kind of toilet paper we use.'

Now that I can tell all, it is, and always has been, of the very harshest grade. But if I slipped through the BBC's vetting net, I didn't fool the

Americans. When I got to Washington the FBI made me register every year as a foreign agent and nothing I could do would persuade them I wasn't.

Chapter Four

NO HARM BEING DULL

I first asked Sylvia to marry me about two months after we met, and went on re-confirming it every month for the next three years. There was a landmark about eighteen months into the relationship when I jovially used the phrase 'honourable intentions' in a bread-and-butter letter to Mrs Rhodes and got back an ecstatic reply saying how refreshing it was to meet a young man who still observed the old convention of asking the parent for her daughter's hand – which hadn't really been what I was fishing for, but I was glad enough to accept it. My mother, when she met them, found the Rhodeses rather overwhelming; but the encounter brought out all my father's gallantry and charm. As usual, he was a great success with the female side of the family and left my future mother-in-law glowing.

With the last exam of my life behind me, the Navy dismissed and a job in hand, Sylvia and I were able to fix the wedding for May 14th 1949, three days before Sylvia's birthday. This gave me about five months to get used to being a BBC trainee sub-editor; for, as I told my admiring relatives, I was going 'to write the news'.

In those days, at any rate, I might as well have said I was going to look after the crown jewels, for the atmosphere surrounding the BBC news bulletins was a compound of holiness, patriotism and the Gold Standard. This was partly due to the disciplines imposed by John Reith which persisted in the Corporation long after he had left, and partly to the role of herald to the nation which the BBC had played, in victory and defeat, throughout the war. It would be naive today to pretend it always told the truth – certainly not the whole truth – but it resisted wholesale lying and emerged as something of a national and international hero. The middle class, which was more select and snobbish than it is today, was also relieved that the Corporation, while providing wholesome listening for the masses, had not allowed much falling away from public school norms of written and spoken English. There was some alarm when, in a democratic gesture, one Wilfred Pickles was allowed to read the news in a northern accent; but this was soon stopped. It was quite clear to my relatives that it would be my duty not only to see that people were told what they could believe but in a manner they should imitate. There was a special pronunciation unit, I found, consisting of two Scottish ladies, whose job it was not only to maintain a card index of difficult foreign names but to sit beside the newsreader advising him on whether to say *contro*versy or con*trov*ersy. One of their most difficult tests came when the Koreans threw up a politician with the unfortunate name of Lee Bum Suk. The ladies, who were not without a sense of humour, suggested Boom Sook, an example I followed many years later when I had to interview a Vietnamese called Captain Phuc.

To begin with, however, speaking was not for me and there was not much writing either. The news division was in the throes of a grand reorganisation which, as usually happens, had led to gross over-staffing. The people who wrote the news in English for the overseas service had been merged with those who wrote it for the home audience and a combined newsroom set up in a building nextdoor to Broadcasting House, known as Egton House. This operated round the clock, churning out bulletins 24 hours a day, and staffed on a peculiarly upsetting rota which had you working three days on, three days off, three days on, three days off, three *nights* on, three days off, each spell on duty being of twelve hours. What was trying about it was not so much the strain of a twelve-hour working day, but that one never got into the rhythm of the night duties.

On any shift there might be up to ten sub-editors preparing items for the bulletins, and each sub had a typist to dictate to, the idea being that this would ensure that the story was speakable by the newsreader; a sound idea, because the style of writing which comes naturally to a journalist trained in print usually makes very bad broadcasting.

Above these rank-and-filers were two NCOs, the chief sub-editor for the Home Service bulletins and his opposite number for Overseas. Classically these were short-tempered Scotsmen with names like Mackinnon and McInnes, who allocated the stories for writing and sent them back when, as usual, they did not like them. Above the chief subs were duty editors, home and overseas, who sat in cubicles reading the newspapers; and over them a head of newsroom and his deputy (known as 'the shopwalkers'), and over them a head of news output (whatever that was – there was a theory that all news could be divided into intake and output) and over him – at last – the editor and his deputy. These last three, who lived on a higher floor as befitted their dignity, had the breathy names of Breething, Hole and Barker. We in the newsroom lived in terror of them, like mediaeval peasants grovelling beneath the invisible Trinity. From time to time their displeasure, but never their satisfaction, would be mediated to us through the chain of command. There would be fearful enquiries and scurryings to and fro with scripts by the shopwalkers, and ultimately the tearful composition by the sinners of memoranda of confession to be entered upon their files. It was actually very difficult to sack anyone from the BBC, and it seldom happens to this day (you have to do something which can be classified as 'gross'), but our lords and masters had refined the art of humiliation and of ensuring that if a crime were committed it was recorded by the criminal in his own handwriting.

Tahu Hole, the editor when I joined, was a massive bloodhound-like New Zealander, a figure out of some black-and-white Hitchcock movie, whose journalistic credentials were a complete mystery to us. It was understood he had been engaged by the overseas services during the war as a gesture to Empire solidarity, began by doing little commentaries to Ministry of Information briefs, and worked his way upwards by the sheer pursuit of ambition – a principle which, if followed singlemindedly, nearly always works. Ambitious people usually reach the top, though they do not always stay there.

Tahu – a Maori name – was a monster in every sense. I am sure he was kind to his wife and his dog, but amongst his staff he inspired nothing but terror, exuding a sinister aroma of power as if he knew something to the discredit of each one of them, as I suppose he took care to do. The only people with countervailing knowledge, and who were therefore immune to his terror, were the Paris and New York correspondents. From time to time Tahu would arrive in their territories 'on a tour of inspection', enjoy a hearty dinner with them at the best restaurants (he was partial to red snapper), and then vanish into the girlie-show district with his black homburg at a rakish angle. Two or three days later he would reappear in the correspondent's office, badly hung over and asking to have his flight home confirmed.

Tahu took good care to make no operational decisions himself for which he might be blamed if things went wrong. Instead he spent hours brooding over scripts which had already been transmitted, looking for errors and heresies. The situation was all too familiar to me from Bags's scholarship form: praise was bad for people because it gave them swollen heads and might be used as evidence for the defence at the next prosecution. The best one could hope for was to attract no attention either way. This was the basic philosophy of Tahu's news division, for if there was one thing the Trinity Upstairs dreaded it was letters from listeners, which usually meant letters of complaint. The idea was to provide a service like the gas, water or electricity: useful, but unremarkable.

Scoops, therefore, were risky and to be discouraged. Nothing was to be broadcast, even if it came from one of the BBC's own highly respectable correspondents, unless it was on at least two news agencies. This was not very enterprising (indeed it was the very opposite of traditional Fleet Street journalism) but in theory it made for the utter reliability on which the BBC prided itself. In practice it made for a pompous and soporific output and involved a great deal of silliness behind the scenes. Information from a reliable source would be held back until a less reliable source had caught up with it. Often it was known that the two agencies which appeared to confirm one another were actually the same man in the field. When I became a foreign correspondent myself I learnt that if I got an exclusive story the only way to get it on the air was to give a carbon copy to my competitor from Reuter's, even at the expense of being thought soft in the head by him.

Above all, the news must not be interpretative or in any way exciting. 'Remember, Priestland,' said one of the shopwalkers as he saw me in despair over a particularly deadly item about last week's national savings, 'there is no harm in being dull.' This seemed to be an appalling doctrine, but it was not difficult to fulfil from the government handouts and diplomatic communiqués which rained down upon our desks. 'The British Foreign Secretary, Mr Anthony A., has left London by air for B to have talks with the government of Transitania. Our diplomatic correspondent says they will discuss matters of mutual interest.'

At the beginning of each shift in the newsroom there would be a couple of tense hours while we waited lest an inquest be launched into the previous day's broadcasting. Any hint of Tahu's displeasure set his lieutenants kicking each other down the line in a frenzy of perfectionism. Not until Hugh Greene became director general – a far greater journalist and an even cleverer man – was the monster finally outmanoeuvred and forced into resigning 'to pursue his other interests' as Greene's announcement intriguingly put it. Some speculated that Tahu was going to pursue a Gladstone-like interest in the fallen women of Paris and New York; others maintained he had bought a chicken farm where he was devoting himself to the care of elderly, wealthy invalids. Certainly he inherited a great deal of money from at least one such invalid and died himself, at a ripe age, early in 1986. I suppose I should be grateful to Tahu for giving me my chances (always while threatening to take them away again at the slightest lapse on my part) but I saw too much humiliation inflicted by him upon my colleagues for any glow of gratitude to gild those memories.

Although I was described as a trainee there was no training at all to be had beyond being told to sit at the bottom desk and 'watch Sammy'. Sammy was a benevolent, grandmotherly old sub who got insignificant scraps of news agency copy and turned them into safe items for the tail end of the bulletin. The first job he taught me was 'how to do the weather'. This came through by teleprinter from Dunstable, at great length and in an unbroken stream of meteorological jargon like an ancient legal document. The scientists who wrote it knew what they meant but felt no call to ensure that anyone else did. It was strictly forbidden to attempt a translation – precipitation had to stay precipitation, not rain – but in order to give the newsreader some hope of making sense of it we were allowed to insert commas and capital letters and tear the scroll into manageable pages. Thus it was that, towards the end of the first week, I was able to rush home and announce to my parents, 'I punctuated the weather forecast!' To my mortification, they had noticed no difference.

Slowly I graduated to the national savings figures, to the comings and goings (by air) of foreign secretaries and even to gem-like half minutes on the activities of the royal family. These were almost compulsory in every bulletin; but it began to grow within me that, historic though it might have been for the people of Cheddar to have their cheese factory visited by the Duchess of Gloucester, the British public in general might have other interests. One day the chief sub deposited upon my desk – on two agencies, of course – the news that the young Duke of Kent would be returning late to Eton on account of mumps. After a few moments' thought I walked back up the room and, rather like Oliver Twist asking for *no* more, said I did not think our listeners needed to know this. The newsroom froze into a Batemanesque tableau – the Trainee Sub Who Doubted Whether the Royals Rated the Bulletin – but as the blood returned to his cheeks, the chief sub was heard to murmur that mebbe I had a point there, laddie; and handed me quite an interesting item about Jugoslavia, at least a minute long. I should like to claim that from that moment I never looked back, but it was not so instantaneous.

With me, at the lower end of the crowded newsroom, were my fellow trainees. They included Mary Edmond who was to spend the best part of a professional lifetime battling her way up through the newsroom in the face of its obstinate anti-woman prejudice; and Geoffrey Godsell, who had been working in the BBC's monitoring service as an Italian specialist. Geoffrey was the most excruciatingly polite person I have ever met – it could take up to half a minute to get in or out of a lift with him, with all the 'No, after *you*,' and '*Prego*' that went on – but he was an extremely able diplomatic journalist and soon broke from the pack to become a foreign correspondent. Being himself a Christian Scientist he then parted from the BBC to become foreign editor of *The Christian Science Monitor* in Boston, one of the few wholly respectable papers in the world, housed in a building that looks more like a bank.

There was also, in our little troupe of trainees, a dapper young man of the sort one could imagine in midshipman's uniform attending an admiral. I forget his name, but he did not stay the course and was later detected in Great Portland Street selling expensive secondhand motor-cars.

The trainees were eyed suspiciously at first by the rank-and-file journalists, who fell into two classes: the lean and hungry ex-servicemen who were desperately trying to make ends meet on their salaries, and the knowing old hacks who had something else going on the side. One of the most courageous was Dan Counihan, supporting a large Catholic family by working all night on the *Daily Mirror* and then working (and sleeping) all day in the BBC newsroom where his chums propped him up every time a shopwalker came by. Dan, too, went on eventually to foreign and diplomatic work, was nearly framed by the Russians in Moscow, but even in retirement is still to be heard from time to time on the World Service. Of the same generation, but more of a shooting star, was the outrageous Russell Spurr – a name that was clearly destined for a by-line in the *Daily Express*. Russell alone had the nerve to put Americanisms in his scripts, depicting 'red hordes pouring into the rice-bowl of China' and 'gun-toting thugs who smashed their way into downtown Saigon', though these only got on the Overseas air very late at night when the duty editor was fast asleep. If fame was the spurr, Russell soon left us to seek and win it in Fleet Street.

The old hacks were not above putting in the occasional shift on one of the papers, but most of them found our newsroom – with its light demands on their concentration – the ideal place for writing books or

One of Uncle Jock Cockburn's unsuccessful neo-Leonardo flying machines (*photo: the inventor*).

The author and cameraman on patrol with US Navy, Saigon River, 1965.

(top) Sylvia and one-year-old Andreas, Pakistan, Christmas 1955 (*photo: the author*).

The author posing heroically outside
Hanuman Dhoka Palace, Kathmandu, 1956
(*photo: anon. colleague*).

Jennet, the author, Nellie and
Andreas (in plaster after his operation), 1956
(*photo: Sylvia Priestland*).

running small businesses. Bookmaking was the traditional preserve of the uniformed BBC office messengers, but the role of office moneylender was played by the most shabbily dressed of all the subs, a man whose journalistic failings were solicitously covered up by the rest of us. One old hack ran a small estate agency from his desk; another, a school of dancing. A duty editor, who wangled permanent night duties, used them to write highly esteemed biographies of the Lakeland poets; and one of the chief subs wrote hard-hitting novelettes set in the world of boxing. Another chief sub, John Beevers, had done rather well on the eve of the Second World War with a scabrous concoction entitled *I was Hitler's Chambermaid* and had drafted a sequel called *I was Stalin's Niece* when the Georgian tyrant entered the war on our side and rendered it unpublishable. Beevers, a huge, boozy Yorkshireman with straw-coloured hair and a heart of gold, quickly identified a fresh market for his talents. He began writing popular lives of the saints and scored such a hit with his *Teresa: The Little Flower of Lisieux* that Catholic ladies' luncheon clubs in the United States implored him to come over and give them a lecture tour. 'But look at me, Gerald, I ask you!' said John, brushing the cigarette ash off his corduroys with the back of his hand. 'How can I go and shatter the faith of thousands? I've had to tell them I'm going into a monastery, I can't stand the heat.'

Another hack, an Irishman called Cyril, wrote little but made ends meet by selling off, in dribs and drabs, his collection of letters and manuscripts by James Joyce, about whom he knew a great deal. What embittered Cyril was that these sales were made necessary by the demands of his ex-wife; or, alternatively, the need to drown the sorrow caused him by her demands. '*The Times Literary Supplement* she wants now! What does a woman want with *The Times Literary Supplement*?' He got more and more pickled, but I was so bored for lack of work that I was glad to write his stories for him.

Another means of fighting off boredom occurred to us: we started a literary review of our own called *Essays* and sold it to other members of the staff to ease the tedium of night-shifts. I wrote about Ravel and the symphonies of Sibelius, and a younger, non-hack Irishman called John Houston wrote about Flaubert. 'I admit it is not really what we are here to do,' said John to one of the typists who complained about taking his dictation, 'but when you think the alternative is me going out and drinking too much and probably assaulting you, you'll agree you're better off with Flaubert.'

For many years the newsroom was part of the grand tour followed by a succession of nubile Australian girls with the minimum of typing skill. On the day shifts they were fairly safe, but at nights they got chased round the desks, fleeced at games of strip poker and put upside down in the giant wastepaper baskets. The willing ones suffered fates much pleasanter than death on the couch in the deputy editor's office. I can only think of one who actually married a sub. Two or three others fell into the clutches of one of the foreign duty editors, a man of mature years and donnish manner who used to entice them out to Strasbourg for sessions of the European parliament, where he completed their educations.

The foreign news department was one of three or four smaller units connected with the newsroom. Its main function was to control the network of a dozen foreign correspondents and to keep an eye on how the newsroom mutilated their work; for, as on most newspapers, there was a constant battle between the subs who regarded the ideal story as a railway accident at Woking with a child's body lying like a broken doll among the buttercups and the foreign staff who knew it was a coup d'état in Paraguay with Our Own Man on the spot. The subs were a good deal better disposed towards the sports room, who came in with cricket and football results; but they were almost as hostile to the parliamentary unit, who came in demanding time for tedious debates which had to be carefully counted up to make sure that Labour and Conservative got an equal number of lines. Finally there were the home reporters, less than half-a-dozen of them and never heard on the news in their own voices because that was held to violate the objectivity of the bulletin. 'The news' was the uninterrupted voice of Frank Phillips, or Alvar Liddell or Lionel Marsden.

The news for the home audience, that is. Overseas audiences, with their exhausting tendency to listen in the small hours, were served by a junior team of whom Jack di Manio was probably the best known and by no means the most sober. Broadcasting House was surrounded by pubs, quite apart from the BBC's own staff club and a number of low dives in neighbouring basements where one could encounter such legendary characters as Dylan Thomas, Louis MacNeice and René Cutforth.

It was the duty of the junior sub on the overseas side to sit with the newsreader in the studio, watching the clock and cutting the script to make sure it came out on time. Many were the midnight hours when I sat on the edge of my chair, mouthing the words and willing my reader to get through without disaster as stumbling-blocks like *Mahabalipuram, helicopter, pituitary* and *extraordinarily* loomed ahead. One

Christmas night, with the reader as sober as an undertaker, a mob of tipsy subs tiptoed into the studio, drew the chair from under his bottom and, as he crouched over the microphone to continue reading, undressed him down to his underpants without his missing a word. Another bulletin went out with six people sitting round the table eating bacon and eggs and drinking champagne. So far as the North American public could tell it was just another dreary catalogue of conferences and communiqués. On yet another occasion, our boxing chief sub, maddened with Merrydown cider, rampaged down Mortimer Street hurling dustbin lids like discuses. The police caught him, there was a whip round the newsroom to buy him out, and we nearly had no bulletin for the morning. Thus it was that we composed the English that set a standard for the nation and the world. It was, I suppose, our way of getting our own back on Tahu and co.

Came May and the wedding day: Sylvia and I were married at the Rhodes family Presbyterian church in St John's Wood, with Richard Donovan as my best man and a full parade of relatives on both sides. Sylvia wore her mother's Edwardian wedding-dress, Paul played the organ, Diana and Gerda were bridesmaids, and the service was conducted by a kindly Canadian minister called Murray-Smith of whose words I cannot remember a single one. I was thinking only that, now I was about to achieve the one thing I had ever really set my heart on rather than been driven to, there was a strange dread to it all: when I tried to look into the future, there was nothing there. I simply did not know what came next, and it frightened me. When I looked at my parents I saw the anxiety in their eyes. I was barely twenty-two.

Our honeymoon was yet another of those disasters. It was clear to me that there was only one place to go. I must introduce Sylvia to the Cornwall of my golden childhood and she would become part of it too. So we spent one week at Porthcurno, near Land's End, and then took the stomach-churning steamer for our second week in the Isles of Scilly. It rained all the time, I ran out of money, and Sylvia – whose family felt about the English Lakes as mine felt about Penwith, and who really wanted to go to Grasmere – vowed she would never go back to Cornwall, and didn't for twenty years. I felt somehow punished, though I was not sure for what.

Back in London we had found a flat in Canfield Gardens, near Swiss Cottage, on the top floor of a redbrick Victorian house behind John Barnes's store. The first time we went to shop there it gave me some confidence to discover a particularly odious Old Carthusian serving behind the haberdashery counter.

Rationing was still on and it was still difficult to find housing in London; we had to bribe the previous tenants with 'key money' to move out in our favour. The landlords were a benign refugee couple named Schönherz, from Hungary. On the first evening our lights went out and when I complained to old Mr Schönherz he beckoned me to a cupboard, pointed out the slot-meter and observed, 'She geefs not credit!' Thenafter we fed her diligently with shillings.

I went back to the shift pattern of BBC news, commuting to Oxford Circus by bus or tube. Gradually I was breaking out of the newsroom, though my first escape was by the macabre route of obituarist.

The BBC prided itself on its handling of death. A committee chaired, I believe, by none other than the Director of the Spoken Word had compiled a list of people who could not be regarded as properly dead unless recorded as such by the Corporation. And there was, of course, a hierarchy of death. There were first-class dead, who rated not only a lengthy biography in the bulletin but also a 'tribute' delivered at the microphone by someone of approximately equal stature, after the nine o'clock news. First-class dead included world statesmen, members of the Order of Merit, the Archbishop of Canterbury and, of course, the royal family. Then there were second-class dead, who got a long obituary written by an expert, but no tribute. Second-class dead included British politicians of Privy Council rank, *knighted* authors, painters, composers and performers, plus *successful* wartime commanders, the Archbishop of York and *reputable* foreign royalty. Finally there were third-class dead who rated about a minute of weighed, polished and approved prose, written by the news division. The third class included sportsmen, film stars, discredited politicians, diocesan bishops and disgraced foreign royalty.

The delicacy of this practice could not be overstressed, so a journalist of tact and style was sought to take charge of it. Nobody much fancied being shut up in a cupboard all day with the dead, but as luck would have it the ideal candidate came to hand. He was a distinguished correspondent, classically educated, who had blotted his copybook in foreign parts and been shipped home by the British Embassy for suitable humiliation. The rumour was that he had fallen in love with a beautiful communist partisan and arranged to be captured by the guerrillas so that he could spend a month of passion in a cave with her. The very man to be an obituarist!

The correspondent, in fact, agreed. Every morning he would check the distinguished invalids column in *The Times*, toss off a few well-turned paragraphs on anyone who seemed poorly, and then spend the afternoon at Lord's while his secretary told any enquirers that he was out doing research. It was a complete waste of talent and after six months he was returned to circulation. The cricket season was over anyway; but the job had to be kept going and so it passed from one of the BBC's most valuable journalists to its least – to me. Perhaps the classical education did it.

For me, at any rate, the job did open certain opportunities, though not those indicated by the soulful eyes of my predecessor's disappointed secretary. Since the scripts had to be approved at the highest level – Tahu or even the Director of the Spoken Word himself – this gave me a chance to show that I could write. I also had to correspond with the famous, asking them, discreetly, if they would care to write advance obituaries on their peers. Some rejected the invitation with horror; others accepted with relish, in which case the choice usually turned out to have been a mistake and the script unuseable. Such was the result of asking the BBC's own director of music, Steuart Wilson, to write about the critic Ernest Newman; for I had not realised that Newman had once accused Wilson of singing with an intrusive *h* and that Wilson saw the chance of getting his own back.

The tribute-payers were a special worry. Not only was it difficult to agree on who deserved whom, but the BBC insisted the tributes would be devalued unless delivered 'live'. This involved the constant checking of transport arrangements to the nearest studio, and the selection of reserve tribute-payers in case the first choice was unavailable when the blow fell. My constant nightmare was that Stalin would die, for the choice in his case had fallen upon Lord Inverchapel, a former British ambassador in Moscow, and getting him to our Glasgow studios involved laying on relays of cars and ferry-boats across the highlands and islands with special provision in case of fog or snow. That was only half the Stalin nightmare; for when at last his lordship was persuaded to let me peep at the script he had in mind, his opening words were 'So Uncle Joe has died on us at last!' I thought this was rather splendid and wrote back that I felt it summed up admirably what the nation would feel; but the higher priests of the Spoken Word were appalled. It was not that they were remotely pro-communist – the BBC simply did not speak like that. A great row broke out with Inverchapel refusing to budge and Tahu flogging me into battle against the vindictive diplomat. I was not sorry when he withdrew altogether, for it enabled me to stand down the ferrymen.

I lasted rather more than six months in the death department, during which I was able to put two or three hundred obituaries on ice, none of them as troublesome as Stalin. When it came to the ex-King Carol of Roumania (distinctly third-class) I was forbidden to describe Madame Lupescu as his mistress, but the BBC felt 'intimate friend' was acceptable. One of the last things I did was to draft my own obituary, quoting the Archbishop of Canterbury as saying, 'This plucky little mortician made a living out of dying, but in the end death got him down.' It is one I shall not be around to hear myself, and in any case the obits are revised annually by my successors, but to this day, when one of my more durable subjects passes away I hear familiar phrases floating through the air.

My next move was to the parliamentary unit which produced Today in Parliament, the one programme which the BBC was compelled by law to broadcast. There were not yet microphones in either Chamber, the job being essentially one of sitting in Egton House and sub-editing from the Press Association and Exchange Telegraph tapes. This had to be done carefully – the MPs themselves listened jealously – and we kept unsociable parliamentary hours; but the work was stimulating and prestigious and the company was a delight. The unit was run by a civilised pacifist called P. L. Ritzema, with Waldo Maguire – a frenzied Ulsterman – as chief writer and myself and an Irish railway enthusiast called Edgar Brennan completing the band. Sybil, a pneumatic blonde with a heart of gold who would have been a shoo-in for the *Carry On* films, typed for us. We were as happy as the parliamentary day was long.

During the evening break I would go round the corner to the Stag, the original Third Programme poets' pub and eavesdrop with wonder on the performances of Louis MacNeice and his cronies. It would be lying to pretend I was a member of the circle – the loan of a match or the helpful passing of a glass was about the nearest I ever got – but as an admirer of Louis's poetry from the moment I read *Autumn Journal* at Charterhouse, it was a rare satisfaction for me to find that the man was as glamorous as his work. He had the classical wit and polish of my idol Kenneth Knowles; something of the physical magnetism, too. His mind, as he expressed it in conversation, was fascinatingly split between romantic Irish and sardonic Scots, each half commenting on the other so that he could launch into a dazzling conversation with himself. It was this that gave him the talent of sheer fantasy that produced some of the best radio plays ever written. They were pure radio, unshackled by scenery, though they would have gained the ultimate dimension had stereo then existed. By the standards of Larkin and the like I suppose he wrote too much; but if I could keep only one out of Auden, Dylan Thomas and MacNeice, it is MacNeice that I would keep for myself.

Also to be found in the Stag or the George was that epic reporter René Cutforth. René, not then quite as battered and bear-like as he later became, got into trouble with Tahu for reporting the Korean War as it really was: the shit, the chaos, the hideous effects of napalm, and not just the headquarters stuff about the Glorious Glosters. René told his own *original* foreign correspondent's anecdotes and was without question one of the half-dozen truly great broadcasters I have known, along with Alistair Cooke, Johnny Morris, Christopher Serpell, Anthony Smith, Studs Terkel.

On dull afternoons René would descend into the depths of a low dive known as the ML Club, which still exists near Broadcasting House, where he would marinate in rum-and-water. Once, an officious reporting organiser, knowing his habits, telephoned him at the bar and called him back for an assignment. 'Can't,' replied Cutforth, 'I'm on a story right now.' The organiser came round in person to find Cutforth lurking in the darkest corner behind a copy of the *Evening Standard*. 'Do you see that man over there pretending to be drunk?' said René, indicating the club's full-time resident alcoholic. 'Well, I've been tipped off by a fellow I know in MI6 that he's waiting here to slip some microfilm to a courier for the Russians. The courier will be a girl – probably a negress. About half the people down here are counter-espionage chaps, waiting to grab them redhanded.'

'But I've got to send someone out to London Airport for the arrival of the King of Sweden, and you're the only one free,' wailed the reporting organiser. 'Tahu will be furious if we miss it.'

'Tell you what,' muttered René, lowering his voice even deeper, '*You* stay here keeping an eye on the man, and I'll pop off to the airport. But you'd better keep drinking or you'll make everyone suspicious.'

'What if he leaves?'

'He won't,' said René, speaking from long experience. 'He'll probably try to sit everyone out, so stick to it.'

Legend (if legend it be) has it that a search party carried the organiser out four hours later, pickled as a gherkin, while René spent a pleasant evening with one of the public relations officers at Heathrow. 'I hear you blew it,' he told the organiser when next they met. 'MI6 were furious.'

It was also told of René that he once emerged from Broadcasting

House to find the police holding back the crowd from a man who had been knocked down by a passing car. 'Let me through to him, officer,' pleaded René, 'it's my duty as an ordained minister of the church.' Whereupon he knelt beside the victim with hands clasped, extracted the information that he was a diplomat from one of the nearby embassies, and earned a few guineas telephoning it to the news agencies.

He had far wilder adventures than these in foreign parts and in his later years he made a living by writing and broadcasting them; as a result of which he made an even better living in the unlikely role of public praise-singer for a certain brand of margarine. None of us realised that René ever touched anything as solid as margarine, but there he was on our television screens bulkily declaring that it had whittled down the waistlines of half Australia and would do the same for us if we took his advice. I was flattered when, on his retirement, the advertising agency offered the role to me, though as a butter man I felt obliged to decline it.

If I was happy in the parliamentary unit the same could not be said for Sylvia. It had never occurred to us to discuss what she would do when we married. In the world in which I had been brought up, husbands went out to work and wives stayed at home resting. If she wanted to pass the time she would presumably get out her paints and paint until the next meal was due; but she had no more incentive to create anything than I had before the BBC set me my tasks, and she did not really find her feet as an artist – as a print-maker rather than an oil-painter – for another fourteen years. Before long the situation was resolved by events like the arrival of our first child, but we rapidly reached a low trough in our relationship and I came home to find Sylvia in tears, sobbing, 'I thought it was going to be so *interesting* being married to you, and now I'm so *bored* . . .' I was full of remorse: it seemed to me that I had tried to climb out of my despair by trampling on the one person I really cared about, that I had tried to nourish my own career by devouring somebody else's. Naturally shy and serene, Sylvia cannot have felt her self-confidence growing when I moved restlessly round the flat trying to save her trouble by doing as much as possible myself. It was the old conviction that women must be happiest doing nothing.

But this was only a low spot and there were many much happier ones on our graph. A friend still at Oxford signalled us that a litter of Siamese kittens had been advertised, in Latin, in the *Oxford Magazine*. We bought one of them, named him Lucretius and smothered him with love. It seemed unromantic to have him neutered, so he was allowed to develop into the local Mercutio, picking fights in the gardens at the back from which he could only be rescued by a mad rush from the top floor, out along the pavement in the front, through an alley and into the gardens where he would still be found, two minutes later, locked in the jaws and paws of the next-door tabby. Sylvia had infected me with catomania. We used to go on cat walks through Hampstead, scoring ten points for an oriental, eight for a white, six for a tortoiseshell, four for a ginger, two for a tabby and one for a common black.

I brought a few friends home from the newsroom for meals, though everything stood in the way of Sylvia's becoming a successful cook. Mrs Rhodes had taken the view that her daughters should not be wasting their talents in the kitchen, and I kept complaining that *my* mother did everything better, or at least differently, which was hardly calculated to inspire confidence. The hub of our social life became the Hampstead Artists' Council and its headquarters at Studio House on Haverstock Hill. When last I saw it, it had become some kind of Hindu temple, the Council having moved to the old Arkwright Road Library where it flourishes still.

We thought very little of Chelsea's claims to being the Montmartre of London, and indeed the Hampstead of the early 1950s did somehow recapture the *vie de Bohème*. The venerable Richard Carline, the Poles Ruszkowski and Jan Wieliczko, Fritz Krämer, Walter Nessler, Klaus Meyer, Morley Bury, Desmond Knight, Alice Lamb, Mary Fox, Vi Reiners, Kathleen Moss and her husband 'Smokey', the indestructible Sidney Arrobus, Patricia Angadi and a host of other artists and their partners made up a society that worked and played with equal thoroughness and very little money. They ate, drank and danced together, exhibited, occasionally sold a picture or two, and talked endlessly not in the abstract jargon of art critics but in the very practical language artists use among themselves about where to buy canvas, how to get framing done cheaply, why that corner of the picture is a mess and what to do about hands if you can't draw them. They were hard-working, competent if never very celebrated, neither *avant garde* nor amateur. Today a few are dead but most are still painting, while Patricia Angadi (the colony's Queen Mother) has suddenly hit the jackpot in her seventies as a novelist.

Patricia was actually brought up in the sort of Hampstead family she describes in her first book *The Governess*. To the family's horror she not only became an artist but married an exotic and unworldly Indian who, having fathered some breathtakingly beautiful children and spread the gospel of Indian dance and music about London, floated back to his village in Karnatica leaving Patricia to cope on her own. With a tolerant sigh, this she did – mainly by teaching – and when the family was on its own feet she reached into her experience and began writing. I can't think of anyone whose pleasure in their late success has been a greater pleasure to their friends.

None of the Hampstead artists could have been called great; they helped, perhaps, to provide the environment in which the very few truly great may grow. At any rate they gave Sylvia and me some of the happiest days and nights of our lives, and if any of them read this I raise my glass to them for the sake of auld lang syne.

In particular, we shall not look upon the like again, I think, of the annual Arts Ball at the Hampstead Town Hall, where I won the costume prize one year dressed as Shakespeare's Globe Theatre, and Ruszkowski won it the next by coming with a pair of disembodied hands round his throat, strangling him. On another occasion I went as the Labour Party, one half of me in cloth cap and dungarees and the other bowler-hatted and pin-striped; and on a fourth I was seen walking through Hampstead with a lighted candle on my head – though as what, I cannot remember. Alas, the ball was progressively taken over by gays who invariably came as nymphs and shepherds. The artists, all heterosexuals to a fault, were relieved when the town hall banned the event forever. We were not yet *that* broadminded.

In 1951 the BBC, which had made no serious effort to train its trainees, decided that I was qualified and began to pay me the rate for the job. We celebrated by getting Sylvia pregnant, taking on a mortgage and moving uphill, socially, to Belsize Park. Glenmore Road, within walking distance of the artists' headquarters and Hampstead Heath, was a charmless street of Edwardian terraces, but inside the rooms were spacious, the prices cheap (with a council mortgage at a mere two per cent), and for Sylvia it had the attraction of being only a couple of hundred yards from where she spent the first fifteen years of her life.

We never really loved Glenmore Road, or its pseudo-highland cousins Glenloch and Glenilla Roads, but somehow they did not seem to expect it. Nobody spoke to their neighbours, lace curtains were *de rigueur*, coal was tipped into the cellar through a coal-hole in the pavement, and the milkman had a horse and cart which spent all day dawdling round the neighbourhood depositing manure in the road-way, which I collected for our tiny garden. Central heating had not yet begun to catch on, though we had a voracious 'Ideal' boiler which ate coke in the kitchen.

There were more rooms than we really needed, so we let off the top floor to a succession of girl typists, some of them Australians from the newsroom. The first of these was Jill Neville.

Jill can't have been much more than eighteen, fresh in from Sydney, a delicious, vivacious redhead who was almost immediately invited out to Strasbourg by the donnish foreign duty editor – an adventure clearly recognisable in her novel *Fall Girl*. Jill was so pretty she had to wear a scowl all the way to the office to stop the men pestering her in the tube; and had I been Sylvia I would not have let such competition into the house. In the event it did not last long, for we turned out to be altogether too stodgy for the parties of merrymaking Australians that went whooping up to Jill's room. One night I had to put on my dressing-gown and suppress a madrigal-singing that had broken out, with Peter Porter in the choir. Goodness knows, one would be grateful for madrigals today in place of the heavy rock and reggae you would probably get from the lodgers. But Jill, now back in Belsize Park again, bears us no ill will and reviews my broadcasts kindly in her column in *The Sunday Times*.

The real trouble with the madrigals was that they might have woken up Jennet. Jennet (who got named after the heroine in Christopher Fry's *The Lady's Not For Burning*, which we thought the greatest thing since Shakespeare) arrived in September 1951 at the Elizabeth Garrett Anderson maternity home. She was born while I was writing the one o'clock news, thus starting a disgraceful tradition of my being an absentee at the birth of our children. The first visitor at Sylvia's bedside was Gerard Hoffnung with a pineapple. When I turned up two hours later I could hardly get to my rightful place on the grounds that 'the father has already been and that's all she's allowed for today'. Gerard, however, made up for the imposture by plying me with chianti from a flask which we drained together sitting on a bench on the pavement outside the hospital. We must have looked like a pair of well-to-do winos.

I had always hoped that our first child would be a girl. In fact all four of our children – a girl at each end and two boys in the middle – turned out to be exactly what I had ordered, though I think none of them was so intimately mine as Jennet. I wanted, I suppose, yet another female to adore me and be adored and the fact that Jennet had my mother's auburn colouring must have made her all the dearer. Everyone doted on her; but I am afraid that as she grew she picked up the anxiety that young parents lavish on their firstborn. Not that she was an anxious baby. Like most babies of the time she was left out-of-doors for hours on end in her pram, red-cheeked, cat-netted, muffled in woollies and mittens, and parked outside every pub in Hampstead at lunchtimes. Jennet was dosed daily with orange-juice and cod-liver oil from the government baby clinic and weaned on mashed kippers and a mush of tomato and grated cheese, which she loved. Rapidly she became quite fat and piggy-eyed.

Fortunately my mother was chief among the doters, parading her first grandchild proudly round Potten End while Sylvia and I took off for holidays in Provence, Majorca or Venice. With rather less enthusiasm my parents also put up with Lucretius the cat; they were really dog people and did not appreciate the seabirdlike squawls that make up Siamese conversation. We reduced the volume by having Lucretius doctored, rather late in life, but it left him with all the burliness and bossiness of an entire tom, and a fierce growl for anyone who dared to cross him.

On those holidays we indulged our taste for big Mediterranean seaports like Genoa, Marseilles, Barcelona. We ate, pottered, made love – in Marseilles once, checking into a seedy hotel, the concierge was astonished when we asked about breakfast next morning: 'Monsieur and mademoiselle wish to stay the whole night?' In Majorca we stayed in a villa rented by a hitherto unmentioned member of the Old Carthusian mafia, the historian Alistair Hennessy (now a professor, I think, at Warwick). Alistair was trying to write a book about a nineteenth-century Spanish radical by the name of Py y Margall, and failing to get much beyond chapter one, page one on account of the sun, the cheap food and a local liquor rejoicing in the name of *estomochal*. His villa was on the edge of the little town of Soller, dotted with English and American scholars snoozing over their chapter one, page ones, and when I produced a little gem-like verse about it, Alistair said it was more words than he had managed to write so far about Py:

> The palm of the island's hand *[I wrote]*
> Displays the town to the arrogant sun;
> The mountain fingers round it stand
> Wrinkled with terraces . . .

But the more I wrote for the BBC – hack-work though it was – the less energy there seemed to be for anything more imaginative. I still indulged in poetry from time to time when I got one of my chest complaints, which were sometimes as bad as pleurisy until I acquired a doctor who treated them with a mixture of antibiotics and antihistamines. Lying in bed with a high fever I slipped easily into the world of fantasy, producing once a series of surrealistic stanzas, and another time a pair of *rhyming* sestinas (which are almost as hard to write as a double fugue). But nobody speaks that kind of diction today – no one gives a damn about Helen of Troy and Deirdre of the Sorrows. There was not much poetry in me after that, apart from foolish clerihews and jingles for children. And for a couple of years I earned my beer-money winning the parody competitions in the *New Statesman*, sometimes two or three in one week under different pseudonyms like Francis Renny or Edward Gascoigne, concocted from various ancestors.

My BBC work became steadily better paid, but I realised that the only really creative and original work was to be found at the very coalface of the news, above all in the job of foreign correspondent. Correspondents actually witnessed the wars and assassinations and then attempted the magic trick of persuading listeners thousands of miles away to imagine *what it was like*. They were the travellers, in an age when travel was still an adventure and not just an expensive bus trip. They actually lived in places like New York, Singapore, Vienna, seldom coming home to where Tahu could cast his shadow over them. From time to time one of them would sweep through the newsroom like an explorer back from the Congo, and a name would by murmured from table to table: Guy Hadley! Robert Stimson! Thomas Cadett! Christopher Serpell, Our Man in Rome, I admired especially because although very little of importance happened in Italy, he made enormous fun out of what there was: allegedly miraculous statues that wept on the roofs of cathedrals, elephants that got loose in spaghetti factories, bank robbers disguised as nuns and long-lost Leonardos that turned out to have been painted on twentieth-century plywood – all of this elegantly written and performed in impeccably BBC tones.

The procedure for becoming a foreign correspondent was nerve-racking. Once a year the shortlist or 'panel' was thrown open and one could apply for admission to it. If accepted you were given a little experience as a home reporter and even sent abroad on limited excursions like a flood in Holland or a small earthquake in Portugal, but there was no promise of a permanent posting and little warning when you got one.

I suspect I got my place on the panel by volunteering for India. Nobody went there willingly – it was a notorious hardship post and communications were so bad that one seldom got on the air – but I was fascinated by the romance of the place and imagined I could hear ancestral voices calling me to the land of my mother's mercenary forbears. In any event, the foreign news department accepted me with the warning that nothing might come of it or that I might end up somewhere totally different.

For a few months I was attached to the reporters' unit which, as I have said, was excluded from the news bulletins and confined to covering very safe stories for Radio Newsreel. The safest of stories were those involving the non-controversial activities of the royal family, and these were the special preserve of Mr Godfrey Talbot and Miss Audrey Russell who spent much of their time jealously ma-noeuvring for the advantage over one another. On one occasion – it was the opening of the St Lawrence Seaway in Canada – I found myself sandwiched between the two of them: Godfrey was at one end of the canal, Audrey at the other, while I was perched on a bridge in the middle. The idea was to describe the stately progress of the royal yacht *Britannia* as she entered the Seaway, passed under my bridge and emerged at the far end. But our two stars had purchased powerful binoculars enabling them to follow the ship for miles. Godfrey pursued her with salvos of ecstatic prose right past my position, whereupon Audrey snatched her from him and carried her on, cutting me out completely. I never got a word in.

What I was allowed to do was exhibitions. Radio Newsreel loved exhibitions and the more obscure they were, the less likely to have dangerously contentious aspects that might raise complaints, the better. My very first assignment as a reporter was to do four minutes about an exhibition of dolls' houses. They were, I reported, very pretty and far too good for children to play with. The reporting organiser shuddered. 'That, Priestland, is your *opinion*. It is not *news*. You may, however, say – if it is true – that in the view of *some observers* to whom you spoke they were too good for children to play with.' Thus I was introduced to that useful but shadowy body, the Royal and Ancient Corps of Observers, some of whom are to be found at any event where reporters are present, ready to give their opinion. Observers believe, *some* observers believe, diplomatic observers believe almost anything that commonsense calls for them to believe; and they are most willing to be quoted provided one does not give their names. (Observers are a shy lot who invariably 'prefer not to be identified'. It will be noted also that they always go round in the plural, speaking in unison.)

Sometimes there were interviews to be done, as when a portion of Sussex was found to be sliding into the sea and I was sent off to ascertain the views of those affected. This was before the BBC had brought itself to embrace magnetic tape recording and the portable recording machine; recordings were still made by cutting gramophone records, and when a reporter went forth to interview he did so in a Humber Pullman limousine the size of a hearse, with a small gramophone record factory in the rear. This was operated by a qualified engineer who also drove the hearse, parking it as close as possible to the scene of the interview and then laying yards and yards of thick black cable into the house. On his expense sheet afterwards, the reporter always entered an item 'To help with cable – ten shillings'.

Interviews in the early 1950s were still very gentle affairs; the victims, who today have seen it all on television and are itching to have a go, were usually paralysed with fear. The roughest one ever got with them was, 'Would you care to make a statement about the coastal erosion in these parts?' Having stopped and started the record factory several times with cries of 'lift' (to lift the cutting head) one secured as near perfect a version as possible, since editing was out of the question on disk, and then made one's way back to the car, reeling in the cable. By now the back seat would be full of the shavings or 'swarf' produced by the cutting head. These would be kicked out into the road, the car driven to safety some yards off and then, with a cry of ' 'ware swarf!' the engineer would toss a lighted match into the heap. The result was spectacular, like an early nuclear test, for the swarf was some kind of highly inflammable varnish that sent smoke and flames high into the air and, on my first encounter with it, removed my eyebrows.

It was fun enough hurtling round southern England in the Pullman, but the innocence of the stories soon palled. I told Sylvia that if something did not happen soon I might think about trying to move over to Fleet Street. It never quite came to that: early in 1954 the BBC told me that for a few months it was sending me to the Paris office to be 'one of Mr Cadett's young men'.

Tom Cadett had been *The Times*'s Paris correspondent before the war, had the satisfaction of liberating his old flat in St Cloud (it had been beautifully maintained by the Gestapo) and was then engaged by the BBC as its principal correspondent in Europe. He settled down to chronicling the endless permutations of government under the Fourth Republic which he understood so well that while he broadcast in

English, he actually *thought* in French and used terms like 'political personalities' instead of 'politicians'.

The BBC maintained a stately office in the Avenue Hoche, near the Etoile, from whose windows one could observe most of the riots and demonstrations of the day. It had become the practice for hopefuls 'on the panel' to be sent over to help Tom in the exercise of his trade and in the hope that they would either break or triumph under the strain.

I lived at the Hotel Astrid, near the office. The routine was that one rose early, bought the morning papers and then telephoned Tom in bed at St Cloud and read him the headlines. 'Nothing that demands my presence *actuellement*,' he would yawn. 'You might do London a piece for one o'clock about the strike on the *chemins-de-fer*. I shall be lunching with a man from the Embassy, so I'll be along about four to do something for Radio Newsreel. Don't forget to answer the telephone in French.'

After a couple of weeks Tom decided that this particular young man would probably do. 'The Corporation owes me a great deal of leave,' he announced, 'so I think I'll push off to my island.' And he departed for the Ile de Ré where he had a holiday cottage.

I was not quite on my own, for I had Tom's secretary, Eva Dreyfus, to hold my hand and there was a steady flow of conspiratorial phone-calls from two tip-off men in the Quai D'Orsay and the National Assembly, paying back Tom's lunchtime investments in them. My temporary posting to Paris made no provision for Sylvia to be with me, but by living stingily I managed to save up enough to bring her over for a week to join me at the Astrid.

She arrived and all hell immediately broke loose. Two French governments fell, and the garrison of Dien Bien Phu, and de Gaulle, who had been sulking, marched up the Champs Elysées to seize power. One could hardly get into the office for riot police. Instead of guiding Sylvia round the cafés and *chansonneries*, I had to spend most nights in the press gallery of the Assembly watching the Republic disintegrate.

'Can't I come too?' asked Sylvia pleadingly. Already I was coming to the conclusion – now a conviction – that work and wives don't mix, but the tip-off man got me a ticket to the public gallery and I pushed Sylvia off down one of the corridors with instructions to ask the gendarmes the way, while I clambered up into the press benches. Looking down into the chamber I was startled to see a door swing open and my wife take a seat – though not exactly *her* seat – among the independent deputies from overseas. She perused the order papers, gave me a little wave and indicated her pleasure at the extraordinarily close view she was getting. After a minute or two there was an agitated twittering among the members around her and Sylvia was politely escorted out, only to reappear in one of the diplomatic boxes. 'There were these Africans,' she told me afterwards, 'they kept telling me 'Trompée, trompée . . .'. 'I think they meant you'd made a mistake,' I said. 'It's a good thing that wasn't the House of Commons or you'd have spent the night in a dungeon.'

After almost a month Cadett came back. 'I've been monitoring you on the wireless,' he said crisply. 'Not bad – not bad at all. Nothing like going in at the deep end if you're going to learn to swim.' Limply I thanked him for the opportunity, and indeed after that baptism of fire nothing was ever quite so terrifying again.

Back in London there were two or three months of anticlimax and then I was summoned to Tahu's presence. 'Richard Williams is leaving Delhi. We would like you to take his place as correspondent for India, Pakistan, Burma and Ceylon.' I said it was an honour; I would do my best to justify his confidence . . . Tahu raised a hand. 'We *hope* you can do it,' he said ponderously. 'You must *believe* you can do it. But until you have demonstrated that you can we shall not send your family to join you. You will be on probation, on your own, for a minimum of six months. We wish you to leave in six weeks' time.'

As it happened, Sylvia was pregnant with our second child and would have been in no condition to travel so soon; but the terms of the appointment were sheer cruelty. It was true that I was only twenty-six, the youngest correspondent that the BBC ever appointed, but if he had not been sure of his judgment Tahu should not have sent me. It meant that Sylvia was left to bear her child while I was on the other side of the globe, and I had to make my reputation in the strangest of strange lands without anyone to come home to at the end of the day. Still, I was in no position to bargain and I knew from observation that correspondents who complained soon fell out of favour. Willingness to go was half the battle, so I accepted on the spot. Explaining the snag to Sylvia was more painful and I again felt guilty about using her as a step-ladder to my ambitions.

But the families rallied round, promising to look after her, and I found reassurance in the shape of my new immediate boss, the foreign editor, Tony Wigan. Tony was a world-weary but humane man with a deeply furrowed face who bore for us correspondents all the sins of the world. Tahu regularly crucified him, but Tony passed little of it on, regarding it as his function to filter out anything that might interfere with us doing our job and to expedite anything that would help. Correspondents are, by nature, prima donnas, all too ready to sniff slights and conspiracies in the wind, but Tony and his admin. girl Audrey (who became his second wife) were skilled at calming us down, tactful in building us up and marvellously reliable in cabling money or collecting children off aeroplanes or shipping crates of furniture round the world (there was one correspondent who could not function without regular shipments of Branston pickle through the diplomatic bag).

And so, in November 1954, I set off to conquer the world; or at least India, Pakistan, Ceylon and Burma. Correspondents nowadays are lucky to fly second class; then it was always first, with free drinks in the VIP lounge, meals served course by course on bone china and invitations from the captain to join him in the cockpit over the Alps. Over the Alps the pressurisation failed and the aircraft, a modest propeller-driven Constellation, spent most of the next day on the ground at Rome while the passengers were taken sightseeing as guests of BOAC. We loitered again at Cairo for a civilised dinner and showers, and reached Karachi twenty-four hours late. Timetables rarely had much connection with reality.

My first sight of Asia staggered me. Crouched along the roof of the terminal building, arms propped on their knees like cormorants drying their wings, were a score of native workmen in rags. They stared down at me, with that neutral Third World stare that gives away nothing; I stared up at them, thinking, 'This is the four-fifths of the world you've never met. Can you come to terms with it?'

Karachi was always a hideous place, with the Sind desert behind it and the stagnant swamps in front. Its most distinguished architecture was the huge shed built to receive airships, which stood empty at the edge of the airfield dropping sheets of corrugated iron so that no one dared go near it. Any spare room in Karachi was crowded with refugee slums wallowing in sewage. The streets boiled with the traffic of three centuries – ancient camel carts, Victorian tongas pulled by emaciated ponies, and the smart cars owned by dealers in import licences. The pavements were stained with blood-red splashes of betel juice. Women walked about wearing dirty-white tentlike burqas. The sun was exhausting. The smell echoed everything you could see in all its corruption.

One stayed, one could only stay, at the Metropole Hotel, where the band kept you awake at night and nobody trusted the water (it was hard to believe any water could be trustworthy in such a city). But the BBC was fussy about paying for beer and I was at a loss how to justify it until I saw an item in *Dawn*, the Muslim League newspaper: 'Three blind beggars found drowned in the Drigh Road reservoir'. I pinned it to my expenses and drank beer ever after. After two or three gastro-intestinal upsets my guts did, in fact, adjust very well to the subcontinent and to this day I can eat my way round it without qualms. Either your stomach can take India or it can't; and if it can't you had better leave before it gets you down. Certainly a foreign correspondent with weak guts will be as useful there as a sewerman with claustrophobia.

Tony Wigan had instructed me in 'setting up camp procedure' and I followed it to the letter. Before anything else – before unpacking – ring up the resident Reuter man in case there is a story going on *now*; ask him to tip you off when there is (after all, you are one of his principal subscribers). Then invite him and his wife out to a lavish dinner as soon as possible, at which you may pick his brains. Next, call up the information officer at the British Embassy or High Commission – a source of evening invitations if nothing else. Third, establish your credentials with the government of the country you are visiting; and check your communications, which will include the radio studio, telegraph office and air freight for recordings or film. In those days, intelligible phone-calls to London were still out of the question from South Asia and telex was unheard of.

Hardly had I put up my professional tent when a story fell into my lap. The Governor General of Pakistan, the now utterly forgotten Ghulam Mohammed, decided to suppress the assembly which after several years' wrangling had still not produced a constitution for the country. Unlike India, where Independence, for all its bloodshed, was very much a transfer of power, carried out with considerable efficiency by the Congress and its hatchet-man Sirdar Patel, Pakistan had never (and still has not) got its act together. Congress India was founded upon some very positive ideas; but Pakistan was based solely on the negative conviction that Muslims could not live with Hindus. When the dust of Partition died down, Pakistan found itself with two wings as widely separated by culture as by a thousand miles of hostile territory; a political set-up riven by feudal loyalties; a desperate shortage of civil servants and technicians; an untenable strategic and economic situation – in short, a legacy of nonsense. Almost the only positive resources it had were religious unity and military tradition, but both of these were overstressed: they were never enough to make the dream succeed. India brooded malevolently in the middle, never forgiving the amputation of her outer limbs and happy to sponsor anyone who would hasten the destruction of the Muslim upstart.

Into all this I waded happily and began filing off dispatches explaining to London what had gone wrong and what Ghulam Mohammed might do next. Wigan reacted protectively: Don't run before you can walk, please take the first plane to Delhi and settle in there before holding forth as an expert. Reluctantly I abandoned Karachi to stew in its own noisome juices and flew on to Delhi and the arms of Mother India.

Chapter Five

THE LAND OF SPICES

Delhi is three inhabited cities and three or four more in ruins on the plains round about. It was a good place for battles. Ignoring South India (as Delhi habitually does) it is centrally placed between the fertile Punjab, the deserts of Rajasthan and the crowded corridor of the Ganges past Benares and Lucknow to Calcutta. The British, who preferred seaports, came to Delhi reluctantly and did not make it their imperial capital until long after they had deposed the last doddering Mogul from his pavilions in the Red Fort. They came to an essentially Muslim city and built their own white man's suburb, the Civil Lines, outside the walls to the north. New Delhi, to the south, was not started until 1911 nor inaugurated until 1931. It has been spreading ever since with a careless profusion of huge international hotels, conference centres and All-India institutes of this, that and the other; but its central composition – Connaught Place, the Viceroy's Palace, the Government Secretariat and the Parliament House – remain altogether worthy of a great nation, a splendid leaving present from its alien mentors. The long avenues were planted with trees and the old forts and tombs were protected as they had never been before. No other capital in modern Asia (with the possible exception of Peking, which I do not know) offers such a picture-book of its own history.

Richard Williams had bequeathed me accommodation in the Cecil Hotel in the Civil Lines. This meant that in order to get to Parliament House or the government offices and embassies one had to drive through the middle of the Old City, which was laborious but instructive. It gave me a daily reminder that India was like a sheet of plywood with a thin veneer of mid-twentieth century glued over layers of the nineteenth, seventeenth and even earlier centuries, all hanging together somehow and forming an amazingly strong and flexible whole.

Jam-packed with bureaucrats and refugees, Delhi had little to spare in the way of private housing, so the international press corps had adopted the Cecil as its professional ghetto and, incidentally, a convenient way of keeping an eye on one another. The Reuter correspondents, Peter and Adrienne Jackson, did have a combined flat and office in the centre of town; and Felix Nagar, the gay representative of the French News Agency, had a classic bungalow hung with tiger-skins near the India Gate; but almost everyone else was to be found on the bougainvillea-hung verandahs of the Cecil Hotel. There were no lifts or coffee-shop or air-conditioning; the place was more like what it eventually became, a Jesuit seminary. No concessions were made to the natives and Indians seldom stayed there – they would probably have been shown to the servants' quarters at the bottom of the drive, for it was assumed that guests would bring their personal staff with them to serve them in their rooms. Dinner was offered by turbaned bearers with white gloves, invariably starting with hot soup (whatever the weather) and working its way down the *table d'hôte* through fish and meat to steamed pudding with custard, welsh rarebit and finally candied fruits with the coffee.

At the tables were to be found Louis Heren of *The Times*, Philip Deane of the *Observer*, Colonel Harold Milks and his assistant Gene Levine of the Associated Press of America, Johnnie Hlavacek of United Press, Kenneth Ames of the *Daily Mail* and, from time to time, visiting firemen like James Cameron of the *News Chronicle* and René McColl of the *Daily Express*. All the resident correspondents were married and had wives with them, and the pregnancy rate gave rise to the rumour that there was something in the water of the swimming-pool that stimulated conception. More likely was the fact that ayahs – nursemaids – were easily come by and everyone was taking advantage of the opportunity while they were in India.

Twice a year we were joined by the Kendal troupe, a family of actors who roved India doing Shakespeare in princely palaces and pseudo-English public schools and were eventually filmed by Merchant and Ivory acting out their own story as *Shakespeare Wallahs*. There was also a large and amiable man called Ted, with a voice like the Man in Black, who professed to be working for a features agency nobody had ever heard of. He would press his service upon you for nothing – it consisted of stupefyingly dull stories that were not worth paying for – and it did not take long to figure out that its real purpose was to provide cover for his activities as a spymaster, presumably On Our Side. Tony Wigan had implored me not to get mixed up in that kind of sideline (I am a little hurt to report that no one ever tried to recruit me), but so many colleagues had been involved in intelligence during the war that I find it hard to believe they all of them gave it up afterwards.

Spying in India cannot have been very difficult, for such Indian secrets as there were could be bought quite easily from badly paid government clerks. Philip Deane (who, being Greek, revelled in conspiracy) used to spread External Affairs Ministry documents on his verandah to photograph them; and I myself had to fight off a little man who tried to win my support for a job with the BBC by offering me Defence Ministry reports on skirmishes between Indian and Chinese border patrols. I was too scared to use them – they would certainly have been denied – but in fact they were perfectly true and finally blew up into the 1962 India-China War. The myth at the time, however, back in 1955, was that Indians and Chinese were brothers – 'Hindi Chini bhai-bhai' as the slogan had it – and that their joint signatures to the sacred Five Principles of Peaceful Co-existence would ward off all evil. In fact the essence of Indian foreign policy was, as it remains, to deprive Pakistan of every possible ally and source of support, or – if Pakistan had acquired any – to make friends with the ally's enemy. Thus if Pakistan allied herself with the United States, India should make friends with the communists; and if Pakistan later secured tanks from the Chinese, India would sign up with the Russians. India went out of her way to ingratiate herself with the Muslim Arabs and would almost certainly have quit the Commonwealth but for the fact that Pakistan did so first.

It is perfectly true that Pakistan operated on the same principle of 'anything you do – I'll do the opposite' and that the succession of military regimes on which Pakistan embarked made her a quarrelsome and unreliable neighbour, intoxicated with the old British legend that one Muslim soldier was worth four Hindus; but there has always been something neurotic about the Indian response, which makes me suspect that Delhi will never feel at ease until Pakistan has been permanently neutralised. The hiving off of East Pakistan as Bangladesh – an efficient piece of work by the Indian Army – has done half the job. The rest might be achieved, as a senior Hindu diplomat once daydreamed to me, by letting the Northwest Frontier Province go to the Afghans, Baluchistan to the Iranians, while India 'resumed' the West Punjab and Sind.

Underlying it all is the almost sexual feeling among Hindus that Partition ravished Mother India, lopping off her limbs so that she almost bled to death. Politically, India never was one until the British united her, and then rather loosely; but that the Muslims should want to secede from her seems to the Hindus a kind of blasphemy. Of all the cultures that have come to India, they feel, only Islam has refused to integrate and become a branch of Hindu civilisation. There is a deep ambivalence here: on the one hand you are reminded that there are more Muslims in India than there are in Pakistan; on the other, 'We are well rid of those trouble-makers across the border'.

The joint neurosis was summed up in the Kashmir problem. At first sight the huge state, with its Muslim majority, ought to have gone to Pakistan. But Jammu province had many Sikhs and Hindus and even the central valley was also the homeland of the upper-crust Kashmiri pundits, to whom the Nehru family belonged. Its mountains were sacred to Hindus and its ruling princes were Hindu or Sikh. The terms of Partition gave the ruler the choice of where his state should go. When the Maharaja understandably hesitated and finally opted for India, the savage Pathans of the Northwest Frontier tried to grab Kashmir for Pakistan. It ended up divided by the sword with India controlling the best bits, Pakistan the outer wildernesses and most Kashmiris hankering unrealistically for a country of their own like Nepal.

Ironically in South India the situation was reversed. The Nizam of Hyderabad was a Muslim prince ruling a Hindu majority; but when *he* opted for a country of his own, the Indian Army marched in and the state was dismembered. That was realistic but not very principled. The ruler's choice was paramount when it suited India, but not when it didn't. Nevertheless, Hyderabad was forgotten while Kashmir grumbled on, providing correspondents with a happy excuse to get away to the mountains whenever the Delhi weather became intolerable. All that was really necessary was to persuade a few newspaper colleagues to come too, so that one's editor in London, studying the papers, would find one's judgment confirmed.

One advantage of Delhi was that it was five-and-a-half hours ahead of Greenwich, so that if you rounded up the day's events at midnight it would still catch the evening bulletins in London. Press cables were still a penny a word, and twice a week I could broadcast in my own voice by borrowing All India Radio's shortwave transmitter for the BBC to pick up and record for re-broadcasting. The disadvantage of this was that colleagues who knew the wavelength could eavesdrop and steal my stories before London had transmitted them officially.

A routine day in Delhi usually began with a visit to the Lok Sabha, the Indian House of Commons, where most of the business was still conducted in English, South Indians in particular being reluctant to use the national but Northern language of Hindi. Nothing much happened in the early afternoon, respected as siesta-time, but about tea-time I set out on 'the rounds': the External Affairs Ministry, the Press Information Bureau (which issued a torrent of handouts including something called the Semi-annual Estimate of Rape – about oilseed), possibly the information department of the British High Commission, and a few Indian contacts. Some of these you kept on a retainer, others were flattered to be consulted for nothing, or even called at your office to deliver their gossip. Among these was the extraordinary Nirad Chaudhuri, who made it his special mission to stop me getting romantic or mystical ideas about Hinduism, of which he was a great debunker.

Above all else Nirad was a *Bengali* gentleman of letters. No one should miss reading his *Autobiography of an Unknown Indian*. But his knowledge of English literature was almost as great as that of Bengali and his written use of the English language almost as elegant. When he at last visited England – by courtesy of the BBC and the British Council – he knew exactly what he would find there and when he returned he announced with satisfaction that it had all been as he had expected. He took the trouble to visit my parents for tea, perching himself upon a small coffee table which they were too polite to tell him was not a stool. It did no harm, since Nirad was about the size, weight (and chattiness) of a starling. Eventually he quit India for good and settled with distinction in Oxford, dressing always as a Bengali indoors and an English gentleman when out.

To my relief I found that cut-throat competition scarcely existed among my Delhi colleagues. The *Mail* and the *Express* were always trying to scoop one another with increasingly outrageous stories (*Mail man arrested stop why you at liberty query* Beaverbrook once cabled his reporter), but the rest of us saw little point in adding to the trials of a trying climate and exchanged notes freely. It was the agencies' job to belt out the facts and figures; the Specials took more leisurely care of the background, interpretation, interviews and colour. In a country as alarming as India, company away from base was very welcome; so we tended to hunt the major stories in a pack, usually organised by Colonel Harold Milks of the American Associated Press. Colonel Milks, a portentous figure with a toothbrush moustache and a dead-pan expression, lived in an apartment in the Cecil Hotel entirely surrounded by skins of tigers, noble creatures which he had personally massacred as the guest of various maharajas. He would also career across the Punjab by night, in a jeep, mowing down black buck and blue bull (or maybe the other way round) which he stored in the hotel freezer and issued to friends when they tired of the restaurant's water-buffalo. Mrs Milks – Evelyn – did not join him in the killing; she stayed with the air-conditioning, playing cards and drinking gin-and-water.

Colonel Milks hated a disorganised rabble. When a press expedition was inevitable he would make all the bookings, buy all the tickets and circulate Roneoed orders, thus: 'Operation Bombay Riots – Correspondents will parade on platform 2, Old Delhi Station at 1800hrs tomorrow for the Bombay Mail. Equipment to include portable typewriter, bedding roll, 2 bottles Scotch (NOT Indian), light reading and cash for poker (minimum stake 1 rupee). NB: Do NOT forget Scotch, Bombay is PROHIBITION TERRITORY.'

It only took me one such trip to learn not to play poker with Americans – and never with Colonel Milks. I had imagined that his deadpan face had something to do with his sense of humour, but after three hours in a railway compartment with him I realised that it had become a fixture from years of poker-playing. I never did get the hang of his sudden announcements that 'red threes are wild!' or 'guess I'll sweeten the freakpot!'

The first such outing I went on was to Madras, where the Indian National Congress was holding its annual convention. Madras issued dissolute Europeans with ration-books for liquor (it still does), so as the junior correspondent I was dispatched to draw the entire party's supply, returning in a taxi with a month's entitlement which took even us a week's hard drinking to get through. Fortunately there was not much news to be drawn from the convention. These affairs were more like colossal folk-festivals arranged for scores of thousands of Indians to 'have darshan' (that is, to bask in the charisma) of their leaders, especially of Pundit Jawarharlal Nehru, Prime Minister and anointed of Gandhi. For the Madras rally a fantastic stadium had been constructed by the Tamil film studios out of old sets of temples and palaces, and around its perimeter various public-spirited organisations had set up pavilions. 'Come inside, dear sir!' cried the man from the All-India Health Ministry, plucking at my bush-shirt. 'Come inside for free syphilis test! By tomorrow you will know the worst!'

One of my first discoveries about India was that in spite of being an obviously well-to-do imperialist entirely surrounded by poverty, one was perfectly safe in these enormous crowds. Nobody stabbed you or robbed you or even jostled you – indeed, if you started giving them orders they instinctively obeyed, and if you marched past policemen in order to get where you had no right to be they usually snapped to attention and saluted. Imperial instincts die hard and it was a constant temptation to exploit them. In one corner of Andhra State, eight years after Independence, I came across an English Collector with his English police sergeant running their district as if the Viceroy were still in Delhi.

After the uproar of Madras I pushed off down the coast to watch Nehru take possession of Pondicherry, the last of the tiny French settlements in India. The French language was spoken widely if not too well and the native police wore gendarme caps, but the only regrets anyone had about changing flags concerned alcohol. I found more serious drinking to be done in the French Club, whose members were polishing off the champagne before the Madras prohibition squad moved in. When Nehru arrived, by train, he was far from pleased with what he found. The reception committee were all tipsy and the police had pushed them to the rear of the platform and were confronting them suspiciously, uncertain whose side they were on. With a little cry of rage Nehru hurled himself at their rear, belabouring them with his swagger-stick, crying, 'All I ever see in this country is policemen's backs!' The reception committee cheered happily.

Even so, Nehru was not quite truthful, for he spent much of his time on ornate rostrums, all over India, lecturing the multitudes on the evils they were so obstinately attached to such as astrology, incantations, dowries, cow-worship, untouchability and the many unshakable prejudices peculiar to their castes and regions. They listened respectfully, understanding hardly a word of what 'Pundijee' was saying (for he spoke to them either in English or bad kitchen-Urdu), and then went on committing the evils he had just denounced. It could hardly be otherwise, for India is not China and never will be; Indians are not Chinese, to be turned in their tracks like vast regimented armies. Nehru might preach the virtues of scientific socialism and five-year planning, and looking about you at the poverty and squalor you sympathised with him; but it was made endurable by traditional Hinduism, and if anyone was allergic to collectivism it was the Hindus.

That may seem a reactionary stand to take. How can you defend casteism (so much crueller than western racism) or the ruthless exploitation of the poor by rich landlords and moneylenders? The answer is that you cannot justify any single case. But in its own extraordinary way the system works, even though it ought not to, and to break it would take a bloodbath. There were times when I found myself writing: 'This country is doomed; if it does not starve to death or perish of the plague it will surely explode in bloody revolution.' But India has done none of those things.

Riots and uprisings have continued at much the same level as under the British. The numbers shot by the army and police have maintained a pretty constant average over the century, for there is no magic formula for governing Indian peacefully – Gandhianism was always a reaction, not a natural product. And who would *want* to govern India? The mood in Britain when we quit was not (as I remember it) one of humiliation but of huge relief. We were too tired to hold her down.

Over the past thirty years the population of India has almost doubled, which seemed impossible. At a modest level it now feeds itself and standards of living have slightly risen, both of which seemed impossible. In a ramshackle way things sort of kind of work, more or less; and far from having fallen prey to military dictatorship or Marxist terror, a corrupt but practical democracy has taken root and will not, I think, be overthrown. All of this not because bureaucrats and party cadres have hammered India into the mould of a socialist people's republic, but because while modern technology has managed to do its best under the circumstances India has remained India, Hindu India, endlessly patient, fatalistic if you will, with each individual keeping faith with his or her immutable destiny and not expecting any spectacular improvement in it. What really matters is the family and maintaining its place in the social and religious framework. There *is* a culture, a civilisation, but there is barely a state, in the Marxist or liberal sense. If those in authority choose to cry slogans in favour of the Five Year Plan it is as well to shout one's approval; but in the end it is an illusion. A peasant in Haryana, near Delhi, once told me, 'I remember when Mahmud of Ghazni came here.' (He meant the tenth century!) 'And then the Moguls, and then the British, and now it is Congress and soon it will be communists – it is all a question of who has the biggest stick and who takes whose buffalo first . . .'

Contrary to the belief of many westerners, India is not a profoundly spiritual country but a profoundly materialistic one. The object of most religious practice is to ensure material success. The twist is, however, that nobody has much confidence that material achievements will last or that attempts to interfere with fate will bring anything but trouble in the long run. Once, in the state of Orissa, I attended the inauguration of a great irrigation dam, and when the speeches and ceremonious sluice-gate openings were over I decided to see where all this water was going; so I followed the grand canal to a branch canal and the branch canal to a distributory channel which eventually came to a stop about a mile outside a village. I walked across and found the village schoolmaster to interpret for me.

'You must be looking forward to the water coming,' I said.

'Oh no we're not,' said the villagers. 'We've seen what happened to the village over there when *they* took it. First, they charge you something called a betterment levy. They say you'll be able to pay for it out of bigger crops. It's true, the crops are bigger; so are your taxes. As things are, we grow just enough to live on. If we grow more, we'll have to send it away to market. The women will have to do that, and they'll go off to the town and spend money on things and get into trouble with men. So we're not having *that*, thank you, Government can keep its water – we're not fools!'

The really extraordinary thing about Hinduism is that, far from producing a grim and depressed society, it produces one that is full of music and dancing, brilliant colours, feasts and festivals. When, later, I was posted to the Middle East I was struck by the drabness and dourness of the Arabs compared with the Indians, and by how much more the Arabs complained in spite of their relative prosperity. I would not wish to be a Hindu myself – anyway, they are born, not made – but Hinduism has served India well. Indeed, it *is* India rather than a religion (in which capacity I find Hinduism defective for *my* needs and experience).

Nehru himself was an old-fashioned Fabian agnostic, really a brown Englishman of the Webbs and Shaw generation. After the death of Sirdar Patel there was nobody of his intellectual class left in the Congress leadership (apart from the abrasive Krishna Menon), and Nehru much preferred European company when he could find it. At press conferences he would perk up when, having politely left the first dozen questions to Indian reporters, the foreign correspondents stepped in with the broader issues he appreciated. It never seemed to me, however, that he had a particularly astute political mind. He was no more obviously brilliant than the average English headmaster or Oxbridge don, whom he so much resembled in conversation. But he had other qualities which, put together, made him the leader his country needed in the dangerous early years of her independence.

I suppose the key word is charisma. Some of it clung to Nehru from his association with Gandhi, the Father of the Nation, at whose side he was so often seen. But they believed in two different Indias, the India of the spinning-wheel and the India of the power-station, and while

Gandhi's charisma was that of a rather wily saint, Nehru's was that of a modern prince. For a start, he was strikingly handsome, even in middle age. Nobody looked more debonair in laughter. His fair complexion and Aryan features established him as an aristocrat among Indians (who are terrible colour-snobs) and his Kashmiri origins put that beyond question. He might claim to be an agnostic, but everyone knew he was also a Pundit, a Brahmin. Nehru squirmed when greeters put dabs of vermilion on his forehead and hung garlands round his neck.

Like the best of the British who educated him, and like his father Motilal before him, he had a profound sense of public service and of duty to his people. I say 'his' people because it seems to me that in a House-of-Windsor way Jawarharlal Nehru developed a sense of *royalty* that was really the essence of his powers. It was as if he had been born and brought up to the job. He knew that he had to do it, that only he could do it, so he did it with modesty yet authority and never failed to be fascinated by the way it worked with the crowds.

Not that he was under any illusion as to its short-lived effect on their behaviour: even that could not deter him from carrying on to the end, for royalty is not brought up to abdicate. And, as we see in Nehru's daughter and grandson, it continues by inheritance. To India nothing seems more natural. The doctrine of a strong, interventionist central government, established by the British Raj, has been intensified. As the quality of provincial politicians has declined, that doctrine has become increasingly necessary; for left to itself Indian politics rapidly balkanises into separate states, each ambitious for its own boundaries, speaking its own regional language and run by its dominant local caste. Majorities in state assemblies are bought and sold like cattle or, if stubborn, whacked into submission by hired thugs known as *goondas*. Two can play that game. During an election campaign in Andhra I was taken round a small town by S. K. Patil, Mayor of Bombay and a celebrated fixer on behalf of the Congress central government. 'Once, Gerald, Congress volunteers dared not show their faces here for communist goondas. Now the communists dare not come – *Congress* goondas!'

It was, I suppose, marginally less outrageous than Pakistan, where I once found the Chief Minister of Sind forcing his budget through the state assembly by packing the benches with uniformed men bearing rifles. They cheered the administration speakers and rattled their bolts when the opposition dared to rise. 'What are these soldiers doing here?' I asked. 'It doesn't look very democratic.' 'Soldiers?' cried the

Chief Minister, 'but those are policemen! You have them in your House of Commons – I know, I have seen them.' 'But they don't carry guns and they don't come and lounge in the chamber . . .' 'Poor fellows,' said the Chief Minister indulgently, 'it is hot. The guns are heavy. They need to sit down.'

Nothing quite so blatant happened in India, or not in my time, though I suppose Mrs Gandhi's Emergency came close to it later. It is hard to imagine her father behaving in so unBritish a way. But for all that I have said, there *was*, deep down in Nehru, a layer of Hinduism which was exposed as he grew older. He patronised a handsome, statuesque young swami who gave public displays of regurgitating jugs of water and being run over by a streamroller; though the Prime Minister went no further than standing on his head occasionally. Indira Gandhi was more thoroughly Hindu. She co-ordinated her politics with her horoscope, built up the swami into something like the Billy Graham of New Delhi, and towards the end of his life persuaded her father to undergo an elaborate 'death-conquering ritual' at the Birla Temple, in which a healing *mantra* was recited over the old man 425,000 times. Nothing would have been more calculated to enrage the Nehru of the 1950s.

Little more than a month after my arrival in Delhi the telegram came announcing the birth of our first son, whom we had decided to call Andreas after the Manx connection. 'Nunc dimittis,' wrote my father, 'for I have seen my grandson.' But it was another four months before London grudgingly agreed that I had proved myself as a correspondent and allowed Sylvia and the two children to fly out and join me at the very hottest time of the year.

I was at the bottom of the ramp when Jennet appeared in the doorway, her head afroth with copper curls, waving one foot at me and piping, 'Look, Daddy, *new shoes!*' I was already in tears by the time Sylvia scrambled down with the bundle that was Andreas, and all his bags and bottles. I had re-engaged Richard Williams's old bearer, Sammy Singh, who awaited us at the Cecil bursting with pride that his sahib had produced a *chota sahib* as well as a mere *chota memsahib*. Jennet (the chota memsahib) took one look at his dusky Indian smile and whispered in my ear that 'Sammy has got a dirty face'. I don't think it is possible to be racist at the age of three.

Besides Sammy, Williams had bequeathed me an office secretary and a driver. The secretary, Mrs Lawrence, was an Anglo-Indian like a little old village postmistress. With her high Welsh accent one could imagine her counting out gob-stoppers and stamping postal-orders five miles from Aberystwyth. The widow of an Anglo-Indian rail-wayman, with two grown daughters on her hands, she knew the favoured days of her community were at an end and laboured hard to get the girls out of the country before they fell into the error of marrying Indians. Off they went to Australia, where their mother eventually joined them and where I saw her, thirty years later, chirruping as merrily as ever, quite ageless.

The driver was probably straightforward Hari Ram, like several million other Indians, but insisted on being called *Harris* Ram in support of his unlikely claim to European blood. Being a Christian, of whom there were not many about in Delhi, he felt he needed all the prestige he could get. Ram was honest enough where money was concerned and drove the underpowered Ford Consul with restraint; but he suffered from an alarming tendency to visions, which he would disclose to me as we ground through the Old Delhi bazaar:

'Sahib, last night one *angel* show me very bad thing going to happen Punjab side.'

'Oh. Really.'

'Sahib, I see *too* many people making *too* much *berludd*.'

'Ah.'

'Sahib, I am seeing coming jungly people shoot-shoot-shooting Punjab side. You make broadcast, tell whole world.'

'But Ram, when is this going to happen, and where exactly? The Punjab is a big place.'

'Sorry I am not yet knowing, Sahib. Happen soon-soon, I think. We go Punjab side tomorrow?'

'Ram, London will not like us wasting time driving around the Punjab looking for jungly people. You find out place and time, *then* we go Punjab side.'

'Very good, Sahib. I pray Jesus-Christ He send one more angel tell me tonight.' But He didn't.

Sometimes I would get Ram to drive me about Delhi as I took photographs of market stalls, holy men, bodies burning on funeral pyres and other images of the East. I found one market near the Great Mosque where household gods were bought and sold as scrap metal, and built up a handsome collection of antique idols for next to nothing. But Ram was disappointed in me. 'Mr Williams, he take *art* photos,' he insisted. 'My photos will be artistic, too, when you see them.' But even then Ram said they were not *art* photos. It was not until we made an expedition to the Central Provinces and visited some very erotic temples at Khajuraho that Ram's eyes lit up. 'Here,' he said, 'Mr Williams take *art* photos.'

They were ecstatic as well as artistic – every imaginable variant of sex giving the greatest pleasure to the greatest number, from basement to pinnacle, but in curious contrast to the behaviour of modern Indians who, in the words of an American colleague, 'seem really screwed up about screwing' and won't even allow the most fleeting of kisses on the cinema screen. 'Why', I asked the official guide at Khajuraho, 'did they put such naughty goings-on all over these buildings; especially on the outside where everybody can see them?' 'Oh Sahib,' answered the guide earnestly, 'in ancient times it is well known such activities keep away lightning.'

Having only just been reunited with me, Sylvia was disinclined to follow the sensible British practice of taking the children up to the hills for the summer; but sweating it out, literally, in Delhi with temperatures of well over a hundred and becoming increasingly humid as the monsoon approached was no pleasure at all. Nor was the lack of privacy in the Cecil, the repetitive food, the endless round of diplomatic receptions and cocktail parties every evening. Newly independent states were touchy about having their invitations turned down (though one learnt to accept many without actually going), and with Indians shy of inviting untouchable Europeans to their homes one relied upon these parties for meeting people and, very occasionally, picking up useful information. Nothing was easier than finding a baby-sitter – we had a Madrasi ayah to do that – but for shy Sylvia the glitter and chatter of the diplomatic merry-go-round was a nightmare.

However, we made particular friends with Louis Heren of *The Times* and his wife Pat, and their eldest child Patrick made an ideal playmate for Jennet. The two families decided to take a month's holiday in Kashmir, sharing a large houseboat on a lake at the edge of Srinagar.

I think the Vale of Kashmir is the most beautiful place I have been to. Its houseboats modelled on the old Oxford college barges, allegedly to get round the Maharaja's ban on Europeans owning *landed* property in his state, were floating palaces. Carved and canopied, full of gorgeous Kashmiri carpets and furniture and staffed by obsequious Kashmiri stewards, they set a standard for holiday-making that nothing in my experience has ever equalled. You could lounge in the stern gallery, casting a languid eye over the gondolas that paddled up to offer anything from fruit and flowers to shawls and jewel boxes. It was impossible to leave Kashmir without a bale of loot lashed to the roof of the car. The lucky Scandinavians in United Nations uniforms who were supposed to be watching the ceasefire line flew out planeloads of carpets and furs under diplomatic privilege. It was the cosiest racket in the world of international peace-keeping.

Or one could whistle up the houseboat's own gondola (*shikara* is the local name) and go splashing off to call on one's neighbours for evening drinks. If two or three members of the Delhi press corps went up to Srinagar, the whole lot would follow; and around 6 p.m. there would be quite a traffic jam of shikaras in the middle of the lake, deciding whom to descend on for the evening.

Ashore there was the romantic wooden city of Srinagar itself to explore, a kind of Himalayan Venice with a castle, the original Shalimar water-gardens in working order and a bogus tomb of Christ (who, Muslims insist, was not really the figure on the cross but fled to the Vale as a wandering preacher after the collapse of His mission to the Jews). Or you could go fishing for trout in the mountain streams, or riding through meadows of wildflowers, or on pilgrimage to the cave of Armanath, twelve thousand feet up, where the devout adored the generative member of the god erected by nature in ice. One evening Louis and I were prevailed upon to go bear-shooting. I had only a dubious shotgun of Ram's, but Louis had borrowed a fine Mannlicher from Colonel Milks. Together we staked out a grove of mulberry trees where a bear was said to feed after dark. Came the dark and came the bear – on Louis's side, thank goodness – but when he peered through the telescopic sight he could no longer see anything and blasted the beast by guesswork. It gave a horrible cry like a scalded child and ran off back into the hills. Weeks later the Kashmiri ghillie, who got paid by results, turned up in Delhi with a bearskin and a story of having followed the bloodstains all the way to Tibet; so Louis had to pay him for the imagination if nothing else.

We spun out the Kashmir holiday by filing a story or two about 'The Problem'. Being Muslims, most of the Valley folk were sympathetic towards Pakistan, but they had had some nasty experiences of the invading Pathans who fancied the beautiful Kashmiri women. India was clearly a better bet when it came to development aid and wealthy tourists, but the roads the Indians were building all led into India and let in hordes of Hindus and Sikhs. Best of all, the Kashmiris would have liked independence, but when their leader Sheikh Abdullah started moving that way, the Indians had him locked up. I managed to gatecrash the bungalow where he was under house arrest and found the Sheikh to be probably the most impressive leader I ever met anywhere: he had all the sulky power of a caged lion and told me, 'I am on Jawarharlal's conscience. Mention my name to him and he will fall silent.' And it was true. Nehru loved the Sheikh deeply, recognising in him a man of his own stature and calling, and there was a touching reconciliation between them just before Nehru died in 1964. At the funeral in New Delhi I saw the Sheikh sitting cross-legged on the grass in the Prime Minister's garden, his eyes full of tears.

Instead of Abdullah, the Indians installed as Prime Minister of Kashmir a crook called Bakshi Ghulam Mohammed, who ran the state for the profit of his family. To my embarrassment I discovered that in Kashmir the letters BBC stood for Bakshi Brothers Corporation.

By this time Louis and I had been joined by Abe Rosenthal of the *New York Times* (later its editor) and the three of us made a formidable reporting team. The authorities hated what we wrote about Kashmir and set plainclothes men to harass us; but with the BBC, *The Times* and the *New York Times* thundering in unison they could not hush us up. Louis, in particular, liked nothing better than a good fight. He fought with authority wherever he went – with General Templar in Malaya, with Adenauer in Germany, with the Kennedy brothers in the United States – the Bakshi brothers were very small beer to him. Rosenthal, a razor-sharp New York Jew, suffered nobody gladly who was not his intellectual equal, so between us we cut our way through the mountains and back to Delhi where the rains were falling.

The next great expedition was to Goa, the last of the European colonies left in India, for the Portuguese had been there since 1524 and saw no reason to give up just because newcomers like the British and French were leaving. This was awkward for the Indians. Having persuaded the British to quit by (more or less) nonviolent means, and being in the business of deploring the use of armed force by everyone else, it would have looked bad for India to turn her army loose on a few thousand Portuguese. The moral argument against colonialism was irresistible, was it not? And if the Portuguese really were the monsters they were supposed to be, surely the Goanese (of whom there were many living comfortably in Bombay) would liberate themselves – nonviolently, of course.

There were at least two flaws in this argument. The first was that the Goanese rather enjoyed having a foot in both worlds – the Indian and the European – and were in no hurry to see their pleasant Catholic homeland liberated by pagans. The second was that the Portuguese were not cricket-playing Englishmen but nasty fascist policemen whose motto, constantly repeated, was, 'Authority must be respected, orders must be obeyed.'

The Indian opposition parties, always short of an issue, taunted Nehru for doing nothing about the Portuguese. In the end he agreed that non-Goanese should be allowed to march peacefully across the border to hoist the Indian flag and tell the Portuguese to go home. The Portuguese made it perfectly clear that any such intruders would run the risk of getting shot, whereupon Nehru dithered and ordered his police to make it as difficult as possible for the demonstrators to get through without actually arresting them. There was much digging up of roads, cancelling of flights and confiscation of buses for having defective brakes. Border towns like Belgaum and Sawantwadi filled up with angry and frustrated demonstrators, sweltering in the heat.

Through this confusion Louis, I and half-a-dozen other reporters bribed and bullied our way to the border. There was half-a-mile of scrubby no-man's-land which the taxis refused to cross, so we heaved out our suitcases and typewriters and staggered off down the track, the Indian Army outposts rattling their rifles at us as we passed. Round a bend in the road we saw the border chain and, parked just beyond it, a Portuguese waggon laden with chilled beer. At the sight of this the foreign press corps broke into a shambling trot, pursued by Indian jeers.

There is no question that Goa was an anachronism and an affront to Indian pride; no doubt, either, that anyone who questioned the divine right of President Salazar to lay down the law there had a very unpleasant time if he or she did not depart for the wider horizons of Bombay, which was easily done. Goa was an economic liability to the Portuguese, and much nonsense was talked in Delhi about how it was being turned into a base for NATO. Everyone, including the Portuguese, took it far too seriously: it should have been allowed, like Macao, to die a natural death. But for reasons of political boredom as much as anything else, the pace had to be forced and people made to die who would have been better off living.

We correspondents, once refreshed with Portuguese government beer, were wafted into the snoozy little city of Panjim and put up in the one hotel beside the River Mendovi. Vinho verde and casserole of goat seemed to be the basis of the menu, but there were champagne cocktails to be had made of Portuguese brandy and Brazilian champagne and these were lined up every evening by the barman as he saw us crossing the river on the ferry at the end of a hard day's demonstrator-hunting. There were no facilities for broadcasting and cables were routed via Lisbon – goodness knows what state they were in when (or if) they reached London.

One could hardly say, in that fine old correspondent's phrase, that 'Panjim tonight was calm but tense'. It was merely soggy. Ferns sprouted everywhere from the walls of red laterite and people shuffled gently along trying to avoid breaking out in a sweat. There was a small square by the river, with a monument to the inventor of hypnotism, where everyone stood to attention as the flag was lowered at sunset. Not far away the Church of the Good Jesus displayed the desiccated body of St Francis Xavier, minus one toe bitten off in a moment of adoration by a voracious pilgrim.

The great day was August 15th, 1955, when according to the Portuguese more than three thousand *satyagrahis* (or 'moral strugglers') entered Goa at twenty-two different points. Most of them got lost in the jungle and straggled home again; but at six places they got fired on and at four some of them were killed, the nastiest incident being in a railway tunnel where the Portuguese, alarmed by the approach of a chanting mob, simply sprayed the passage with machine-gun fire. Perhaps twenty people were killed altogether. The Portuguese contented themselves with arresting a few ringleaders and booting the others back into India.

I went charging up and down the border in a rented jeep and managed to find three groups of about forty satyagrahis each, just after they had been intercepted. The first consisted of militant Hindus who squatted sullen and rebellious under the carbines of the police. The next was a group of communist peasants, poorly dressed and utterly dispirited. Then, herded around the altar of a village temple, I found a batch of socialists from Rajasthan – one of them dead, shot in the back. It was a tragedy of incomprehension: the satyagrahis had been trained to believe that provided they did not use force, no one could resist the rightness of their cause; the Portuguese had been trained to believe that anyone who did not obey the law could, after due warning, legitimately be shot. Neither could understand the convictions of the other. So the satyagrahis marched straight ahead, shouting that India and Goa were one, and the Portuguese after shouting 'Halt or we fire' fired in the air, fired into the ground and then aimed to kill. Each now protested against the stubbornness of the other.

There was little more for me to do than count the casualties as best I could, put down the last champagne cocktail and footslog it back into India. I made my way to the satyagrahis' headquarters at Sawantwadi where I found them in total confusion. Some wanted to make more and more martyrs until the government of India was forced to send in the troops. Others confessed the movement had got out of hand – had never been *in* hand – and one leader told me, 'We had never realised it would be quite like this. Both sides are not playing by the same rules. Perhaps Gandhi's techniques are not valid in international disputes.'

But the rank and file satyagrahis had no such doubts. Many were still determined to march, kicking against the restraints of their leaders and equally bitter against Salazar and Nehru. When word got round that I had just got out of Goa, scores of them crowded round to ask what would happen when they met a Portuguese patrol. Was it true that unarmed men had been killed? Yes, I replied, it was. But, they insisted, those were peaceful men, they could have given no provocation. All I could do was to repeat what I had heard so often in Panjim: 'Authority must be respected, orders must be obeyed.' The satyagrahis still would not understand. However rash they may have been and however much their sufferings were of their own making, they were brave men.

After a few more futile plunges into the jungle, it all petered out. Goa was left alone for another six years; until, goaded on by Krishna Menon who had become defence minister and wanted the exercise, Nehru's patience was declared at an end, nonviolence was explained away, and the Indian Army rolled ponderously over the colony like a streamroller. Was it worth it, even then? The following year, in 1962, the war with China broke out and Krishna Menon's army was shown to be a paper elephant facing the wrong way.

Menon was a dangerous mixture of charm and malice. As a westernised South Indian he had a few friends among the Congress establishment, mostly Northerners who had gone to jail while Menon was being lionised in London; yet when he sought British company it was usually to vent his spleen against British imperialism. He particularly disliked the BBC – 'a bunch of bloody pukka-sahibs' – though he never seemed to miss a news bulletin and was always making complaints to me which, when it came to chapter and verse, he could not substantiate. Stories about his sexual hangups were many: how he leapt from the bed pounding his groin and crying, 'No, no! This stands between me and my greatness!' – for like many Indians he believed that ejaculation weakened the brain. In Delhi he was ill-at-ease with the opposite sex and made a number of promotions in the armed forces which seemed to have more to do with the good looks of young officers than with their military competence.

Soon after the Goa adventure Sylvia and I began to have worries about Andreas. He had started trying to walk and then given up. Our doctor (whom we were to meet again almost wherever we went around the globe) was Mollie McKenzie-Pollock, whose husband Jimmy was an epidemiologist with the World Health Organisation. She X-rayed Andreas and diagnosed the trouble: 'You can see the outline of a cystic tumour in the hip joint, eating away the growing point of the femur. Eventually, if nothing can be done, it will break and the leg will cease to grow. There's no one here in India who could operate, and not many in London.' And Mollie explained there was a risk that similar cysts might break out elsewhere. In the skull it would be fatal.

There was nothing for it but for Sylvia and the children to fly back to London while I resumed my role as a bachelor correspondent. To cut a long and rather gruesome story short, Sylvia – by refusing to take no for an answer – found a surgeon at Hammersmith who did a pioneering operation of great delicacy upon so small a patient, and did it with complete success. Andreas today is well over six feet tall and a good squash player. The risks, particularly from keeping a fourteen-month-old child under anaesthetic for so long, were considerable; and for many years after the boy was nervous and hypersensitive to pain. All I could do was to cast my vote for operating by telegram. The huge burden of the decision had to be almost entirely Sylvia's, and I at last began to realise what a remarkable person she really was, what a reserve of toughness there was under her gentle appearance. She was *not* going to allow this child of ours to be crippled, even though London's leading orthopaedic hospital said there was no help for it.

As if to take my mind off the drama, the operation coincided with the coronation of King Mahendra of Nepal – the first time the mountain kingdom had opened its gates to a mass invasion by the foreign press and diplomatic brigade. Kathmandhu hardly knew what had hit it, and the invaders were knocked all of a heap by Kathmandhu.

India, which regarded itself as Nepal's big sister, sent a rather dreary delegation in Gandhi-caps. China, which fancied taking over that role, sent an even bigger delegation in blue Mao-suits. The Americans sent a delegation in striped pants, swallow-tails and top hats. But the British, entering into the spirit of the occasion, sent a mixed bag from the theatrical costumiers. There was the Earl of Scarborough (who was Lord Privy-something-or-other) in the robes of the Garter, Lord de Lisle and Dudley in a cocked hat and several pounds of bullion on his chest, and the author of the only dictionary of the Gorkhali language in the most exotic of academic dress. Having had an excellent lunch at the Embassy, they were loaded into the howdah of an elephant and paraded through the streets of Kathmandhu with an escort of British Gurkhas playing 'Cock o' the North' on the bagpipes. It was theatre of a high order. American film directors cried 'Git that lord!' to their camera crews; the Indians and Chinese looked as sick as teetotallers at a booze-up; and the inhabitants of Kathmandhu, who are terrified of Gurkhas, barricaded themselves behind their wooden shutters.

The ceremony took place in the central courtyard of the Hanuman Dhoka palace, a structure so richly ornamented with erotic fantasies that there was hardly anywhere the American film crews could safely point their lenses. It must have been the most lightning-proof palace in the world, and the press set to work taking art photos for its private collections – men, women and donkeys in multiple combinations, all carefully retouched in garish colours for the occasion.

Rumour had it (and there was nothing more authoritative to be found) that the coronation itself was going to be pretty sexy. Wasn't the king supposed to be an incarnation of Vishnu, and wasn't he the guy whose prick was on show in all the temples? Say, just what *was* the role of the queen going to be? But Mahendra, a scholarly looking young man in a vaguely Florentine outfit, seated in a little hut decorated with banana leaves, displayed nothing more than intense boredom as a pack of rather scruffy priests made up the service as they went along, with much whispering as to what to do next.

In the square outside the Nepalese Royal Guard in uniforms which might have been abandoned by the D'Oyly Carte Opera Company during a Himalayan tour lounged about under yet more erotic carvings and wholly ignored the Nepalese General Staff when it drove up, late, in a 1930 Austin Seven. I pottered off into the Kathmandhu post office to see if there were any letters. 'You may seek, you may seek!' cried the postmaster, waving a hand over the ankle-deep envelopes on the floor. I ran into Desmond Doig, a celebrated Calcutta journalist who was reputed to know all about Nepal. 'Come along,' he said, 'I've just got a tip-off that somebody has the dried skin of a yeti.' 'A what?' 'The Abominable Snowman – somebody shot one and skinned it, and this fellow's offering it for sale.'

We wove in and out through noisome alleys, past hideous idols and eyes painted on doorways, escorted by relays of little boys who professed to understand what Desmond was asking for. At last we clambered up a staircase into a low attic where a very old man lay gasping on a string bed. Desmond spoke to him, very slowly and deliberately, in his best Nepalese. The old man sat up, drew a black tin box from under the bed and unwrapped something. It appeared to be a dried artichoke. 'Damn,' said Desmond, 'I must have got the wrong word for yeti. I think that's an aphrodisiac.' 'Should we buy it?'

We didn't, and Heaven knows why the Nepalese should need it with all those carvings to excite them. That was the end of the yeti story for the time being, but there were plenty of others to occupy our time, most of them equally unreliable. Peter Jackson of Reuters, who occasionally got fed up with having his brains picked by idle 'specials', spread the rumour that the celebrations had included a royal elephant fight in which the queen's elephant had killed the king's elephant, thus casting an evil omen upon the reign. Two Fleet Street correspondents filed it, and all the rest of us – including Peter – got call-backs from London asking why we had missed the story.

Kathmandhu is now full of tourist hotels and restaurants, but in those days there were only two: the Snow View, where mountaineers stayed, and a draughty palace surplus to the requirements of the Rana family run as a hotel by a white Russian named Boris Lissanovich. Boris was said to have danced for Diaghilev, which was hard to believe, but it was easier to believe the rest of the story, which was that while running a nightclub in Calcutta he had been recruited by the Nepalese nobility to come and run a reliable gin-still in Kathmandhu, on condition that the nobility got their gin free. This he did; but since everyone in Kathmandhu made their own hooch, no one bought Boris's and he was thrown into jail for non-payment of excise duty. Everyone came to visit him there and the parties in his cell were noteworthy, but still it cramped his style. Till the coronation was announced and a deal was struck: Boris would do the catering provided they let him out of jail. His hotel, full of crocodiles which had been stuffed the simplest way by filling them up with concrete, became famous for its bar and restaurant, the Yak and Yeti.

The celebrations continued for some days. The Chinese gave a really poisonous party at which everyone got ill on the Chinese Scotch. Boris's parties were utterly reliable, I am glad to say, and there was much singing and dancing. A *Daily Telegraph* correspondent called George Evans turned out to have been a Gurkha officer once and went completely native, dancing far into the night with a little drum strapped round his waist and Gurkha folksongs on his lips. It is hard to remember much more.

Meanwhile, back in London, the operation on Andreas had been a success and Sylvia was making her mind up about something. She had not been enjoying life in Delhi and half contemplated not coming back. But as she looked around her and compared the ordinariness of London life with the adventures she had had in India, feeling also the old-fashioned call of duty which was so strong in her family, she made up her mind that when Andreas was healed and she did return, she would throw herself into becoming the best foreign correspondent's wife in the business, as indeed she did.

I flew back to London for a month's leave with her, and found that the two of us had not only grown up but grown together during our separation. Our love-making was very sweet during those few weeks and our second son, Oliver, was conceived at Potten End where my parents had moved into a charming little flint-and-brick cottage called Stone House. It had a rickety barn, a tiny farmyard with a weeping ash in it, and an orchard. Sylvia and I resolved that, back in Delhi, we would quit the Cecil and find a bungalow of our own.

But until the family rejoined me I could wander as I pleased. Keeping on the move seemed to keep at bay those pursuing Furies that I sensed behind me during moments of depression. So I got off the plane in Karachi, took the train up to the Khyber Pass and, as good luck had it, found that the British Deputy High Commissioner in Peshawar was about to leave on a tour of the legendary Malakand States. Would I care to keep him company?

There followed one of the craziest excursions it has ever been my pleasure to make. I think the altitude had something to do with this, for once above seven thousand feet I feel permanently two Scotches ahead, without even opening the bottle.

Nothing much had changed in Malakand since Winston Churchill wrote his first book, *The Story of the Malakand Field Force*, in 1898 – indeed, we used it as our guide and could see exactly where the Gatling gun had held the bridge against the revolting tribesmen. The tribesmen today are charming, but they are divided between three very different states called Swat, Dir and Chitral. The rulers have since been deposed, I am sorry to say, but at that time Swat was ruled by a Wali who was positively progressive and ran one of the nicest little hotels in the subcontinent. The surrounding hills were fresh with running water and smelled like Harris tweed. Dir, on the other hand, was dusty and deeply reactionary; education was not merely discouraged but banned. I forget what the ruler called himself but he sent the crown prince down to the guest house to dine with us. He was a fat, debauched-looking youth whose conversation crackled with such gambits as, 'Tell me, Mr Priestland, which do you think the better – Gordon's gin or Booth's?' I could hardly wait to get over the Lowari Pass into Chitral. Chitral was ruled by a Mir who was only eight years old, and it was my honour to lift His Highness into the saddle of his pony. Already we had had to abandon the Deputy High Commissioner's Humber for a jeep, and now the jeep had to give way to horses which stumbled along foot-wide tracks across shifting screes. All around us the high peaks peered down through cloudy veils, 25,000 feet of Tirich Mir dominating everything. Where were we going and why, and did it matter? The furthest we got was a tiny hamlet surrounded by poplar and apricot trees, containing a polo ground and a bath fed by natural hot springs. The bath was in a crumbling shed much favoured by scorpions. The choice was either to jump in and get boiled alive or stay out and get bitten; after which, polo – played without any intelligible rules and to the frenzied music of drums and oboes. It was apparently some kind of festival, a gathering of local tribesmen, and it gradually dawned upon me what we were doing there.

Travelling with us as our official escort from the government of Pakistan was a Pathan whom I shall call Mohammed Afzal. He had once been a junior officer under the Raj, but upon being captured by the Japanese had defected to the traitorous Indian National Army, which he shrugged off as the sensible thing to do in the circumstances. In any case it had been forgiven him and we bore each other no ill will. Now Mohammed wore smart European dress and was clearly a man of some mysterious authority. The word Intelligence came rapidly to mind.

One night, after the Deputy High Commissioner had turned in, Mohammed and I and a dozen Chitrali tribesmen were sitting round a fire under the stars, sipping whisky, smoking hubble-bubbles and gossiping in Pushtu (or rather, they were gossiping and I was waiting for Mohammed to spare me a translation of it). After a while he said, 'Do you know what I am saying? I am telling them, Look! Over the mountains there is Afghanistan; and just the other side of Afghanistan is a big Soviet air base. Now if you will bring me one Russian officer from that air base, I will pay you ten thousand rupees. Only *this* time he must be alive.' One of the tribesmen who understood some English chortled at this. Mohammed scolded him in Pushtu, then continued, 'Once before they bring me dead Russian. Very dead. Not nice after ten days coming to Peshawar.' 'Mohammed, who's paying for this? Is it us?' But Mohammed would not say. I am inclined to think it was the Americans.

We visited the Chitral Scouts, the mountain troops raised by the British to give the tribesmen some organised war-games to play instead of shooting up one another. A portrait of Queen Elizabeth still hung in the mess and the silver was inscribed with the names of its British donors. On the tiny parade ground, between two ancient mountain-guns, the Deputy High Commissioner inspected the garrison which was promptly ordered by the colonel to race across the valley, up the mountain opposite and back again – last man home to polish the silver. I doubt if it made us popular, but they scampered off like goats, lugging their ancient Lee-Enfields. We sat back to wait for them, quart bottles of Murree beer at our elbows. 'Damn fine chaps,' said the colonel, watching through his binoculars. 'Lick the pants off the Hindus if they ever came this way – lick the pants off anyone except Gurkhas.'

We made our way back to Peshawar, making a detour to visit the valley of the Black Kafirs, a people said to be descended from the stragglers of Alexander the Great's army. They lived in villages that clung to the cliffs like swallows' nests, reachable only by tiptoeing along the brinks of irrigation channels. When we got there the women danced for us, sadly and two by two, wearing baggy brown dresses and cowls ornamented with cowrie shells, even though it was seven hundred miles from the sea. They did not look very Greek but, as in Kashmir, the women were so much more handsome than the men that you might have thought them separate races. No wonder there was once a flourishing slave trade in women from Chitral, but not men.

In Peshawar I recorded all the talks I could about the trip, which London seemed to enjoy when I airfreighted them home. Correspondents had never been given the time or encouragement to analyse and describe what they saw – that would have been dangerously subjective according to the old BBC tradition – but things were transformed in 1955 when Roger Lazar of the foreign news department invented From Our Own Correspondent. Somehow he persuaded Tahu to let him edit a programme in which the correspondents could explain *what it was like* to be where they were, picking out not the formal diplomatic stories they would have submitted for the dry news but the life, the colour, the humour that nobody in London could get from the agencies, yet would attract the listeners' imaginations far more. It was Roger's genius that although he never failed to shoot down second-rate work he left it to the correspondent on the spot to decide what was interesting and at what length to write it. He allowed me to do thirteen minutes about the Malakand States, which I think is still a record for the programme. I am afraid that after Roger retired From Our Own Correspondent became more like an exam paper, with contributors answering the questions set them in the allotted time.

I had become hooked on the mountains, especially the remote Karakorams where Indians, Pakistanis, Afghans, Russians, Tibetans and Chinese manoeuvred, gasping for breath in the thin air. I went to Rawalpindi and persuaded the Pakistanis to fly me to stranger places still, like Gilgit and Hunza and Baltistan, carved out of the top of the Maharaja of Kashmir's empire.

The aircraft were the faithful old DC3 Dakotas flying without pressurisation or oxygen at nearly twice their normal operating height. At one point they would fly straight at a mountainside, counting on the *usual* updraught to lift them over it – one tried not to think of engine failure.

Within half an hour we had left the dun-coloured plains behind us and entered an immaculate world that made me weep with its majesty: it was as if the waves of the sea or the flames of a furnace had been frozen. The whiteness of the peaks seared my eyeballs. I remember thinking how it made washing-powder adverts seem like blasphemy; for here was the absolute, eternal white.

Our first stop was Gilgit, just over an hour from 'Pindi, though by mule it would have taken a fortnight if the mule track had been open. Gilgit was a shipshape little town with a bazaar which used to be the terminus for the caravans out of Sinkiang, until the communists closed the Chinese border in 1949. When I saw it, instead of silk and tea and porcelain, the bazaar was trading hurricane lamps and streptomycin and plastic combs. In the orchards the apricots – Gilgit's one and delicious export – were exploding joyously into blossom.

Then we took off for Skardu, the village capital of Baltistan, another fortnight by mule but only half an hour by plane – yet what a half-hour! The mountains reached up like sharks' teeth to tear the belly out of the plane. To starboard we passed Nanga Parbat, a scarred brutal-looking hulk over 26,000 feet high. To port, Rakaposhi, still unconquered then at over 25,000. And far away in the distance, the sublime K2 – 28,000 feet. The aircraft barely skimmed the lower ridges and plunged into the gorge of the Indus to find Skardu. This called for a terrifying manoeuvre, a sharp S-bend within the gorge, with the mountains looming above us on either side offering absolutely no escape if things went wrong. After seeing that from the co-pilot's seat (and where *was* the co-pilot if the captain had an understandable heart attack?) I find scheduled airlines a bit dull.

Skardu was nothing much to write home about, though there was a great joy about the place as if everyone there felt grateful to be alive and the bazaar teemed with a fascinating assortment of faces: Chinese, Tibetan, Pathan, Mongolian and goodness knows what. Their music was punctuated with wholly irrelevant blasts on five-foot-long trumpets, and on March 21st they celebrated their New Year by fighting with hard-boiled eggs and racing them down hill; a ritual which I next encountered at Easter on the White House lawn in Washington DC, though I can't imagine how it made the migration.

After that I took the airlift which was the sole link between the east and west wings of Pakistan – one country divided by a thousand miles of hostile territory. But in fact it was never one. East Pakistan had not yet become Bangladesh but it was quite clear that it would some day, for it had nothing whatever in common with the west wing except for religion and a consequent dislike of Hindus. Above all, East Pakistan was Bengali, not Punjabi or Pathan, and it disliked the boot-stamping, bullshitting manners of the West Pakistan military establishment. 'Volatile' is the standard description for East Bengalis, and who can blame them in that dreadful climate? At moments of tension they hovered between laughter and fury; the smallest irritant might tip them either way. Dacca (or Dhaka to give it the proper breath) was full of non-studying students on the lookout for something to demonstrate about. At the drop of an insult they would riot, set fire to the bazaar, get shot and then paralyse the city for days while a monument was built and dedicated by the authorities to their 'martyrs'.

If I had thought India was doomed, East Pakistan was in hell already. Underfed, grossly overcrowded (for Bengalis are convinced there can never be too many Bengalis) it seemed well on the way to proving the correctness of Malthus's theory of population; and yet it never has, thanks, I suppose, to the generosity of its river system. East Bengal owes as much, if not more, to the Brahmaputra-Ganges as ancient Egypt did to the Nile and for much the same reasons: it waters, fertilises, renews and provides transport.

There was something endlessly fascinating about the life on its waterways. People really did live on them and off them. Like all great river economies, Bengal had evolved its own breeds of boat ranging from little sampans with stern timbers rising into a horseshoe to seventy-year-old paddle-steamers like floating grandstands; and there were steam launches called *Cecilia* and *Primrose* that looked as if they had been built for English comedy films. Some of them still had Scottish chief engineers down below.

Rafts of jute and bamboo were constantly on the move like floating haystacks. On one of them, drifting casually without power, I saw two pretty tribal girls, bare-breasted and smoking pipes. 'Jungly people!' said the Bengali master of my launch, eyeing them contemp-tuously. Personally I thought they were rather nice, but Bengali Muslim women were hardly ever seen in public, let alone naked to the waist. The bamboo raft was on its way to a new paper-mill – quite the most evil-smelling process I have ever endured and, once again, supervised by Scots.

I had covered most of the subcontinent by the time word arrived that Andreas was out of hospital and ready to return. By way of a holiday I arranged our reunion in Ceylon and booked rooms at the Mount Lavinia Hotel, justly famed in my view as the most gracious hotel in South Asia. Originally the marine villa of a colonial governor it made one see the real point of having an empire: not the strategy or the profits but living like a prince for the price of a holiday in Blackpool.

Coming out of India, Ceylon was a breath of fresh – if rather humid – air. It was clean, it was healthy, there was everything in the shops and the local press and radio still used immaculate English. In short, it was too good to be true. Lovely Ceylon had got its independence without a struggle because India, Pakistan and Burma were getting it. Brown Englishmen, many of them astute Tamils, kept things running as they had been in 1948 and the natives in the villages seemed happy enough living off the fruits of tropical bounty.

We pottered about the island, pausing at the well-kept rest-houses for cold beer and incandescent curries. Andreas learned to walk again at the old British naval station of Trincomalee. It seemed to us that Ceylon – which only a few extremist politicians then called Sri Lanka – was an unique achievement in pretending to go independent while keeping things just the same. None of the tea-planters had panicked (ah! that was the life on the old verandah, looking out over the bush-lined hillsides and the bright saris of the underpaid tea-pickers); there was horse-racing on the downs at Nuwara Eliya, and the *Little Hut* nightclub at the Mount Lavinia swirled with handsome Ceylon Burgher couples bearing Dutch or Portuguese names. It was the best stop for tourists between Cape Town and Singapore.

What went wrong? The economy was in surplus and the death-rate had been halved since 1939 – but that was part of the trouble: the tea and rubber industries offered limited employment and the island could no longer support the rising expectations of its people. The removal of the British referee loosed the easygoing Sinhalese majority and the ambitious immigrant Tamils at each others' throats. If any two religions ought to have been able to tolerate one another it was Hindus and Buddhists; but I have noticed, in other parts of Asia too, that Buddhism contains a suppressed violence and intolerance (the very opposite of what it professes) that make its adherents the deadliest of fanatics when the breaking point comes. Even among themselves, Sinhalese were liable to go berserk with machetes over disputed coconut trees.

I was back in Ceylon for the elections that finally shattered the mould. Down in Colombo nobody believed that it would happen; surely Sir John Kotelawala would be returned to keep the streets clean and the trains running on time? But unlike most of my colleagues I took a car away from the capital and saw what was happening in the villages: the swarms of apprentice monks fiercely campaigning for Mr Bandaranaike's People's United Front. Solomon West Ridgway Dias Bandaranaike, yet another of those pipe-smoking Oxford Fabians, had cobbled together a coalition of discontent – Buddhist fundamentalists, Trotskyists, practitioners of folk-medicine, those non-studying students and failed candidates for the civil service who had been outclassed by clever Tamils, and persuaded them that Sri Lanka – Sacred Ceylon – was being eaten up by Hindus and Christians and foreign imperialists. They were all too ready to believe it: Ceylon had to have its attack of the anti-colonialist fever like everyone else, though delayed. Not that it did the island much good. The tea-gardens and British trading houses were nationalised, the all-too-Anglicised press was gagged, and the Royal Navy and RAF obliged to bow out of their bases. But the economy went to ruin, S.W.R.D. Bandaranaike was assassinated by a disgruntled monk and the Tamil problem worsens to this day.

One irrelevant memory stands out from that campaign. *The Times* posted Louis Heren to Bonn and replaced him with Roger Toulmin. Roger had served his apprenticeship in Paris while I was Tom Cadett's 'young man' there – indeed in many respects he was my counterpart on *The Times*. Handsome, cultured and perceptive he was, nevertheless, not a fluent writer and used to spend hours hammering his copy into the properly tortuous *Times* style. His nerve as a correspondent eventually broke – and who can blame him? – when a plane he was taking from Delhi to Karachi crashed on takeoff, leaving him strapped to his seat in the tail while the rest of the fuselage careered down the runway, burst into flames and incinerated its passengers. After that, Roger joined the Eastern Services of the BBC in London; then the DHSS as an ideas man; and finally retired early to wrestle with his Catholic conscience. Through it all, Sylvia and I have shared with him a nostalgic friendship. But back to my irrelevant memory of Ceylon . . .

One weekend, Roger and I took the diesel train down the coast to the port of Galle where we stayed in an old hotel which had once been a Dutch officers' barracks and served the hottest curries in the orient. On the Sunday morning we wandered down to the harbour, hired an outrigger across the bay to a little beach where the East Indiamen used to fill their water-casks from a stream, and there borrowed underwater goggles from some obliging Sinhalese. As we floated face down, spying on the reef fish in their multicoloured blazers, we had the amazing experience of being *caught* with a shoal of mackerel. Some fishermen cast their nets around the shoal, and we were in the midst of it. For several minutes we shared in the undersea drama – the leaping, the flashing, the dashing to and fro, as if we were particles in some atomic implosion. Neither of us ever forgot it and we seldom meet without one of us starting, 'Do you remember, at Galle, at Watering Point?'

Back in Delhi I had found a bungalow, though the moment I had made the first down-payment the landlord celebrated by commencing work on his own residence on my roof, which was not particularly restful. Sylvia would bare her breast to start feeding the baby, and look up to see a row of upside-down workmen's faces peering in at the top of the window, watching the show. The baby was Oliver, our third, warning of whose imminent arrival in Delhi was flashed to me while I was covering an election campaign in Madras. I bluffed my way onto an aeroplane by pretending diplomatic privilege and arrived a couple of hours too late, to find Sylvia in a smart modern nursing home entirely surrounded by miserable sweepers' shacks. Some of the sweepers worked in the nursing home, mopping the floors by hand and even washing the patients' grapes for them, but Oliver survived. He was born there on the same morning as a Russian baby and a Chinese baby, but there was no doubt which was ours: from the start Oliver was a lady-killer.

The garden of our bungalow looked out on the tomb of one Khan Khana, a statesman of the Mogul period, resembling a rather motheaten Taj Mahal in red stone instead of white. It added great distinction to our view, a roost for flights of raucous green parrots and, on hot days, the coolest refuge in the suburb. One of my successors, the incomparable Mark Tully, settled only a few doors away; so that when I visited him years later, it was like coming home.

There in the suburb of Nizamuddin East, with a Khan at the bottom of the garden and a Muslim saint in a shrine across the road, we set up the complete post-imperial household. There was Mrs Lawrence and Ram, Sammy the bearer (or butler-valet), Ali the cook, Christine the ayah and a low-caste sweeper who by custom was not permitted to touch anything above floor level. One could as soon require them to step outside their traditional roles as try to interfere with trade union demarcations in a Scottish shipyard. *Then* there was the visiting staff: the mali, who was the gardener but would not water the flowers; the bheesti, who watered them from a leather goatskin; the dhobi, who took the washing away to the banks of the Jumna and thrashed it on the rocks; the durzi, or tailor, who squatted on the verandah with his sewing machine, making clothes; and the mistri, or handyman, who mended things. We drew the line at appointing a chowkidar or night watchman, partly because Abe Rosenthal lived three doors away and had a ferocious Gurkha with a kukri, who was reckoned adequate for the entire neighbourhood. This must seem appallingly extravagant, but in fact they cost very little, the cook and the bearer topping the payroll with about seven pounds a month each – which, in turn must seem exploitive, but Europeans paid what Indian employers considered extravagant rates. I quietened my conscience by reckoning that, including everyone's wives and children, I was supporting forty-seven Indians. Besides pay they got food and clothing and around September they usually borrowed money in the sure knowledge the loan would be forgiven them at Christmas.

Correspondents came and went. Robert S. Elegant came in for *Newsweek*, with his Australian wife Moira and a pack of little Tibetan terriers. Bob was really a China specialist who could not get into China and was maddened by the inefficiency of Indians compared with Chinese; indeed, a good many Americans – to whom China really *is* their India – felt that way and found it harder to keep their tempers than the British did. I tried to preach the doctrine that if one managed to achieve one thing per day – a ticket booked, a question answered by a ministry – that was the ration and nothing more should be expected till the morrow. Anything extra was supererogatory grace. Trying to force two, three or four things out of India on the same day was the road to madness through sheer frustration.

Bob took hardly to this, but Moira calmed him down and they became favourite company of ours and have remained so despite lengthy separations. After a spell in Hong Kong, beating in vain on the gates of China, Bob became a tax-free 'creative writer' on the coast near Dublin, where he turned out a series of massive historical novels on Chinese themes – *Dynasty, Mandarin, Manchu* – which have had much the kind of success among Americans that epics on India have enjoyed among British readers. In the end, though, even freedom from taxation did not compensate for the intellectual soddenness of life in Ireland. The Elegants moved to a manor near Windsor where Bob writes to the iron discipline of a set of 'Rigid Rules for Robert' nailed up over his desk by Moira.

And there were Russian correspondents in Delhi, Messrs Orestov, Efimov and Egerov representing respectively *Pravda, Isveztia* and *Kosomolskaya Pravda* (which was said to mean *The Kiddies' Pravda*). News to them was evidently not what it was to the rest of us, for while they were always to be seen at the diplomatic receptions they seldom turned up at the obvious news events and seemed to be in no hurry whatever to file their stories. On the few occasions that I did see them *pretending* to be businesslike reporters it was perfectly clear they did not know which end of a typewriter was which. I have always assumed that Russian correspondents are KGB agents, but these ones were so terrified of India that it is hard to believe they found out anything worth knowing. Maybe they were trying to find out about *us*, for on one occasion, when Sylvia was keeping the children cool in the hill-station of Kasauli and I was passing the weekend with them, a nervous little Russian called Sitnikov hitched a ride with me back to Delhi and spent four hours, across the Punjab, pumping me for my views on the monarchy. 'Tell me,' he queried breathlessly, 'your Queen: is she very tyrannical?' Sitnikov had been an interpreter with the Royal Navy in Murmansk during the Second World War. He had been on an embassy outing to Kasauli and missed the bus home, or so he said. Anyhow, he brought his wife to have tea with us in Nizamuddin East. They had a single child and Mrs Sitnikov confided to Sylvia that she was having no more 'for the state to take away and bring up instead of his mother'. I waited hopefully for offers of gold in exchange for royal gossip, but none was made.

India, I think, is too set in its Hindu ways to be fertile ground for communism. Certain intellectuals in corners like West Bengal and Kerala have fallen for it, but in the end the theories of class warfare have not been able to rise above the realities of caste warfare, and the

Nehru-Gandhi Congress has always managed to outmanoeuvre the Indian communists. Not that Moscow has given them much support: why should it when the Nehru-Gandhis have made themselves personal friends? Though not, I think, stooges. India's 'non-aligned' foreign policy has been a lopsided affair, relying upon being able to kick the West in the teeth without fear of losing Western goodwill, but in selfish terms that has been sensible enough. If Tweedledum has the good conscience to help you anyway, why not flatter Tweedledee to see what you can get out of him – especially when it is important to stop Tweedledee fraternising with those Pakistanis next door? The Russians, as is their wont, have given India more flattery than aid (and the West have given more aid than flattery), but over all, with the exception of some bad miscalculations about China, the non-aligned policy has paid off well. For her size India has to spend relatively little on defence and is remarkably self-sufficient.

Part of the price for this was the great B. & K. circus of November 1955, when Nikolai Bulganin and Nikita Khruschev – Prime Minister and First Secretary of the Soviet Union – set forth on a state tour of the subcontinent that almost killed the accompanying press corps. Bumping ahead of them in a rented Dakota, getting about three hours' sleep a night for seventeen days, we pursued B. & K. down a triumphal avenue of engagements that stretched from Delhi to Bombay, Madras and Calcutta with added attractions like Kashmir, Agra, Bangalore, Poona and Ootacamund thrown in. The Indians had been much pleased by the reception laid on for Nehru when he had visited Russia the year before and they were determined to outdo the spectacle on an even grander scale.

No place can lay on a spectacle like India. Even when nothing has been arranged it is colourful enough. With a bit of effort it becomes a human kaleidoscope, deafening, dazzling, totally overwhelming. At every stop there were crowds by the *lakh* – the hundreds of thousands. They would have turned out for anyone, so powerful is the urge to 'have darshan' of the great. Bands blared, showers of marigolds poured down, triumphal arches sprung up, elephants lowered garlands over stubby Russian necks and 'dancing-girls re-enacted the amorous adventures of the love-god Krishna' (a phrase I had to give away to my colleague of the *Daily Express* because I knew the BBC would not stand for it).

The day before we arrived in Bombay, there was a minor civil war in the streets and the police shot twelve people dead and wounded a hundred more. A truce was declared for the Russians. B. & K. were puzzled by the prevalence of Scottish bagpipes and statues of Queen Victoria in liberated India, but they carried on relentlessly; or rather Khruschev did while Bulganin retired for the occasional nap. They put on oriental headgear and made long speeches, Bulganin reading from a prepared script whereas Khruschev ad-libbed. According to the English translation they were using Indian hospitality to attack Anglo-American militarism and neo-colonialism, so we of the Anglo-American media stirred up a great fuss, upsetting the Indians. But I doubt if the crowds understood a word. To them it was all a great *tamasha*, a festival. At Agra Khruschev was shown the Taj Mahal at dawn – one of the world's great wonders that does not disappoint. But instead of praising it he denounced the exploitation of the workers who had built it. No one was going to catch *him* admiring the extravagance of an emperor.

He was at it again when we flew on to Burma. Pious Prime Minister U Nu had spent a great deal of money constructing, out of concrete, an enormous hall in which scores of Buddhist monks had been set to work revising the sacred scriptures. The holiness and magnitude of the task was explained to Khruschev, who looked around him and announced, 'But the roof leaks.'

The truth was, I think, that by this time everyone was getting tired and peevish. The Burmese were not as skilful as the Indians at keeping the press away from their visitors, so that we managed to run Khruschev to earth, unprotected, at the foot of Rangoon's Shwedagon pagoda – a great gilded trumpet, three hundred feet high and alleged to be two thousand years old. Through his interpreter, Khruschev reminded us that England had not existed till 1066 and that her monuments were less than half the age of Burma's; yet (he maintained) the English called the Burmese savages and barbarians. Mind you, he went on, tapping accusingly at the inches of gold leaf on the pagoda, in the Soviet Union architects who wasted public money on unnecessary ornamentation got criticised pretty severely.

At this, a tame Soviet architect in the party assured everyone that such criticism was thoroughly healthy and deeply appreciated. 'Have a care!' cried Khruschev. 'The Americans and the French will try to make you defect!' I do not know why the French were dragged into this, but a French correspondent promptly joined the argument and pretty soon we were all being denounced as paid slaves of monopoly capitalism 'who would die of starvation if you ever dared write the truth about the Soviet Union. You should go red with shame!' The Frenchman retorted he would sooner stay the colour he was. 'You can turn black for all I care!' shouted Khruschev. It was all rather childish and, from the perspective of thirty years later, supremely insignificant; but we cabled off thousands of words about it and the Burmese were even crosser than the Indians with us for rocking the boat of peaceful coexistence. They got their own back by allocating us the oldest plane in Union of Burma Airways: the engines leaked oil which spread along the trailing edge of the wings and got ignited by the exhausts so that we flew over Burma like a blazing cross in the sky.

Our skirmishes with the Russians continued through a splendid regatta on Lake Imlay – where they raced enormous longboats by standing up and working the paddles with one leg, men and women; it blazed up in Taunggyi, where Khruschev took a savage dislike to a fur hat I was wearing (I suppose he thought I was mocking the Russian style of headgear, but I wasn't, it was bitter cold); and finally the row fizzled out at a place called Maymyo where we found a better story. Tactlessly the local communist guerrillas chose that moment to kidnap a doctor belonging to the World Health Organisation. He was an Italian who turned out to be married to the daughter of an Australian jockey and a Burmese aristocrat, by the name of Princess Rose-Belami. She was, in the words of Philip Marlowe, the sort of girl to make a bishop kick a hole in a stained-glass window – as half-Burmese women tend to be. Finding the world's press in town, the Princess summoned a news conference and announced that she was about to set off, alone and unarmed, into the jungle to find the kidnappers. And should there be no other way, she was prepared to surrender her body to the bandit chief in exchange for her husband's release. Khruschev was swept from the front page overnight and I think we would all have plunged into the jungle after the princess had not the pilot of our flying coffin refused to wait for us.

There were many more such expeditions. Chou En Lai came to India (and was very gallant to Sylvia at a New Delhi reception), the Shah of Iran, Marshal Tito, President Eisenhower, the Dalai Lama and many much dimmer potentates. The Indians evolved a sort of top people's package tour, with a nice balance of historic monuments and locomotive factories. They left up the triumphal arches as a permanent feature and simply changed the slogans hanging from them: 'Long live the friendship of the Indian and BLANK peoples!' Frankly, when you had seen one grand tour you had seen them all.

Sylvia was not the only member of her family in the subcontinent. Her eldest brother, Bill Rhodes, was working as a doctor at a Church of Scotland medical mission at Jalalpur Jattan in the Pakistan Punjab;

so one Christmas we set out from Delhi, together with our children, to bring him good cheer. This consisted of such goodies, unobtainable in Pakistan, as bacon, Scotch whisky, Colman's mustard and gripe water. Bill had tried writing to his mother in England for them; but the local postmaster used to steam open the letters and substitute requests of his own which he would extract from the returning parcels. Mrs Rhodes could never understand why her son needed so many woollen mittens and views of Buckingham Palace.

The journey took us through Lahore, in my view the most ill-done-by city in South Asia, the old capital of the Punjab endowed by the Moguls and the British with all the parks, monuments, bazaars, clubs and hotels necessary to furnish a place of importance. It would have been the capital of Pakistan had it not been vulnerably close to the Indian border. Once, when I steamed into it from Amritsar, I found the entire railway station had been taken back to the 1940s and renamed Bhowani Junction: John Masters' novel was being filmed, with Ava Gardner and Stewart Grainger, and that great Jewish actor Abraham Sofaer was leading mobs of Pakistanis through the streets dressed in Gandhi caps and shouting, 'Quit India – long live Indian National Congress!' I settled into Faletti's Hotel – Lahore's equivalent of the Cecil – where the cast and I had to beat off the attempts of the Royal Court of Jordan, on a state visit, to evict us from our rooms. Mine, I found, had been allotted to the Master of the Revels, but I pulled rank on him and he ended up in a tent on the lawn.

Sylvia's visit to Lahore was less theatrical. We moved on, after a day or so, to Jalalpur: a baked and battered town where the whole of life was viewed through a buzzing bead-curtain of flies, water was hauled up out of the ground in bucket-chains operated by camels, and the most celebrated inhabitant was the last harem eunuch (or so it was said) in Pakistan who stared dolefully at his visitors.

The medical missionaries wanted a pictorial record of their work, so I spent a week at the hospital taking anything but art photos. Every patient was fed and nursed by a live-in escort of relatives, camped out on the floor round the bed; it would have shocked the Royal College of Nursing but was good for everybody's morale and gave the staff a chance to teach some elementary hygiene. Whatever qualms I had about watching operations vanished as I glued my eye to the view-finder and snapped away at caesarians, duodenals, piles, hyster-ectomies, whatever came along. It was a century behind the London Clinic, yet the success rate – let alone the worthwhileness and the gratitude – seemed no less.

Came Christmas Day and Bill Rhodes put on his pastoral hat. We climbed onto camels and lurched out into the countryside to visit the handful of Christian villages out there. Sylvia clutched her saddle with one hand and the latest baby with the other. Jennet was carried off on the saddle-bow of some galloping deacon. I swayed miserably in the rear on a sex-mad male camel which kept turning its head and inflating its tongue at me; camels are the vilest creatures I know, suffering from halitosis at one end and incontinence at the other. Somehow we brought the good news to the scattered flock: the experience has stayed with me ever since as a reminder of what the first Christmas must have been like, not electric lights and wrapping papers on the sofa, but flies and dust and dung.

Bill went on to become medical superintendent of the Christian hospital at Nagpur in central India, then took to theology and was eventually made Dean of Theology at Serampore, a celebrated Baptist foundation on the banks of the Hooghly near Calcutta. I think I might nominate Bill for sainthood, except that I am not sure an intellectual can ever qualify for that distinction; but I am quite sure he would never have survived without his amazing wife Helen. Helen was a former Edinburgh policewoman who could have given Princess Rose-Belami a run for her money and will always bring a smirk to my lips when anyone mentions missionary wives. She is the only missionary wife (or policewoman) *I* know who normally wears a red rose behind one ear.

Our time in India was drawing to a close, for the normal tour in a foreign station was three or four years. I had volunteered for Delhi partly because I wanted to trace my family roots on my mother's side; I was there at precisely the right place and time. For 1957 was the centenary of the Indian Mutiny, which had broken out not far from Delhi and found its focus in the siege of that city. In the midst of it stood the remains of the East Indian Company magazine where my ancestor, George Alexander Renny, had won his Victoria Cross. The British had erected a pompous inscription describing how their heroes had defied the 'rebels and mutineers'. After considerable thought Delhi City Council added a polite postscript, in no way obscuring the original, which read: 'The persons described as rebels and mutineers in the above inscription were Indian members of the army in the service of the East India Company, trying to overthrow the Foreign Government.'

Nothing could have been more objective, and it was typical of the attitude towards the British Raj in Nehru's time. He took the view that history ought not to be tinkered with, for years opposing the removal of the many imperial statues that punctuated the Delhi road network. When the centenary turned this into a welcome stick for the socialist opposition to beat him with, Nehru reluctantly agreed that the statues should go – but gradually and tactfully so as not to create ill will. The first to depart, furtively by night, were General Nicholson and General Taylor, posturing outside the walls of the Old City which they had stormed a hundred years earlier. But when we left India, a year later, Queen Victoria was still presiding over her lapful of pigeons near the Great Mosque, and the equestrian Edward VII still pranced above a plaque proclaiming, 'His reign was a blessing to his well-beloved India; an example to the great and an encouragement to the humble; and his name shall be handed down from father to son throughout all ages as a mighty emperor, a merciful ruler and a great Englishman.' Edward has now ridden off into the imperial sunset; but he had a longer innings than he had any right to expect.

Several officially sponsored books on the Mutiny came out, but none of them accepted the communist theory that it had really been the First War of National Liberation. On the contrary, declared the most authoritative of them, the English had been effecting a social revolution which the mutineers would have set back; it was the death-throes of Ancient India, not the birth-pangs of the New. I found Indian historians scrupulously fair in recording the atrocities committed on *both* sides. 'It was a fight between people driven insane by hatred and fear,' wrote one of them. 'The Mutiny hit the white and the black alike.'

Today the scene has been badly chewed up by civic development, but in the 1950s the battlefield of the Siege of Delhi had altered very little in a hundred years: the Ridge, Flagstaff Tower, the Observatory, the Kashmir Gate, Hindu Rao's House and Subsimandi Market were all there and still had the same tactical significance. What a fantastic situation it must have been, though: the British, constantly harassed by heat and disease, taking on with supreme confidence a hostile city and a well-equipped army ten times their size. The more one thinks about it, the more one is inclined to put it all down to sheer morale, a conviction – perhaps on both sides – that the sahibs were bound to win in the end, as they had done ever since Plassey.

Things were equally untouched at Meerut, forty miles away, where the Mutiny had begun on May 10th 1857. The town still had a garrison, but with the British gone their residential quarter had lost a good deal of its grace and affluence; it was a straggling, tumbledown neighbourhood. But I could still identify the large, cool bungalow of Colonel Carmichael Smyth who caused all the trouble by taking such a harsh line over the greased cartridges which so offended the sepoys; and in the same road was the two-storey home where Captain Craigie, Lieutenant Mackenzie and their womenfolk held out. In the railway goodsyard at the back I even found the remains of the small Muslim tomb where they eventually hid.

The Church of St John, where the British troops mustered for Church parade on that fateful evening, was still spick and span, a distinguished Georgian piece with a classical portico and spire. Nearby was the cemetery, asking for an elegy to be written in it, crowded with portentous monuments evidently built by Indian masons, for instead of crosses there were little shrines with domes on them after the Mogul fashion. The graves of the Mutiny victims were down at one end, their inscriptions recalling all too vividly the passions aroused by their fate:

> Donald MacDonald, Captain, 20th Regiment
> Native Infantry, aged 35, who was killed
> by his own men on the 10th May, and
> Louisa Sophia his wife, aged 30 years,
> who was barbarously murdered the same
> night while trying to make her escape
> with her three infants from her burning house.
>   'Avenge Thou my cause, my God'

Meerut was putting up its own monument in another part of the town. The inscription was in itself a monument to Indian delicacy. It read:

> 'In memory of the 1857 martyrs.'

Chapter Six

STARS AND STRIPES AND CRESCENTS

The Priestlands quit India early in 1958, before the hot weather started. Today we look back on it with nostalgia, but at the time it was a relief. The climate was an ordeal for young fair-skinned children, but Sylvia and I were opposed to the English fashion of sending them home to boarding schools. Neither of us had happy memories of boarding. We argued that we had not produced our young for other people to bring up, and that families were born to enjoy one another, not to fly apart at the earliest opportunity. However, Delhi was not doing us any good physically. The boys had inherited the Priestland chest which caught infection easily, especially when carried to and fro between air-conditioned bedrooms – necessary if we were to get any sleep at all – and the searing temperatures outside.

Delhi's summers offered every sort of torment, at first intensely hot but dry, punctuated by choking dust-storms off the Rajasthan Desert; then getting more and more humid as the monsoon approached and tempers frayed; then a few weeks of glorious rain which petered out and left the city to steam until October. The thudding of the ceiling fans went on for more than half the year and my instinct upon entering any room – an instinct it took months to shake off after we left – was to reach out for the switch that turned them on.

During the dry season we lowered huge bamboo blinds, known as chicks, all along the verandahs and hired monstrous machines called desert coolers to blow moistened air through the house, but these became worse than useless as the natural humidity built up. Air conditioners extracted the moisture, dribbling a constant trickle of water out of the windows in which they were wedged, but they used a great deal of electricity and Delhi was short of power which had to be rationed. Before moving into the Nizamuddin bungalow Sylvia had to go off to the electric controller and cry all over his desk until he gave us an extra unit for the children. Then we paid the meter-man to put in a bigger meter than we were entitled to, and finally we put in heavier fuses than we were supposed to, which gave us enough to run two air-conditioners and a refrigerator. Since most of Delhi was engaged in electrical jiggery-pokery it was not surprising that blackouts were a nightly event.

If anything, the bureaucratic climate was even more exhausting. In my work I always ran scared, terrified of missing a story or of being thought idle by London. But trying to research a story from Indian official sources was like trying to borrow money from a miser. Officials suspected, not always without reason, that you wanted the information in order to expose their own inefficiency. Stupid 'press wars' broke out between the government and the foreign correspondents, with Krishna Menon brooding malevolently over carbon copies of our dispatches, telephones being tapped and mail steamed open and then clumsily resealed with crusty Government-of-India glue. In my case this got so bad that Tony Wigan wrote to the government's chief information officer, offering to send copies of all our correspondence directly to the secret police to save trouble. The quality of the glue then improved, but the police got their own back by refusing to issue permits to visit interesting border regions like Assam, Kashmir and Ladakh. To do them justice, permits for foreigners had been introduced by the British; but once introduced a regulation is seldom abolished in India. To this day you have to get a permit to travel from Calcutta to Darjeeling by train, and it is a terrible crime to photograph a bridge that may have been standing for the past eighty years.

London proposed transferring me to Washington, as number two to Christopher Serpell, one of my heroes, who had at last been prised reluctantly out of Rome. My place in Delhi was to be taken by Charles Wheeler, one of Grace Wyndham Goldie's bright young men from television. Charles came out married to the beauteous Katie Dove, a television colleague, but soon lost her to John Freeman. Never mind; in Delhi he met and married a Sikh lady, Dīp, and a happy and distinguished-looking couple they make to this day.

Washington has always been acknowledged the plum posting among correspondents. It seemed to me no comedown to get there as somebody else's assistant. We were to fly back to London for a few weeks' leave while our baggage made its way by sea to Southampton whereupon baggage and Priestlands would sail together to New York. It would be a great adventure for us all.

The first thing to do was to send for the Chinese packers, acknowledged as the most careful removers in Delhi, for there were intricate BBC regulations as to the amount the Corporation would pay for, calculated according to size of family, length of service abroad and sundry other factors. In our case it seemed to work out to the equivalent of two or three trunks. Furniture was out of the question – one usually hired it wherever one went – but we reckoned to turn any place into a home by dressing it with familiar books, pictures and ornaments. The Chinese contemplated our treasures and announced they would occupy twelve packing cases of Central Provinces teak. Fortunately they estimated the weight – which was what London wanted to know – in Hindustani units of maunds, seers and tolas, which so baffled the BBC that we got away with it. The Chinese moved in, lovingly packed everything in little birdsnests of hay: not a thing was broken when we opened the crates on the other side of the world, though the alien hay horrified the US Department of Agriculture and we nearly had to burn the lot on the pier in New York.

Our last night in Delhi a lavish wedding procession passed the house with three bands drumming, braying and squealing. Out among the ruined Delhis the jackals whooped it up like drunken teenagers. We left behind some good Indian friends, especially among All-India Radio: I remember with affection Iqbal Singh (who got exiled to the station in the Andaman Islands), Amita and Iqbal Malik (unusually, she was a Bengali Hindu and he a Muslim from the Northwest), and P. C. Chatterji, known as Tiny, the philosopher Director General of AIR who fought bravely – if, in the end, unsuccessfully – to prevent a great organisation from becoming a purveyor of sycophantic propaganda.

For one thing I shall always be grateful to AIR, its concerts of Indian classical music, which I learned to love almost as much as I love European music – though perhaps it has more in common with improvised American jazz. Once you get used to the curious timbres of the instruments – so redolent, anyway, of the whole atmosphere of India – you can enjoy it (I find) without necessarily understanding all the rules and structures that underlie it. Gradually you get the hang of its logic, the thoughtful exploration of the relationships between the notes of the *raga*, the discovery of something close to a tune, the competition that develops between the soloist and his drummer. Sincerely, I revere the playing of Vilayat Khan, Ali Akbar Khan, Mysore Chowdiar and Panalal Ghosh (the greatest of *bansari* flute-players) as much as I do that of Heifetz or Galway. But I do draw the line at the bleating and mewling of Indian vocalists.

So we left India (and yet have never left it). The isolation had scared me out of my wits at times, but although I realised that America, with its permanently floodlit stage, was going to test me even more, I was glad to be moving on. It was as if I was shaking off something that was in pursuit of me. It or they would turn up in Delhi to find me no longer known at that address – gone away.

When we arrived in London Jennet looked about her and pronounced, 'Mummy-Daddy, this is *our* country, isn't it?' But it was no longer really our home. We had sold the unlovely house in Belsize Park and had to live in a rented flat which Mrs Rhodes found for us on the Finchley Road – the top floor of a house curiously named 'The Shack'. Grandparents fussed happily over the children and we renewed contacts with members of the Carthusian mafia and the Hampstead Artists, but it was a holiday in limbo, transitory and unreal. For Sylvia there was the constant problem of what the children could do. I spent some of my time 'on consultation' with the foreign news department, which actually meant very little but pottering about chatting to old friends and realising that I was both respected for my work and regarded as a visitor from another planet who would soon go back where he came from. The most human reaction came from one of the bookmaking office messengers: 'Always knew you'd do well, sir,' he cried, 'though you were a miserable-looking bastard when you first came here.'

Somehow life became real again as we climbed aboard the liner *United States*, holder of the Blue Riband for the fastest crossing of the North Atlantic and an extremely noisy ship with a rude American crew. In order to attract government subsidy she had been built for quick conversion into a troop carrier, so there were few of the trimmings of decadent luxury one would have expected in a Cunarder. Attempts to eat one's way through the menu were not merely discouraged but denounced by the stewards, but this did not prevent the children from ordering themselves banquets of hors d'oeuvres while Sylvia lay groaning in her bunk and I sat holding her hand. *Batter-batter-batter* went the ship, all day and all night, until the classic scene was unveiled of Manhattan and the Statue of Liberty – a forbidding lady who always seems to me to be holding the immigration regulations under her arm.

Anyhow, they let us in – *and* our dozen crates in Central Provinces teak – and we passed the next day being stupefied by the contrast between the world's poorest country, which we had left, and this, the world's richest. We had seen almost no television before. All our friends in London were clinging to the pretence that they could not possibly find the time to watch it. But here in New York there was not only unlimited TV, it was also beginning to appear in colour. On the set in the BBC's New York office, tidal waves of red and green poured down the faces on the screen and provided the BBC representative there with a full-time job adjusting the controls. Except in country areas Americans seldom bother with proper aerials and seem content with standards of reception which would send the average Briton to phone his rental company; among the skyscrapers of Manhattan the pictures might have been beamed from Mars.

Black-and-white was somewhat less disturbing. We became instant addicts of Have Gun – Will Travel and a flock of other cowboy sagas. The children also learnt the words and music of the commercials, singing them as if they were nursery rhymes: 'Take Tums for the tummy – T U M S – the digestives with the happy hole – keep them handy in the pocket roll!' Or, 'Call Roto-Rooter – that's the name – and away goes trouble down the drain . . . Roto-Rooter!' They knew I worked for the radio and were disappointed I didn't write the jingles. 'We could sing them for you.'

Still dazzled by New York and the splendours of Grand Central Station we took the train down to Washington – an unlovely route through the back lots of chemical factories, until you reach Phila- delphia – where we were met by the man I was to replace: Douglas Willis. Douglas eventually drank himself to death in Nairobi: there is a long story about how his ashes were flown home to the BBC, taken to his own memorial service and left on the bar of the George before being rescued and filed under *W* in somebody's office. He never went anywhere without a small portable bar, containing Scotch and bour- bon, presented to him by his admiring fellow-boozers among the engineers at the Washington CBS station. How Douglas, with his hairline moustache and his fake Australian accent, was ever selected for the gentlemanly corps of BBC foreign correspondents I do not know. He flatly refused to speak any foreign language and behaved like the prototype of the Flash Harry tabloid reporter. Almost all the well-known anecdotes of the profession have been attributed to him, one or two of them correctly. The best-known is probably that of the unpronounceable Polish military attaché who was said to have appeared, month after month, in Douglas's entertainment accounts until found to be unrecorded in the Washington diplomatic list: 'The fellow is clearly an impostor – I shall never trust him again!' wrote Douglas when exposed. Less well-known, and with some basis in fact, is the story of Douglas and the loss of the submarine *Truculent*, in the Thames estuary. The tale goes that he submitted the item 'To hire of tugboat to visit scene of disaster – £100.' The administrative officer rings up a tugboat company and confirms that a day's hire might indeed be £100. So the admin. man signs the expenses and decides to take in a newsreel cinema during his lunch hour – there was one at Oxford Circus, just down the road. There he sees a report on the *Truculent* disaster and, amidst all the action, a shot of Douglas Willis at the oars of a rowing boat. Douglas is sent for and asked to explain what the admin. man has just seen. 'Thanks mate,' says Douglas, pulling the expense sheet towards him, 'I'd forgotten.' And he pencils in, 'To hire of rowing boat to reach tugboat – £10.' An alternative version has it that there really was a tugboat and that Douglas had sold places on it to all the other reporters at £50 a head.

He survived Washington through sheer effrontery and the benevolence of Christopher Serpell. I witnessed an example of the former within twenty-four hours when Douglas, having taken me for a belting session at the bar of the National Press Club, drove through three red lights in the complicated traffic system behind the White House and was brought to a howling halt by a fat cop on a motorbike. Almost literally, Douglas had not got a leg to stand on, but he climbed out of the car, laid a fatherly hand on the policeman's shoulder and began talking. To my amazement, cowering behind the windscreen, I saw the policeman lower the pad in which he had begun writing a summons, then fold it, then put it back in his hip pocket, and finally, with head lowered as if in grief, give a little gesture which could only mean 'Get the hell out of here'. As we did so I asked, 'Douglas, how on *earth* did you talk your way out of that? You're sloshed. You're pickled.'

'No getting round it, dear boy. I didn't attempt to. Putting on my best British accent I said to him, "Officer, I confess I am inebriated. Tomorrow I have to leave this great country of yours – the Land of the Free, the Home of the Brave – for ever, and my sorrow is such that I have been seeking comfort to an admittedly excessive degree. I have done wrong, I admit. Let justice take its course. But I want you to know that here is one Englishman whose feet are bound to take him wherever duty calls – but whose heart will always be here in your great nation's great capital." Not a dry eye in the house.' And we went through another red light, in Foggy Bottom where the State Department is.

Douglas's rented home, which we were to take over, was in

Jennet on her wedding day, 1972.

Patricia Rhodes, London 1971
(*photo: Jennet Priestland*).
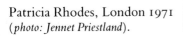

The author outside the US Capitol, 1965.

Thornapple Street, in the Maryland suburb of Chevy Chase, just over the District of Columbia boundary. Like all the houses in the area it was well built in an agreeably folksy style and stood in a spacious garden surrounded by lofty trees. In the autumn these deposited tons of leaves upon the ground, which suburban mores dictated had to be promptly cleared up. The trees knew this and would drop their loads one tree after another, waiting for one lot to be removed before dumping the next in its place. Nor were you allowed to burn the leaves: you had to pile them in the gutter for the county leaf-chomper to devour, or rather for passing traffic to scatter up and down the road. Still, the trees kept the house cool in the summer, when the garden was haunted by cardinals, cat-birds, grackles and occasional humming-birds. When we had unpacked the twelve crates of Central Provinces teak they made a sturdy playhouse for the children among the dogwood bushes. Sylvia at last learned to drive – all the examiner was really interested in was, could she park – and we bought a nine-seater station waggon called a Country Squire, with fake Tudor beams.

Douglas departed boozily to become assistant in Paris, a transfer which he regarded as a plot to make him learn French and for which he sought his revenge by insisting that the BBC pay for the shipment of his motor mower. This, he claimed, had been a major investment, not to be written off just because his Paris flat had no grass. When he and the machine were later appointed to the lush lawns of Kenya, Douglas was triumphant and insisted that vast sums had been saved by his farsightedness.

I had a whole new world of politics to master and for Sylvia the adjustments were even greater. In Delhi we had our miniature caste-system of servants, but in Washington we had only Bernice, the coloured maid, who came twice a week and preferred working for British families because she reckoned they treated her as an equal; to our India-bred offspring it seemed the most natural thing in the world to have a brown face about the house, though Andreas shocked the neighbours by announcing that when he grew up he was going to marry Bernice. The massive shop at the supermarket once a week took a bit of getting used to – there were no shops round the corner to pop out to – but after a while Sylvia got the hang of American house-keeping, its convenience, efficiency and gadgetry, and the absence of all those servants with their lurkings and pleadings turned out a positive relief. No longer was half one's time taken up with the problems of Indian man-management.

The natives were friendly. No one could ever resist Sylvia's serene innocence (she is incapable of deception or malice) and our taste for Jewish companionship was instantly served by our over-the-road neighbours Sid and Leila Asher and their children Barbie and Warren who matched our elder two nicely. Sid, a chortling butterball of a man, was an arbitrator for the Labor Relations Board. Leila, more tense and worrying, was a professional artist who taught at Howard University, one of the four universities in Washington, established primarily for the negroes. Politically the Ashers were liberal Democrats supporting do-good organisations like the Urban League and the League of Women Voters. It was quite difficult in Chevy Chase to make friends with a really reactionary Republican.

Washington was beginning to have stirrings of conscience about civil rights and integration. Blacks could not actually afford to live in Chevy Chase but the local primary school made a gesture by hiring two black teachers – *British* West Indians with respectable English accents. The school provided a natural reservoir of friends for our children, who soon acquired the protective colouring of American clothes, American habits and American accents. There were few hedges in the suburb to hinder the restless tide of dogs and kids that swept through the houses once school was out.

In my view there is no substitute for the resident foreign correspondent living in his territory with his family and drawing on their experiences as much as his own (nowadays I would certainly add 'or her own', but there were very few women correspondents in my day: Elizabeth Partridge of the old *News Chronicle*, Taya Zinkin and Hella Pick of the *Manchester Guardian*). It is an old, probably sexist, joke of mine that 'You cannot be a good foreign correspondent without a good foreign correspondent's wife – preferably your own', but I firmly believe it. Being a foreign correspondent's wife is a highly skilled occupation. My little joke has a sting in its tail, for not every marriage can stand the long separations, the unpredictability, the temptations. I could name three correspondents who had to give up because their wives could not stand the strain, and three more who changed wives in midstream.

It is not only the safe house that a wife can provide amongst the encircling strangers, or the telephone messages she takes or the meals she lays on for important guests or homesick camera crews. She and the children have to integrate themselves with the community, making friends with people who are not necessarily government officials or diplomats or journalists; and from the experiences they have, the gossip they pick up and the human touches they add, the resident correspondent assembles a very much better picture of what it is like being an American or an Indian or a Lebanese than any visiting fireman, jetting in for a quick raid from a downtown hotel. That is why people like David Willey (who really *lives* in Rome), Mark Tully (who really *lives* in Delhi), Anthony Lawrence (who really *lived* in Hong Kong) are worth listening to.

All praise to the BBC for remaining one of the few news organisations to keep an extensive network of resident correspondents, for they and their communications cost a great deal of money. Newspapers like the *Mail* and the *Express*, which once had equally extensive networks, have virtually given up trying. Again, the flying squad reporter favoured by television, who never sees the territory in its normal times as well as its abnormal, has little hope of understanding and then communicating *what it is like*.

It was May 1958 when we arrived in Washington, finger-printed and pledged not to plot the violent overthrow of the United States government. After India there was nothing much the Washington summer could do to frighten us, though it seemed that the flora and fauna were even more hostile. Americans were disappointed to hear that we had never seen a tiger and that the only cobras we had met had been in snake-charmers' baskets, but they warned us earnestly against poison oak, poison ivy, black widow spiders, skunks and venomous snakes.

When our first November came round we determined to celebrate Guy Fawkes' day. I looked up fireworks in the yellow pages and found a dealer who was happy to sell off some of his stock left over from the Fourth of July. 'There's always one or two goddam English come in around now asking for fireworks – can't think why.' We stuffed a Guy, lashed him to a stake in the garden and invited the neighbours round, greeting them with salvos of cheap but effective rockets. Their reaction was dubious. We were almost certainly violating some sort of county ordinance – the anti-smoke laws at the very least – but what did this effigy represent? Some kind of lynching? A British branch of the Ku Klux Klan? As I related the history of poor Guy – I realised that was precisely what it was, especially when one of the neighbours summed up: 'I see – so it's kind of an antye-Catholic demonstration . . .' That was our last Guy Fawkes' day in those parts. Our support for the legitimate monarchy had to be confined to the Queen's birthday party on the lawn of the British Embassy: strawberries and cream and a band playing Gilbert and Sullivan.

It was a half-hour bus ride into town to reach the BBC office, which at that time was in the National Press Building along with *The Times*, the *Telegraph*, Reuters and most of the other foreign and American bureaux. There was alcohol on the top floor in the Press Club bar – where PR men for unlikely lobbies were happy to foot the bill – and alcohol on the ground floor, in the Press Liquor Store and yet another bar which specialised in paralysing mint juleps. In between was, I suppose, the greatest news distillery in the western world, where we sat chewing up acres of newsprint and miles of agency tape. From time to time the teleprinters would summon us to a press conference, whereupon dozens of newsmen spilled out into 14th Street and commandeered taxis for Capitol Hill, the White House, the State Department or the Pentagon. Today I can remember very little of what it was all about, but at the time it seemed thrillingly important that the world should know – and fast! News on the hour, every hour from NBC, CBS and ABC made it hard to miss anything, but very difficult to relax.

One day the teleprinter summoned us to a rare briefing at the US Post Office. The Postmaster General wanted Congress to pass legislation forbidding the circulation of pornography through his mails, and in order to stir up support had mounted an exhibition of the sorts of things being sent. We were all invited to a very private view. The American papers, anticipating the unprintable, sent studious young reporters with law degrees; but the hardened hacks of the foreign press, scenting headlines like WHAT THE POSTMASTER GENERAL SAW, abandoned their typewriters *en masse* and pelted up Pennsylvania Avenue to the Post Office. At their head was the redoubtable Suzanne of the *Agence France Presse*. At first she was refused admission altogether on grounds of modesty, then allowed a quick trot round all by herself 'provided you don't look behind the screen'. Suzanne was dragged out after three minutes, protesting, 'But I demand to see behind ze screen! Zeese are no more than ordinary brothel pictures!'

Alas, they were not even that. Pinned up round the walls were pages from Danish nudist magazines, that well-loved view of most of Miss Marilyn Monroe, some saucy calendars and some tattered books on spanking. Henri Pierre of *Le Monde* led the way to the screen, behind which were displayed two little whips and a number of uncomfortable-looking rubber objects. We turned, disappointed, upon the Postmaster General who announced that if the squeamish would like to leave the room he would show us some film.

First came a scratchy printed entitled *Rover Does His Daily Chore* featuring a lady and her Alsatian dog, in an apparently endless loop.

When that had run for a while the PMG reluctantly gave the signal for the main attraction, a 1930-ish piece about a girl who hides in a cupboard and watches a couple amusing themselves in a manner now considered fit for public display by Mr Jeremy Irons in his Proust film. 'Haven't we seen enough now, men?' quavered the Postmaster as the girl was dragged from the cupboard and the possibilities began to open out. Silence. 'Men?' Some heavy breathing, then a clatter and it was announced the projector had broken down. The Americans did not dare write a word but the Europeans enjoyed themselves immensely and Christopher Serpell turned out one of his most elegant and allusive dispatches for the BBC.

Christopher was one of a generation of correspondents now only to be heard in their retirement on the World Service; men of deep education and culture, fluent in many languages, who took diplomacy seriously and would themselves have made worthy ambassadors. I think also of Leonard Miall, Christopher's predecessor in Washington, who first spotted the kite flown by Secretary of State Marshall for the Marshall Plan, and of Kenneth Matthews, F. D. Walker and Guy Hadley. Christopher's treatment of me was generosity itself. As I sat looking at my first American dispatch, wondering if it was good enough to show him, he walked into my office and offered me *his* script for *my* approval. He introduced me to all his contacts – something of which correspondents are often rather secretive – and welcomed Sylvia and me into his home and the company of his wife Jean and their four children. They lived in a state of uproar and an old wooden house, of which Christopher managed to be both the most intellectual and the most practical inhabitant. He could never resist the gadgets with which Americans love to clutter their desks. Prominent among these was a small black box with a switch on the top boldly labelled 'Do not throw this switch'. When you inevitably did, the whole box heaved and groaned, the lid flew open, and a small green hand emerged and turned the switch off again. That was all it did.

One of my earliest appointments was to go along to the White House and apply for my credentials. The White House press pass was issued then to relatively few and was reckoned to be the most prestigious form of identification anyone could hold. Getting it involved a vetting process that took some weeks while the Secret Service (a body which eschewed espionage and confined itself to protecting the President against assassins and the currency against forgers) made enquiries in all the countries you had ever lived or worked in; for the pass was going to entitle you not only to enter the office wing of the executive mansion but to crowd round the President's desk and shoot questions at him – when he felt like calling the press in. Roosevelt and Truman did that frequently but Eisenhower preferred the set-piece news conference, and even vetted the transcript afterwards. His views came to us mostly through the mouth of his Press Secretary, Jim Hagerty, whom I consider the best of his kind since the Second World War.

Hagerty told very few outright lies – though you had to watch out for dodgy phrases like 'at this time' or 'I can neither confirm nor deny that'. He was very close indeed to his master, and if a foreign reporter showed himself serious about his job Hagerty allowed him a fair crack of the whip. Understandably there was an inner circle of the top American correspondents who got special briefings, but if I managed to find out where they were meeting and elbowed my way in Hagerty would insist I be allowed to stay. He was good company and I liked the man.

The machine he ran was highly efficient and handled press expeditions even better than Colonel Milks. Wherever the President went transport was laid on, hotel rooms were booked, luggage was collected and delivered and telephones were installed by the dozen. That was part of the joy of working in America – everything worked and nobody cared what you wrote, since no foreigner could be as hard on the Americans as they were on themselves. When important heads of government came to Washington Eisenhower liked to hold his talks with them at his mountain lodge Camp David, near Gettysburg. Hagerty would commandeer the Gettysburg Hotel for the press corps, who would while away the time by touring the battlefield where 43,000 Americans had slaughtered each other during the Civil War.

Hagerty Tours Inc. excelled themselves in December 1959 when Eisenhower, who was really more of a monarch than a prime minister, took it into his head to visit eleven countries in twenty days in a kind of jet-propelled royal progress. For the record, it went Rome-Ankara-Karachi-Kabul-New Delhi-Teheran-Athens-Tunis-Paris-Madrid-Casablanca and home: almost twenty thousand miles mostly in Boeing 707s, one for the Secret Service, one for the President, one for the White House press corps and a fourth for the luggage and steadily accumulated loot. It was even more exhausting than the B. & K. tour (which I suppose it was meant to eclipse), and before long it was literally a matter of, 'If it's Tuesday this must be Afghanistan'. You could look that up in the guidebook Hagerty provided, which not only outlined the political issues at every stop but told you when to have your suitcase packed for removal to the next country and added useful tips like 'American cigarettes not available. Taxi drivers untrustworthy. Do not touch the native women.'

Impossible to make any sense of what was going on. In Teheran the motorcade drove over miles of Persian carpets and there were lashings of caviar and duck cooked with walnuts to eat. At Karachi Mohammed Afzal appeared among the security men and gave me a massive wink. At Kabul the driver of the press bus had clearly been standing to attention all night and we had to sing to him to stop him falling asleep at the wheel and driving us into a ravine. In Delhi it was Eisenhower who fell asleep during the Indian classical dancing display, and the US Army doctor sent along to keep the press corps fit caught Delhi belly himself and had to drop out. At Athens we were put aboard an American aircraft carrier, next to the nuclear bombs, and ferried across the Mediterranean to Tunis. 'Our man there recognisable', signalled the BBC, 'by bowler hat rolled umbrella and toothpaste.' And, by God, he was. As my helicopter descended into the waiting crowd I could spot the bowler easily – and the brandished brolly – and after we had shaken hands I noticed that, just as some people take snuff, this fellow kept taking furtive sucks at a tube of Macleans from his waistcoat pocket. I met him again at Casablanca, where I spent the night in the company of a French medical team singing rude French medical students' songs; after which I tottered back to London with a small dose of pneumonia and recorded some broadcasts in bed.

Heaven knows what good it did for international peace and understanding. Earlier that year Eisenhower had lost John Foster Dulles, his Secretary of State since 1953 and regarded by many as the architect of the Cold War (though I think he was no more or less of an abominable No-man than Vyschinsky and Gromyko). With Dulles gone it may have been that Eisenhower was trying out the effects of his personal charm as a substitute; for certainly people did 'like Ike'. He was honourable, better at delegating than most professional politicians, and if he did spend a fair amount of time on the golf course at least he was doing less harm there than presidents who lock themselves up in the Oval Office for week after week. Dulles, who had been in the American delegation to the Versailles peace conference, grimly resisted anything that smelled of appeasement, and if he never succeeded in rolling back communism at least he never lost anything to it. Of his monuments NATO still survives, but there is little or nothing to show for his Asian alliances, CENTO and SEATO. Dulles was actually a jollier man in private than his public appearances led one to expect. He liked to drink rye whisky and water, stirring the mixture with his finger even when a swizzle stick was provided.

It did look, for a while, as if Eisenhower's personal diplomacy might get somewhere. Khrushchev (solo this time) did a knockabout tour of the United States, refusing to be impressed by anything but the pigs in Iowa. I am glad to say I avoided covering that; but Christopher, who took it on, staggered off the plane at the end crippled with arthritis – these epic tours had a high casualty rate. May 1960 brought Khrushchev and Eisenhower together again at the Paris Summit, but that was wrecked by – ostensibly – the shooting down of Gary Powers in his U2 spy plane over the Soviet Union. The Russians must have known these flights were going on for some time, and have been humiliated by their inability to stop them. To have it revealed at that particular moment outraged their sensitivity to contempt. Today equally good pictures are taken by both sides from satellites and nobody objects.

A good deal of my time was taken up with space stories, for the Russians had scored a first with Sputnik and were heading for another with Vostok (the first manned spacecraft) and the Americans were desperate to get ahead. It was somewhat unnerving to find Wernher von Braun and his merry men, who had made life so uncomfortable for Londoners with their V2 rockets, being promoted as heroes of the United States. One of the Americans' handicaps was that the Army, the Air Force and even the US Navy insisted on developing each its own launch-rocket, the Navy having a peculiarly dud model whose countdown usually went '. . . five . . . four . . . three . . . two . . . one . . . Darn it!' I was once asked by the British Embassy in Washington how I was getting such good information about the American space programme, to which I replied that I was only doing what presumably the Russians were also doing – piecing it together from the boastful adverts of the aerospace manufacturers in the technical journals. If anything, Christopher was even more fascinated by this new technology. He was convinced the Americans were working on a Doomsday project called Project Omega. What it was precisely we had no idea, but whenever we got into conversation with a Pentagon official or defence scientist we would remark casually, 'But I suppose it all depends on how Project Omega goes?' Or, 'Well, that's cheap compared with Project Omega.' We never got back anything more than blank incomprehension and *I* don't think there ever was a

Project Omega; but pretty soon the whole of Washington was referring to it darkly at cocktail parties and I hoped the Russians enjoyed it.

At least I enjoyed the Russians. They had the usual band of unlikely journalists in Washington, one of whom was told off to sound me out, which he did in a series of luncheons at the very best restaurants in town. Glad to avail myself of the KGB's hospitality fund I ordered none but the choicest dishes and met all his probes with expressions of astonishment that he should regard NATO as a threat to anyone: twenty-five-year-old lorries, tanks that the Nazis had been able to puncture like cans of orange-juice – he couldn't be serious! 'But what,' demanded my host, dropping his voice to the lowest line on the bass clef, 'about Project Omega?' 'Old stuff. Obviously it's been made totally obsolete by Project Nightmare.' But Nightmare evidently proved a dud – I didn't have time to spread it around enough – and my free lunches came to an end.

Occasionally I would be sent up to New York to help out at the United Nations during crises, of which there were plenty. In 1958 we had the fall of the Iraqi monarchy, and a massive upheaval in the Middle East which brought the US Marines crunching ashore in Beirut. The next year we had Castro's Cuban revolution – Fidel began well and was mobbed by the secretaries in the National Press Club when he visited Washington; but then blotted his copybook by committing the sin against the holy dollar of nationalising American property. Then we had Khrushchev in person, hammering his desk with his shoe, and on top of that the savagery of the Congo. There was seldom a dull moment – though in fact the whole value of the United Nations, and especially of the Security Council, is that it *does* make things a bit dull, removing the issues from the operatic stage of real life and transposing them to a kind of chess congress, conducted in clinical surroundings with immense formality and much paperwork and translating. There were times when one felt like standing up and shouting, 'But don't you realise people are *dying* out there?'; and then you realised that a certain pressure was being applied on governments to behave better, and that almost all the delegates were enjoying themselves too much to allow the game to fail utterly.

The BBC was one of the first news organisations to seek accreditation at the UN, and had been rewarded with its own studios overlooking the Assembly and the Security Council and a glorious office looking out onto the East River where, during intervals in the argument, you could admire the traffic of boats and barges and helicopters. F. D. Walker was the resident correspondent, succeeded by John Crawley and Tony Wigan himself, and their secretary was a lady called Joanna Vandamm who had known the UN and its staff since it was so-high. There was nobody and nothing Joanna could not get hold of if you wanted them – cans of cold beer, recordings of speeches, advance texts . . . Once, with a deadline creeping up on me, I muttered that I wished I knew how the French delegate was going to end his speech. In a flash, Joanna was out of the cubicle, to reappear in the front row of the French mission taking notes from the speaker's text over his shoulder.

By tradition the Washington number two was the runabout man: I ran about the United States from New York to Chicago, to California, Texas and the Deep South. Canada, too, though Ottawa was about as exciting as an English cathedral city. Montreal could be fun, but it was important to establish that you were not from the US and could understand French. In the winter months, though, it seemed to me that most of Canada was beyond the boundaries of human inhabitability. In fact most Canadians of any enterprise seemed to recognise this by emigrating permanently south of the border; those who remained were pleasant enough and for a week or two I rather welcomed their lack of aggressiveness, but whatever province I went to the atmosphere was, frankly, provincial.

New York, on the other hand, had all the glitter and glamour of the wide screen. It bestowed on one the energy to do all there was to be done there. Chicago was almost as splendid, one of the few American cities with a distinct personality and a view of life that challenged that of Washington and New York. Whenever I thought I had got the hang of American politics I would come to Chicago and revise my ideas. I remember spending one night touring the strip joints in the company of Vicky, the cartoonist, an earnest little central European who kept sketching away and demanding – as we sank lower and lower down the scale of depravity – 'But ees zees ze *classical* striptease?' We ended up in Cicero, Al Capone's base camp, where a girl pranced along the top of the bar stark naked, pretending to pluck pubic hairs and deposit one in each drink. Studs Terkel, the Mayhew of Chicago – who built up what must be the finest oral history library of any city in the world – supplied me with a map showing which were the black areas, which Polish and Irish, and which were strictly no-go.

California for me meant San Francisco rather than the endless suburbia of Los Angeles. San Francisco is one of the most beautiful cities I know, and witty too. At the foot of its statue of Christopher Columbus someone had written 'Poor Chris! Standing on a shore you never touched, staring at an ocean you never saw – (signed) Friends of Sir Francis Drake.'

But my introduction to the place came in a particularly gruesome way. A man called Caryl Chessman was on death row in San Quentin jail, convicted of unnatural rape. Unpleasant, but not an offence that normally carries the death penalty and no longer did, even in California; but by lodging an ingenious series of appeals Chessman had managed to keep himself alive for eleven years after his original conviction. Now he had exhausted his final chance and his appointment with the gas chamber was booked. Knowing the power of the press in America I cabled the Warden of San Quentin requesting a D-Day-minus-one interview with the condemned man. I had not really hoped for the permission that came instantly back ('California has nothing to hide from the press of the Free World').

The case intrigued me. There had been a number of such assaults in the Bay area at the time and it was obvious the police had been desperate to convict somebody of them. Chessman roughly fitted the descriptions given of the assailant but although he had a criminal record it was not for that sort of crime: I believe he *could* have done it, but I am still not convinced that he did. Moreover there were some imposing moral issues far greater than the man himself, for Chessman had turned himself into an expert on the futility of capital punishment, admittedly with the object of saving his own life – but fate often has a warped way of presenting worthy issues through unworthy people. And surely there should have been some kind of statute of limitations; this was no longer the man who might have committed the offence so long ago.

It was a weird encounter, the warders treating me with all the courtesy of a four-star hotel staff, Chessman himself looking like the hired killer in an old B-movie, me wondering what on earth I was doing in this production. Chessman walked in wearing an open-necked shirt and boiled denims, his skin shining with that sweaty look prisoners get, sat down at the table and rattled off the answers he had given so often before; somehow he seemed two-dimensional, unreal: 'They can turn me off tomorrow – this time I guess they really may – but sometime soon some guy will do exactly the same thing. It's pointless. It's not Caryl Chessman I care about any more – the one I was then or the one I am now. I just want society to realise that it's just trying to prove how virtuous it is by rubbing me out. And it won't make a shit of difference.'

The day after I talked to him they gassed Caryl Chessman in the presence of the ladies and gentlemen of the press and the representatives of the civil power. There was an open line to the governor's mansion in Sacramento, but it remained silent. Outside the grimly anonymous shed the sun sparkled on the waters round San Quentin peninsula and on the pretty flowerbeds round the prison walls.

They taped a stethoscope to the prisoner's chest, strapped him into a kind of dentist's chair in a glass and steel kiosk, and told him that when he heard the cyanide pellets plop into the bucket of nitric acid under the chair, he should breathe in deeply. It was like asking him to commit suicide, please, after all he had done to stay alive. When the pellets plopped he held his breath for as long as he could, and when he had to breathe he could not breathe deeply because (as he mouthed through the glass) they had belted his chest 'too tight'. He could manage only short gasps. Chessman had arranged with a girl reporter from one of the San Francisco papers that he would keep looking at her and nodding for as long as he was in pain. He nodded for what seemed like a couple of minutes. I have never witnessed a hanging, but with a reasonable drop it sounds a good deal better way to die.

When no more heartbeats could be heard through the stethoscope they turned on the fan and vented the gas through a chimney rather like the one that sends out smoke signals from the papal conclave. The girl at whom Chessman had nodded was telling everyone, 'They said it would be instantaneous. But it wasn't. It hurt. It hurt like hell.' 'It doesn't do any good. It doesn't do *any* of us any good,' said the Warden as we walked towards the car park with bowed heads. And before I had left San Francisco there was yet another sodomy-rape.

Excursions to the South meant always the same things: civil rights and school integration. The Supreme Court had long ago ruled that 'separate but equal' schooling for blacks and whites was a fraud, and now added that the two races should be brought together 'with all deliberate speed' – whatever *that* meant. To Eisenhower it seemed to mean deliberate lethargy. He did not really understand the South, which was traditional Democrat territory, did not want to sour his popularity by reawakening the bitterness of the Civil War, and anyhow had been brought up in a US Army which in his day had kept blacks and whites in separate units. He must also have known there were parts of the North where race relations were even more precarious than they were in the feudal South.

What forced the President's hand was the uproar that broke out in Little Rock, Arkansas, when a handful of black children tried to get into the Central High School in fulfilment of their constitutional rights and were turned away by the Arkansas National Guard under the orders of Governor Orval Faubus. For the first time since the Civil War the President was obliged to send federal troops into Dixie to enforce negro rights, to the fury of the white South.

Arkansas was a poor, rather scruffy borderline state with none of the faded dignity of the true South, and Faubus was more like an Ulster Protestant than a fine old southern gentleman. Once, at a press conference, I asked him how he could reconcile his racial prejudice with his evangelical Christianity; whereupon he preached for ten minutes on a text from Genesis IX, demonstrating how the 'niggrahs' were descended from Ham, who had been punished by God for spying on the nakedness of Noah and were therefore condemned to be the servants of the whites who were descended from the virtuous Shem and Japheth. The governor's chaplain sat beside him all the while, wagging his head in approval and ejaculating 'Ay-men'.

On my way out I met a delegation of tiny tots coming up the steps of the capitol to present an address of support. 'We wanna preserve the purity of the white race in this state,' their diminutive leader declared proudly. 'But surely none of *you* is likely to marry a negro?' I suggested. 'It's our grandchildren we gotta protect!' piped the spokeschild. It was not easy being an outsider in the South. Once I had established that I was not one of those hated East Coast liberals but English, I had to cope with the widespread assumption that since most white southerners were of English extraction and the English had imported the slaves in the first place and were protestants, I would be on their side. 'We hear you have problems, too,' they added pointedly. I am afraid that in reply I usually prevaricated. Prevarication and dissembling are vital parts of the foreign correspondent's survival kit.

Quite apart from the problem of what to do with the children I never felt able to take Sylvia with me on my assignments out of Washington. Frankly one is too busy thinking of oneself and the service to have time for anyone else. However, we did manage at least two long touring holidays: one across the Middle West to Colorado, Utah, the Grand Canyon and Yellowstone Park; the other to Niagara Falls (which looked and smelled badly polluted) and on into Canada round the Gaspé and the Maritime Provinces. French Canadians flattered us by supposing we came from Paris (but then almost any accent sounds sophisticated compared with theirs). Nova Scotia plied us with lobster and wrapped us in fog. Prince Edward Island sandblasted us on its beaches until the children whimpered with pain and refused to go bathing any more. There is nothing like a long-range motelling holiday to impress on you the vastness of North America, its variety and the isolation of its great inland from the rest of the world. But it can be very trying with a waggon full of pent-up quarrelling children whining to pull up at every bogus Indian Trading Post, Santa Claus summer camp and Slurpee Saloon. I still have a badge proclaiming 'Yes – I have Slurped', and if I remember rightly it was a snowball drenched in raspberry syrup.

Christopher Serpell's hip got steadily worse and he decided to take his children home to England before they turned into Americans. Radio News was getting more adventurous, thanks to a wily editor called Steve Bonnerjee who saw a place for Christopher as presenter of the newly invented World Tonight: the BBC had never before dared to give any journalist such power to interpret the news 'live' on the air. His replacement in Washington was to be Douglas Stuart, another of the older generation, about whom I knew little except that he had been expelled from Cairo at the time of the Suez crisis and was reputed to have an explosive temper which changed the colour of his face as the pressure built up. In the event he never let it loose against me; but after a little while it became clear that he had his own way of seeing America, considerably to the right of mine, and I was not going to stand much chance of modifying it. I was approaching three years in Washington, so I wrote to Tony Wigan suggesting it was time to move on. He agreed. It was lucky that he needed a new posting for Erik de Mauny who could take my place. Erik, besides being an astute correspondent and brilliant linguist, was a man who could get on well with anybody, even Douglas. As for me, I was offered the choice of South Africa – where Tony thought my sympathies with the American negro might be tested – or the Middle East or a new post the BBC was thinking of opening in Japan.

I plumped for Japan. It sounded a complete contrast with anywhere I had been before, and Sylvia would like the art. I am sorry, in retrospect, that I did not go for Africa which I still do not really know; but the Sharpeville Massacre had just taken place in which seventy people had been killed. I feared there would follow the kind of bloody upheavals which would make it no place for my wife and children. This made the Middle East my second choice, and when the BBC decided to *stop* thinking about Japan because of the expense, the Middle East it became by default. British organisations were still not welcome back in Egypt, so the base had been moved to Beirut, not because there was much news there but because its communications were good and the censorship minimal. As well as the correspondent's office the BBC maintained a small production centre recording music and pop songs for its Arabic service, though to my ear they were vastly inferior to Indian music.

My last big assignment in the US was the elections of 1960. Richard Nixon received the less-than-enthusiastic endorsement of Eisenhower as the Republican candidate, while John F. Kennedy – or rather the Kennedy family machine with its manpower and its money – captured the Democratic nomination, outwitting the old pro from Texas, Lyndon B. Johnson. Johnson campaigned on the catchy slogan 'All the Way with LBJ', but he only got half-way and had to be content with the vice-presidential place.

I am an unashamed addict of American electioneering: it goes on too long, it is outrageously commercial and it is quite likely to produce the wrong man, but golly! it's fun, and everyone can join in. The candidates criss-cross the country, towing planeloads, busloads or trainloads of reporters behind them. Bands play, majorettes strut and twirl, showers of ticker-tape cascade from windows; or rather, they used to, for during the Kennedy-Nixon campaign the PR men decided that too much valuable TV exposure was being wasted on ballyhoo. There was an era when conventions came to a halt for half an hour while carnivals took place on behalf of some utter no-hoper who simply wanted to go to his grave with a smile on his lips at the memory that once upon a time he had been proclaimed as 'Florida's favourite son – the next president of the United States – Governor Hiram K. Hoosit!', whereupon a torrent of plastic oranges rained down from the ceiling to ricochet off the Kennedy-ribboned straw hats below. But the Kennedy men, with their walkie-talkies and stopwatches and direct lines to the TV networks put a stop to all that. They weren't having their man pushed onto the air at two in the morning. They were there to launch him into prime time with all the accuracy of mission-controllers shooting for the moon.

I must confess I preferred LBJ to either Kennedy or Nixon. LBJ was a rogue – they still laughed at how 'Landslide Lyndon' had polled the graveyards of Texas to get into Congress – but at least he had visible heart. Nixon, when you met him, had a veneer of polished sincerity but under that – what? He would never let you find out, pulling back suddenly from any advance, lowering the shutters that concealed a dark, suspicious mind that was working to get even with those who he knew despised him. I believe the key event in his life was when he failed to make it into his college football team. It was an affront to his

All-American manhood. Very well, then, he'd play dirty. He'd score on his own, and they'd be sorry.

John Kennedy was a man whose impact improved with distance: the further you were from him the more he looked the handsome prince to whom Americans flocked to 'have darshan'. Close up, there was something cold about him – it showed in the eyes and in the strange lack of intimacy one sensed between him and Jackie. When he was elected President one old hand in the White House press corps murmured to me, 'All John F. Kennedy needs to do now is fall in love with his wife,' but when I quoted that remark in the first book I wrote, the BBC made me take it out as *lèse-majesté* – about the only time I was censored by the Corporation and a curious example of how the British had come to treat the Kennedys as royalty. Nevertheless most Washington insiders knew the JFK was a womaniser. J. Edgar Hoover of the FBI kept his job because of what he knew (Hoover preferred the company of well-built young agents himself), and the sort of thing he knew is on public display in Alan Drury's political novel *Advise and Consent* in which Kennedy is clearly visible as the young senator who flits up and down Washington hotel corridors late at night.

What made Kennedy run was the will of his racketeering, British-hating father Joseph, who trained up the whole family as a championship team in the power game. When his eldest son died, John was promoted willy-nilly to be striker. Like many second sons he did not feel born to it personally, but he did accept the *family* destiny and he did have an instinct for choosing and trusting his key advisers – notably his younger brother Bobby who was the toughest of the whole clan. I cannot claim to have been an intimate of the Kennedys – they did not waste their time on foreign journalists who could influence no American votes; and I positively disliked their inflated rhetoric. But then American public speaking has little in common with the British parliamentary style, much more with the biblical cadences of the evangelical pulpit.

There is no doubt that the Kennedys used the media skilfully to stir up impatience with the Eisenhower lethargy and march the voters towards the rising sun crying, 'Let's get America moving again!' But I sensed that not everyone, perhaps only a bare majority, was packing for the New Frontier. My eve-of-poll article in the *Listener* was headlined *Kennedy to win by a narrow margin*, and that is how it turned out. In a total popular vote of 67.3 million, Kennedy had a majority of just over 100,000 which could well be attributed to the negroes.

So just before Christmas 1960 we left for Beirut by way of London.

Sylvia was already pregnant with our fourth and final child. Louis Heren and his family had caught up with us in Washington, so we bequeathed them our magnificent red long-haired cat, Orlando, a stately creature whom it was impossible to think of as being *American*. He simply had to stay in British hands. The coloured maid, Bernice, was equally relieved to find another post with the British. She was now 'by appointment', as it were, to the BBC, *The Times* and Reuters. 'Guess I've kinda got used to the accent,' she explained. But it had worked both ways: when we got to Beirut people asked, 'How is it you are English, yet you have three American children?'

It took us a little while to find a flat in Beirut – a separate house was virtually unobtainable – but when we did it was in a commanding situation near the American University, looking out onto the Mediterranean over the Corniche with a citrus grove between. Money was pouring into Beirut from the oil sheikhdoms in the Gulf and the pleasant old Ottoman houses were being torn down as each sheikh tried to build a more luxurious block than his neighbour, preferably blotting out his neighbour's view. The days of our orange grove were clearly numbered, but it was pleasant while it lasted.

In fact it was to last barely a year. From the start I felt unstable there. Life in Beirut was cheap, tax-free, everything was obtainable including servants and the climate was agreeable for almost all the year. You could, if you were that sort of person, go ski-ing at the Cedars in the morning, bathing at the beach in the afternoon, dine upon roast woodcock and Bekaa Valley wine, and then gamble the night away at the casino. There was a British Club, a British School and a large community of British businessmen, diplomats and journalists. Even our doctors from Delhi, the McKenzie-Pollocks, turned up.

Of the journalists the most conspicuous, if hardly the most active, was Kim Philby, officially working for the *Observer* and the *Economist*, who was perpetually drunk and rather pathetic. He and his American wife Eleanor were to be found in the bar of the Hotel Normandie from eleven o'clock in the morning onwards. In the evenings they would go round the cocktail parties, where Kim took a particular liking to Sylvia, once holding her hand on a balcony overlooking the Mediterranean while he recited Keats's 'Ode to a Nightingale'. Then he wandered off, bleating for Eleanor to take him home.

Very rarely he would talk about his friends Burgess and Maclean, blaming everything on the dastardly Maclean and lamenting that he (Kim) had been found guilty by association so far as those *brutal* men in Security were concerned. At least one very senior intelligence man in the British Embassy still took an interest in Kim (most of the Beirut embassies had intelligence men bulging out of the windows); but when Kim eventually vanished behind the Iron Curtain most of the rest of us found it impossible to believe there was still anything in him of value to the Russians. None of us realised the cynical pleasure he must have taken in splitting his personality in two so successfully.

Lebanese politics were in a state of suspended animation. There were at least a dozen identifiable communities, power being shared between them according to constitutional formula. With the money rolling in it was in none of their interests to rock the boat. The Palestinians were multiplying in their refugee camps but until King Hussein threw their fighters out of Jordan they lacked the firepower to make themselves heard in Lebanon. Most Lebanese groups were in the pay of some foreign patron – President Nasser, the Syrians, the Saudis, the French, the Americans – and would have sold the country to the highest bidder, except that no one was sure they had yet heard the highest bid.

There was the occasional bombing or assassination, as likely to be due to the drug trade as to politics: there was hardly one Lebanese story a month that would interest London, so the bulk of my service had to concern neighbouring Arab countries and was gleaned from local agencies which translated the Arabic press or monitored Arab radios. My scripts had to be stamped by the Lebanese censor, an elegant young man who lounged at his desk above the telegraph office, polishing a pearl-handled automatic; but he found everything I submitted 'trop ennuyeux' – too boring – to be worth more than a perfunctory glance. His only concern was not to annoy Nasser, and the one real fight I had with him was when Syria walked out of her short-lived union with Egypt. This, I wrote, would be a severe blow for President Nasser. 'You cannot say this blow,' declared the censor, tapping the offending word with his pistol. 'To an Arab leader it is a physical insult.' 'Setback, then?' I suggested. 'That is perfectly acceptable. A setback is abstract.'

I never learnt more than a few pages of phrasebook Arabic, getting around adequately on English, French and my oriental-taxi-driver accent (telegeraff offiss – Bereetish Embassee – 'otel), but I came to realise that Arabic has moods and naunces which can be drastically misunderstood in translation. A British ambassador once said to me, 'You know, Priestland, the Arabs believe things they know to be untrue,' but I think he was being insufficiently subtle. Arabic some-times tries to say, 'Would it not be nice if this were true? It ought to be true. It is unpatriotic to deny it is true. It is *morally* true.' English spoils everything by translating, 'It is true.'

Something else I learned was that you never got your way, as you could in India, by coming the old pukka sahib and shouting at them; that only made Arabs nastier and more obstructive. I spent a great deal of time in Arab consulates applying for visas, to which the first response was invariably no – because if the applicant accepted it and went away a great deal of tiresome paperwork would have been saved. The determined applicant should not be so easily put off. He sank back in his chair with a disappointed sigh and an expression of sympathy at the difficulties faced by the consul – the need to be careful, to sort out the wheat from the chaff, to exclude those whose activities were not what they seemed on the surface . . . thank you, a cup of Turkish coffee would be most hospitable – the consul's country was, of course, noted for its hospitality and one had been looking forward to experiencing it at first hand . . . So the courtship went on, patiently, if need be until closing time. There is an Arab tradition of paying one's respects to a high official by just sitting quietly in his presence, implying that this in itself is a privilege. Quite apart from what a newsman may pick up from the comings and goings of other clients of the great man, there is a good chance that eventually he will break down under the weight of his obligation to you – for a whole morning he has been the sole object of your flattering attentions – and he will give you what you want. 'Very well, I will give you visa – but only for one week!' Such generosity! Such authority! Naturally His Excellency had to be sure of one's sincerity – there were some who sought visas with no intention of actually using them, who wasted His Excellency's time . . . 'OK. I give two weeks. Now office closing.'

Having got your visa with such assurances, it was as well to use it or there might not be another. The trouble was this often meant visiting a country for the sake of the visa rather than for any active story. Active stories in the Middle East tended to be coups d'état, which happened without warning and invalidated the visa that you might have extracted from the regime now overthrown. I was constantly dashing to the Syrian border to find the gates slammed in my face and only a trickle of information leaking out through them. After one of these crises I eventually got through to Damascus and asked my principal contact there what he had thought of my output. 'Pretty good,' he remarked, 'in fact almost as well informed as the Voice of Israel.'

I liked Damascus – its fabulous bazaar, where you bought gold by weight; its great carpet-filled mosque which was once a Christian basilica; its elegant museum, organised by the French, which included one of the oldest synagogues in the world. But the United Arab Republic, with Egypt, was not proving a success: government departments were full of Egyptians moaning about the incompetence of the Syrians and Syrians moaning about the arrogance of the Egyptians. The Arabs have a yearning for unity and it is considered bad form to reject the most incongruous of marriage proposals. The mistake Nasser made was to attempt consummation instead of leaving it as a spiritual gesture.

Nevertheless the threat of Nasserite takeovers kept the entire Middle East in a state of jitters at that time – still more my headquarters in London which kept sending me off to watch for rumoured coups as far afield as Teheran. The Shah still had twenty years to run and was steady as a rock so far as I could see, thanks to the diligence of his infamous secret police, *Savak*; but I had no objection to viewing the Persian antiquities, gossiping with world-weary Iranian intellectuals and lunching on vodka, toast and caviar. Teheran is the only place in the world where I have been able to afford *enough* caviar, for, as one effete young second secretary at the British Embassy remarked, 'There is nothing more squalid than too much *second-rate* caviar.'

Normally I did not rely very much on our embassies for information: an active correspondent has greater freedom of movement and choice of contacts than the average diplomat. But with a dozen countries on my beat I had little choice in the Middle East. Some embassies were less helpful than others, however, and the one in Teheran was notoriously snooty towards journalists, refusing to allow them in its swimming pool or to get beyond the information office at its gates. There were actually two embassies: one behind high walls in the middle of Teheran, and a summer embassy in the hills outside, shaded by tall plane trees and watered by its own subterranean *qanat* which fed a network of tinkling streams and provided an idyllic setting for the Embassy Players' production of *A Midsummer Night's Dream*. I *was* invited to that, but not, of course, in the best seats.

Walled gardens were one of the joys of Teheran. One of the most spectacular belonged to the Iranian correspondent of the United Press news agency, and as you were admitted through its gateway and progressed up a winding path towards the house you could not help being struck by a series of lifesize plaster casts of a naked woman posing among the flowers and bushes. It was something of an embarrassment, when you got there, to have the door opened by (very obviously) the model – his wife. And she knew you knew she knew.

Baghdad was the greatest possible contrast. It had taken me days to get a visa, and when I arrived at the airport they tried to confiscate my typewriter on the grounds that I might use it to circulate subversive propaganda. When I pointed out that it did not even type Arabic they admitted it only on condition that it be granted its own visa, which they inscribed in the space labelled 'Accompanied by his wife'. For months afterwards immigration officers were demanding to see Mrs Olivetti Priestland.

The suspicion continued. My room in the Baghdad Hotel was bugged, and the bathroom, too, via the telephone which emitted a gentle frying noise and babbled when they wound the tape back at the other end. Information was practically unobtainable, for the army junta which slaughtered the royal family had cultivated a fanatical hatred of foreigners and very few Iraqis would speak to me. It was no comfort to hear that on the day of the coup a mob had descended on my hotel and driven away a coachload of German businessmen who were never seen again.

The climate was appalling. When the sandstorms cleared the sun beat down like a sledgehammer, driving you into the ground. But at least the embassy was friendly – glad to be visited by anyone, even a journalist – and allowed me into its swimming pool where I floated side by side with the ambassador while he told me of their daily humiliations which included the regular heaving of dead dogs and donkeys over the compound wall. About the only other relaxation was to wait for sunset and visit the open-air cafés on the mudflats of the Tigris, where you could get charcoal-broiled catfish – the nearest thing to a Baghdad delicacy – and watch Iraqi television, trying to guess whether the flies you could see were on the screen or in the studio. If the actors twitched you knew it was the studio. The shutdown of TV was always marked by the showing of a speech by the Leader, Abdul Karim Kassem, whose appearance was the cue for the abrupt disappearance of everyone in sight. One of the eeriest pictures in my memory is that of looking along those mudflats over rows and rows of empty tables and rows and rows of ranting Kassems on flickering screens. There was a poetic justice about his end; for two years later they shot him – 'live' as they say – on TV and propped his body before the camera for several hours while the ratings soared.

Perhaps to get rid of me the Iraqi authorities did grant me a permit to visit the port of Basra for one day. It was an alarming flight, tying with Union of Burma Airways for sheer laxity of procedure: so far as the Iraqis were concerned small *female* children did not count as passengers and were left to roll up and down the aisle as the aircraft climbed or descended. When I protested to the pilot – an American who had been defrocked by some obscure mid-western airline – he urged me to write in about it, 'But not till you're out of the country. The last foreigner who complained got beaten up by Passenger Relations.' Anyhow, we made it to Basra where, incredibly, I was given a hotel room looking out onto the riverside wharf where a Russian freighter was unloading a shipment of tanks. This was news.

But how to get the story out? It was not worth trying to cable it, and on the one occasion when I had tried to broadcast in voice to London it had been quite inaudible and my script, heavily censored, had been followed intently by an army officer with a revolver. The only hope was to use my miniature recorder – out of earshot of the hotel bugs – and airfreight the tape back to London. Even so it would have to be passed by no fewer than three different censors – the information department, the foreign ministry and the army. Gambling on the chance that they would not know about twin-track machines I recorded my dispatch about the tanks on one side of the tape, turned the reel over and recorded a version of the introduction to the catalogue of the Mesopotamian Museum on the other and (for the benefit of London) absentmindedly hummed a few bars of 'Roll me over in the clover' at the end. It worked, and London got the message. If the censors *had* asked to hear both sides I could still have fooled them by keeping my finger on a switch that cut out the loudspeaker. Fortunately they could not have played my tape on any machine of their own, but they were surprised I should have come all that way to write anything so dreary. 'It's for what we call the Third Programme,' I explained. 'Very learned, very boring.'

One drawback of having been to Iraq was that I now could not get into Kuwait. The Iraqis had decided that Kuwait really belonged to them and the sight of an Iraqi visa in one's passport was a mortal affront to the Kuwaitis. Not for the last time I defaced Her Majesty's property by covering the offending page with Lebanese excise stamps, overprinted smudgily with a rubber stamp marked *Urgent* and finished off with an illegible signature. No one ever asked what it was and I got into Kuwait in time for a state visit by the King of Saudi Arabia.

Kuwait was hardly ten years into the oil business and although the Americans, Europeans and Japanese were all drilling away like mad there was still something left of the old Gulf culture: the shipyards where the dhows were built beside the quicksilver sea, the low courtyard houses, the desert on the doorstep trying to sneak in. The new Kuwait was coming up in steel and concrete but the main symptoms of it were four-lane highways going nowhere, whose frequent roundabouts betrayed their British design. The oilfield workers were mostly foreigners from as far away as Pakistan. The main occupations of the native Kuwaitis seemed to be driving taxis and watering the doomed saplings that some city planner had decreed along the four-lane highways. If you wanted a bottle of Scotch in Kuwait you went to the sheikh who held the concession – Jock al-Ghaneim – the only sheikh in the Gulf (he boasted) with a Glasgow accent.

The King of Saudi Arabia turned up with a triple escort: on the fringe, a pack of American-trained gangsters in tropical suits and dark glasses; in the middle, a squad of fairly up-to-date soldiers with submachine guns; and, surrounding the royal person, a horde of tribal bodyguards festooned with muskets, bandoliers and curved daggers, men who were plainly after the king's heart and mainly (it was said) the fruit of his own loins. Some of them, dressed in crimson and very dirty, were described as minstrels and court jesters. They did not amuse the Kuwaitis by slaughtering sheep on the promenade and defecating in the gutter.

The royal tour consisted of dashing across the desert from oilfield to oilfield in a fleet of Cadillacs, one of which really did have gold-plated trimmings but looked disappointingly drab. From time to time the leading Cadillac would hit a sand-drift and go careering off the road, where it was simply abandoned to be looted by Bedouin. High spot of the visit was a banquet in the ruler of Kuwait's new marble palace, though in some ways it was more like an orgy with the tables piled high with food. The centrepiece of each table was a roast baby camel stuffed with a sheep which in turn was stuffed with chickens which in turn were stuffed with hard-boiled eggs. Naturally enough, I was seated amongst the court jesters and what jesters like, above all, is hard-boiled eggs. In a trice they were on the table, hauling out the sheep, tearing apart the chickens and fighting for the eggs. From time to time one of them would wander up to the top table, murmur a jest in the king's ear – at which he never even smiled – and potter back again. I ate little myself.

Habits were cleaner at the royal court of Jordan, in fact they were up to Buckingham Palace standards. I say this as a result of attending King Hussein's wedding to Miss Toni Gardner, an English soldier's daughter, which provided yet another of those press expeditions full of colour and uproar but signifying very little. *Royal* weddings, especially those with the Cinderella touch, attract hordes of Mediterranean photographers – Corsicans, Sicilians, Maltese and Cypriots – beside whom the conduct of Fleet Street's lowest seems positively Wykehamist. The mob that descended on Amman snarled with rage when the royal public relations man told them they could *not* witness the signing of the marriage contract: '*Eh bien,*' snapped one of the Corsicans, '*on va forcer!*' And force it they did. As the king bent over the document to affix his signature there was a tinkling of glass and a long lens came through the dome overhead. The Corsicans paid for it, though, with a beating at the hands of the Circassian Guard.

Marrying an English girl might have been the cue for Hussein's overthrow, which was why most of the press were there. But the king packed the town with his loyal Arab Legion and carried it off with his usual guts. Afterwards, in the bar of the Philadelphia Hotel, I was drinking with Alan MacGregor, a wry little Scots gnome who reported for almost everybody in the Middle East at one time or another, including the BBC, until he removed to Geneva. One of the flying squad from Fleet Street – clueless as ever – asked anxiously if we knew what presents the royal couple had given one another. 'I hear Toni gave the King a swimming pool in lapis lazuli for the royal palace,' said Alan solemnly. Frivolously I added a bikini in solid gold thread as Hussein's gift in return. And there they were in black and white two days later when the papers arrived from London.

As he grew older Hussein added a fine sense of diplomatic balance to his courage. The fanatics will get him one day, I am afraid, but I cannot think of any other ruler now living who has stood for so long in the same hair-raising place without getting run over. The way he manages to juggle the hostile powers around him and the rival factions within is breathtaking. Hussein was always ready to keep his British connections in good repair by granting an interview to the BBC and there were times when one had to dodge the invitation to invite him. 'Unwant interview little chief yet again' as London once cabled me.

Amman, an honest enough small town, was far from glittering. I used to broadcast from the back seat of an old Southdown bus abandoned by the British Army and converted into a studio by Cable & Wireless. In the evening there was always the floor show at the one and only night club, but this tended to consist of adagio dancers 'straight from their fantastic success at Homs, Syria' or an alleged fashion parade which was really an excuse for Jordanian gentlemen to stare at untalented English girls in their underwear. On the eve of the royal wedding they gave a huge ovation to a young lady in bra, panties, bridal headdress and bouquet who glided across the stage to Mendelssohn's Wedding March.

MacGregor and I decided there would be no coup and left for Jerusalem, where the Old City was still under Jordanian control including the American Colony Hotel, which is not in the least American and remains one of my favourites anywhere. Alan had promised to introduce me to the jolly fellowship of the British School of Archaeology, under Kathleen Kenyon, excavator of Jericho. Each archaeologist kept a bottle of gin on a side-table in the dining hall and jealously marked the level with a chinagraph after pouring out a drink; visitors gained popularity by donating a bottle and declaring it free for all.

Alan sent me off to explore the holy places. 'I'll be interested', he said, 'to see what they do to you.' What they did, as he expected, was to shock me profoundly, especially the Church of the Holy Sepulchre. The alleged Tomb was like a large, dusty tea-caddy and the church around it was falling down because the warring denominations could not agree on how to restore it (though they have now). Greeks tried to shout down the mass of the Latins, Copts and Armenians tripped up one another's processions and clobbered each other with crucifixes. There were decoy banknotes on the slab where the body of Christ had lain, and the poor Ethiopians – who lived in exile on the roof – chanted raucous psalms through the skylights of St Helena's Chapel. Even the supposed site of the Crucifixion was divided down the middle between the Greeks and the Latins. The whole place was hung with tinsel like a Christmas bazaar, and there was not a decent northern protestant presence to the seen. I told Alan how appalled I was.

'Do ye not think,' he suggested, 'that it's a microcosm of the Church on earth – with all its quarrels and divisions? Does it not remind ye too that, originally, Christianity wasna meant to be the cold intellectual thing we've made of it in the north, but a religion of the east and the south – hot-blooded and human?'

He was right, of course, and on subsequent visits I came to see it that way, too. But I never came closer to my God, my Jesus, than away from the crowded shrines, sitting out under the stars among the olive trees of Gethsemane or at any of the rival 'Shepherds' fields' outside Bethlehem. The Church of the Nativity convinces me as well: of course the stable was a cave – you can see beasts stabled in caves all over Judaea.

After a few days I came to love the old Jerusalem, with its honey-

SOMETHING UNDERSTOOD

coloured stone and its aroma of pine and pepper vines. The British archeologists explained how it was not and could not be the Jerusalem of the Bible, but it stood for it very well, apart from the Tomb and Calvary. General Gordon's Garden Tomb and Golgotha, behind the bus station, are certainly bogus but somehow they carry more conviction than the authentic ones.

It was tough luck on the Jews, excluded from their own equally holy places and watching resentfully through the barbed wire; but for a Christian pilgrim Jordanian Jerusalem was pleasantly snoozy and remarkably free of commercial pollution. I shall provoke howls of rage from my Jewish friends by writing this, but if only it could have become a neutral, international city of all faiths it would have been the holier for it.

Though the BBC had been thrown out of Cairo as a residence it was once again possible for its correspondent to go there as a visitor. Egyptians are tolerant, friendly people, scarcely Arabs at all, and I encountered no hostility whatever among them. Cairo is a huge, seething city, not as variegated as it used to be when there were large communities of Greeks and Jews and French there, but still far more worldly-wise than Baghdad or Teheran and less newly-rich and provincial than Beirut. It was shabby and rather pissy-smelling under Nasser, but seemed to be saying that normal service would be restored as soon as possible. Meanwhile the great Museum remained the grandest junk-shop in the world, stuffed with riches that had never been properly labelled or catalogued; you could still take a luscious tea at Groppis; and behind the pyramids there was a nightclub in a carpet-hung marquee where you got kebabs, a Nubian floor-show and a bottle of genuine Dimple Haig for about five pounds. No belly-dancing, though. Nasser considered it degrading and had imported a team of Russian folk-dancing instructors to devise something more decorous. The belly-dancers had been ordered to wrap up their bellies in gauze, which defeated the purpose of the operation, so they had gone on strike.

Shepheard's Hotel having been burned down by the mob some years earlier, I used to stay at a second-rate place called the Metropolitan. It had originally been the Cosmopolitan but under the nationalist revolution that was deemed to have unEgyptian overtones. Despite the reputation for luxury that I may have acquired with the reader by now, the fact is that I prefer shabby hotels: generally you get no less than you pay for in them and they are more likely than the Intercontinental Sheraton-Hiltons to let in occasional whiffs of the country

—— *186* ——

they are supposed to be in. What really counts, from the foreign correspondent's point of view, is communications. Do the telephones work, and is there an efficient concierge who dispatches and delivers your telegrams smartly and passes on the gossip (particularly about other correspondents)? The concierge at the Metropolitan had earned the devotion of the press corps by sheltering it while the mob was burning Shepheard's and, when it moved on to the Metropolitan demanding to lynch the *feranghis* turning it away with a rhetorical, 'You don't think foreigners would stay in a crummy place like this, do you?' So we stayed for years afterwards, even though one woke in the morning to find the ceiling had snowed flakes of whitewash all night, and the family that lived on the roof opposite watched one dressing, and the lift was XIIIth Dynasty and there were Bulgarians in the dining room breakfasting on beer.

Alan MacGregor, who had mysteriously managed not to get expelled from Cairo, was the BBC's 'stringer' or part-time correspondent there as well as everyone else's. He would start by writing his story for *The Times*, because that was the longest, and then compose parodies of it in the house style of all the other newspapers he served, which ranged as far apart as the *Daily Mirror* and the *Economist*. His output was phenomenal. 'There's an auld precedent here for making bricks without straw,' he would say, 'but the real trick is making them without mud, either.' He introduced me to a number of good bourgeois restaurants, one of which specialised in spitted pigeons, while the street pigeons peered in innocently at the window.

Cairo's cheapness was embarrassing. Before leaving Beirut I used to visit the moneychangers in the Rue Hamra and turn sterling into whatever rials, piastres or liras I needed. On visits to the more obscure Gulf states it was advisable to take some of the enormous Maria-Teresa silver dollars, recently minted but always dated 1780, which gave a satisfying clang as they were counted out. The Beirut foreign exchange market was completely free of controls and most of the currencies I purchased were extremely cheap. Back in London, however, the BBC accounts department insisted on applying Bank of England rates which were fixed and more in favour of the foreigner, with the result that I made a large profit on almost every trip, especially those to Turkey and Egypt whose banknotes were regarded as little better than toilet paper on the Rue Hamra. I always owned up to this in my accounts, accumulating huge surpluses which the BBC – alarmed that I must be doing something illegal – refused to acknowledge. It took me months to persuade them even to split the difference with me. I found myself arguing that I actually *had* to eat caviar in Teheran in order to make the books balance. It was not the first time the BBC had got me into a financial mess. The salary it paid me was not large compared with most newspaper correspondents; but in line with the diplomatic service the Corporation paid any income tax I incurred abroad. In Delhi, where anyone with more than about £50 a week (a fortune by Indian standards) paid punitive rates of tax, the foreign correspondents had a cosy agreement with the head of the civil service that they would declare only a portion of their incomes. When I explained this to London I was told it laid me open to official pressure and I was to declare *everything*; with the result that the BBC had to pay a huge sum on my behalf, all the other correspondents had to fall into line and none of them would speak to me for months.

I welcomed expeditions to Turkey, not because it was madly gay (Ankara was grim and my *Daily Express* colleague used to fine his paper double expenses for sending him there) but because it had quite a different flavour from the Arab world and a whole new set of political factors from which Islam was officially excluded. The Turks seemed to have more in common with Central Asia than the Middle East and their language whose one-two-three-four-five went bir-ikki-ooch-dert-besh, whose yes was evvet, whose no was hayir, which said yok for there isn't any and made me wear a badge saying basin instead of press? Much of the time I found myself retreating into German: the Turks felt an affinity with our late enemies and many of them had done a stint in the Volkswagen works.

Still, I could not help respecting them if not quite loving them. Somewhere in the Turkish character lay a streak of savagery that had ridden out of Mongolia with the galloping hordes. Kemal Ataturk, the Father of Modern Turkey, had commanded them to become Europeans and they sweated conscientiously at it – you could still eat in restaurants where Ataturk had set the tone by doffing his fez, donning his spats and indulging in *thé dansant* – but from time to time the effort was too much and they reverted. Something of the kind caught up with the wretched Prime Minister Adnan Menderes, who was overthrown by the army and put on trial for high treason and corruption.

The trial took place in an army gymnasium on Yassiada Island, not far from Instanbul, where the foreign press were invited to witness the sentencing. It was a mass trial of the ex-government; the accused were marched in by batches, and when the former premier's group came in we could see he was not there. He and two of his ministers were condemned to death but there was no Menderes to be seen. After a moment's murmuring in the press gallery an officer appeared and tapped myself and the Reuters man on the shoulder. 'Follow me!' Which we did, to a small house at the back of the island where we were shown Menderes lying unconscious – tubes up his nose, tubes down his throat, tubes in his veins – as the doctors fought to bring him back to life. He had saved up his sleeping pills for two or three weeks and swallowed them all at once.

Back to life they brought him; and a few days later, when he was fit to stand, they killed him properly. They dressed him in a white sheet, put a placard round his neck describing his crimes, and hanged him rather slowly – strangled him, really – from a tripod, along with his two colleagues. The photos appeared instantly in the Istanbul papers. 'Like you English,' said the colonel at the information office, 'we believe in justice for all, no matter how exalted. Also democracy. Very soon there the army will withdraw and there will be free and fair elections.' And there were. I toured Istanbul, Izmir and parts of Anatolia (where, incidentally, there really were flocks of turkeys in the fields) and those elections were as free and fair as any I have seen. Menderes sympathisers emerged as the largest single grouping, and the army managed to bear it (though Turkish soldiers seldom grin). It matters little now, but once again I managed to forecast the result correctly, unlike colleagues who sat it out in the agreeable fleshpots of Istanbul. Now there is a great city: there is more peace under the domes of its mosques than in any Christian cathedral I know.

Somewhere amidst these wanderings I got a telegram ordering me to 'proceed Belgradewards' to cover something called the Nonaligned Nations Summit – a kind of mutual admiration society of the power-less. Crazily, the quickest way of getting there turned out to be to fly to Geneva, change for Zurich and then take the Orient Express, a dilapidated skeleton of its former self. Each country it passed through maintained it was the next country's job to provide a restaurant car: so there was no food, apart from what one could grab through the windows from platform vendors. The company, instead of being romantic secret agents, was mostly other, equally frustrated, foreign correspondents. I spent most of the journey listening to a recital by the garrulous Jean-Jacques Servan-Schreiber who at that time was a prominent member of the BBC's slender repertory company of approved English-speaking foreigners, a kind of one-man political and diplomatic brains trust.

Still, Belgrade had its faded charms. We were put up in an Austro-

Hungarian period hotel where the food was excellent and a Serbian band played wild gipsy music late into the night. The bar contained little but slivovitz and as there was a great deal of hanging about and consequent stress-deprivation, the press corps was continuously hung-over for the duration of the conference. We contrasted shabbily with the world's nonaligned (which meant anti-American) leaders: they were all there, from Nehru and U Nu to Sekou Touré and Tito (who, with the sumptuous Madame Tito, was playing host). The Titos plainly saw it as their answer to the Congress of Vienna, with the minimum of conferring and the maximum of banquets and recep-tions, and their guests entered into the spirit of the thing; the more insignificant the nation, the more gorgeously costumed its delegates.

At one of these receptions I bumped, literally, into the King of Nepal and struck up a conversation about his unforgettable coronation in Kathmandhu. 'Those carvings,' I said, 'is it true they keep away lightning?' 'We lose more pagodas from lightning than any other cause,' said His Majesty. He seemed pleased to have found someone he could talk to, chatted about the merits of Eton or Harrow for the Crown Prince, and – as the distinguished guests began moving towards the banquet hall – drew me along with him. I found myself parading between two rows of presidential guards behind whom my colleagues (for whom an economical buffet had been laid on the verandah) shook their fists and gnashed their teeth. Arrived at the table, a few chairs away from the Titos, I managed to ease myself into one of the places set for interpreters and enjoyed (I suppose) the most elevated company of my career – at any rate I enjoyed the banquet: better caviar than even Teheran had to offer, sturgeon meunière, wild boar shot by Tito in person – the vegetarians among the nonaligned shuddered and picked at their salads. I picked up enough confer-ence gossip to make an entertaining piece for From Our Own Correspondent – oh, vanity, vanity! But it was fun.

In fact these expeditions were punctuated by the occasional week or two in Beirut with Sylvia and the children. Now we were six: for in April 1961 – in fact on Queen Elizabeth II's birthday – our fourth child Diana was born, in the American University Hospital. Like Jennet, her elder sister, she was a redhead and a great beauty. The hospital gave her a birth certificate in Arabic, so I hurried round to the British Embassy and got her registered as authentically British.

We had engaged a dark Lebanese girl called Camelia as nursemaid, and an Assyrian cook named Despina, so that Sylvia had help enough in the home while I was away. But it was becoming very clear that this was no way for any of us to live if we intended to be a real family. Jennet and Andreas were going to school, where they made friends, but Oliver was a hyperactive little boy for whom our flat was not big enough. Once, driving home down the lane, I met him– his face red with rage – running away from home at the age of four. Goodness knows what would have become of him if he had got very far into Beirut.

In effect Sylvia, with a new baby at her breast, was having to bring up a one-parent family, and though she coped magnificently in the best Rhodes tradition, the unfairness of it bothered me deeply. My ceaseless movement round the Middle East in search of stories to satisfy London helped to keep my mythical 'pursuers' at bay, but at the cost of bitter guilt when I came home. The conflict between the urge to travel and satisfy my masters and the urge to stay at home and satisfy my family became intolerable. I wrote to Tony Wigan that my mind felt like an old radio set that had been kicked around and could no longer pick up intelligible signals – only a long howl; once again, I could see no joy and no future.

Tony wrote back understandingly: he had to have a medical report first, but it looked as if I should come home. In any case, it would be a good idea for me to get some experience of television which was becoming more and more important to the news division. So I went to see the elderly Swiss doctor with whom Mollie McKenzie-Pollock shared her practice and virtually dictated him a letter recommending my recall. In fact he could find nothing wrong with me, as he told Sylvia, but I was adamant that I could not stay: two more years of this restless, rootless life, of intermittent marriage and children who seemed hardly mine, seemed to me a sentence of death. A superstitious dread seized me that I would never complete my forties if I stayed in the Middle East.

Was I taking an easy way out? Hardly, for it was a professional defeat and a matter of deep shame. The one job I had longed for, that of the dashing foreign correspondent, had proved too much for me, but only after it had unfitted me for anything else. I knew from the experience of others how hard it was for a returned correspondent to settle down again to the humdrum routine of shifts in the newsroom, and how stay-at-home colleagues regarded him as out-of-touch and rather spoilt. I managed to take Sylvia for a weekend in Jerusalem, but had to tell the British archaeologists we would not be joining them for their dig at Petra. 'A pity,' they said. 'We'd reserved a special cave for the baby.'

Chapter Seven

ON THE BOX

Though a little shocked at our extravagance in producing a fourth child, my parents were glad to see us back in England again. They had missed having grandchildren to dote on in their declining years, and now they were readily to hand. Jennet was my mother's favourite and helped her at her kitchen crafts, while Andreas solemnly understudied my father in the garden at Potten End. Each of the elder children grew up to resemble its grandparent both in temperament and appearance. Mrs Rhodes, whose seven children supplied her with upwards of twenty grandchildren, petted them all equally and was scrupulous in avoiding favourites. The two grandmothers became known as Country Granny and London Granny.

It was the London Granny who came to our rescue as we looked for somewhere to live, for we had retained no place of our own and there was no question of settling anywhere but in London. My parents may have dreamed of having us near them in Hertfordshire, but it was too far from the studios for my liking and I knew that Sylvia – for whom civilisation ends at the North Circular Road – would have been miserable in Cooper country.

With an eye to providing a retirement home for Bill Rhodes, who was still a missionary in India, his mother had purchased a small cottage in Hampstead Garden Suburb. It was vacant at that time and we could just squeeze into it, grateful yet miserable, for it was a hard winter with snow on the ground and all of us fell ill: Sylvia caught mumps and I contracted yet another of my chest infections which extended this time to the painful complaint of pleurisy.

As I had expected, the BBC did not really know what to do with me, though it seemed logical to assign me to television news which was just beginning to spread its wings. For a short time foreign news had tried to make its correspondents double as cameramen by equipping them with a 16mm tourist camera as well as a tape recorder and

The author interviewing Lal Bahadur Shastri, Nehru's successor as Prime Minister of India, Delhi, 1964.

The author and ex-Archbishop Lord Ramsey, 1981.

typewriter, but that was mercifully stamped on by the cameramen's union. As a result I had to learn vision journalism from scratch. A place was going on a staff training course in television production, so that seemed the ideal solution to the problem of what to do with Priestland. The trouble was, TV production called for faculties of imagination I simply did not have.

Those were the days before the universal adoption of the zoom lens, a flexible device which enables you to frame almost any size of shot with the same lens. Its drawback is that in most positions it has a rather shallow depth of field, so that as two people speak to each other at different distances from the camera, the focus has to drift nervously to and fro between them. But in 1961 BBC cameras were still fitted with a turret of three or four fixed lenses, each with a different angle of vision, which had to be selected in advance. One spent hours with a chart of the studio floor working out the lenses and movements of the cameras – something I found it very hard to visualise.

Things were no easier when it came to the action, because contrary to my dream of the TV director as a captain on his bridge with a clear view of the sea, the director usually sees nothing of the studio, his sight being blocked by banks of monitor screens each giving the blinkered view of one particular camera. Where the brutes really are, one can only guess. *My* cameras backed into one another, took pictures of each other or of unwanted corners of the studio, knotted up each other's cables and shunted into the scenery like bulls in a boudoir. In despair I tried to devise a script needing only one camera, but was ruled out of order. Some of my fellow students produced ballets, cookery demonstrations, horror stories, and went on to become heads of BBC departments; but my final exercise – a demonstration of telepathy which actually demonstrated nothing – was so disastrous that half my cast froze with terror and the other half burst into tears. I was sent back to the news division with a strong recommendation I stick to radio. 'I don't think you're quite ready for the latter half of the twentieth century, Gerald,' said the chief instructor wearily.

But radio did not want me, either. I was assigned to Alexandra Palace, the BBC's original centre for all its television though now big enough only for its news operation. The Palace was easily accessible from Hampstead Garden Suburb and despite its outward appearance of being a reproduction of Gormenghast it was actually a pleasant place to work in, oddly detached from the rude world it was presenting to the viewer. After the hurly burly of Beirut it was positively relaxing to sit there, at the top of a tower, looking out over wooded parkland with a race-course at the foot of the hill, a boating lake at the back and such diversions as a bowling alley, a roller-skating rink and a number of pubs and bars to hand. One could even pop out in the lunch hour, auction one's car and stake the money on a horse.

In human terms, Alexandra Palace TV news was one of the happiest ships ever to sail under the Corporation flag. It owed much of its success to the presence in its midst of the BBC Club – a large hall with a bar and a buffet where, every lunchtime, the editor propped himself in a corner, accessible to everyone from the dispatch-rider to the diplomatic correspondent. Unfortunately that spirit collapsed when the news moved to its custom-built high-tech wing at the White City, where the news people found themselves lost in an ocean of actors, musicians and top-of-the-poppers. News esprit-de-corps never recovered from it. It was a mistake that commercial television's ITN avoided by segregating itself in its own West End building and having nothing to do with anybody else.

One might have expected television news to be run by someone from the old cinema newsreels, but the BBC hated importing outsiders. The first editor I encountered was Pat Smithers, a former organiser of radio reporters. Next, if I remember rightly, came Stewart Hood – a dark, tormented figure from some John le Carré novel – followed by Michael Peacock (known as 'the Young Master') who hurtled through on his way to higher things like founding BBC's Channel 2 and breaking his neck on the slippery slopes of commercial TV.

My own job at Alexandra Palace was to liaise with the foreign correspondents, advise on the importance of events abroad and write commentary for the film that came in from overseas. This meant acquiring the entirely new skill of telling the story with pictures: not so bad as the training-course nightmare, for there was something you could hold in your hands and look at. Or rather, you crouched over the film editor as he spun it through the viewing-machine, selecting the shots, timing them with a stopwatch and then writing the commentary to fit.

And here lay the danger, the *trahison des clercs*. For Alexandra Palace was full of highly intelligent journalists who had been brought up in print or radio, were determined to show they could master vision as well and were carried away by its possibilities, sometimes to the ruin of the truth. All too often the medium perverted the message. For if the camera cannot lie, the cameraman, the film editor and a complaisant script writer most certainly can, and with great conviction.

It is not simply that the moving picture is bound to distract attention from what is being said – that you cannot prevent people from wandering off after the thought, 'How tired he's looking,' or 'Whatever is that car in the background?' Television has derived its grammar from the cinema. It cannot resist trying to entertain; and though all journalism must strive to entertain in the sense of being interesting the sort of programmes that surround the news on television force it to play their game or appear dowdy and dull. Pace, colour, action and good looks assume an importance they do not really deserve. BBC news, which is much more closely integrated with the entertainment machine than ITN is, constantly fiddles with its sets, its opening titles and its presenters because of this urge.

Which is not to say that all television news is corrupt. It is up to the reporter on the spot, who directs the cameraman and usually supplies the commentary, to see that the story tells the truth. But he, too, will be tempted to heighten the drama in order to get his report on the air, and he cannot be sure what will happen once it has left his hands and arrived in the news factory beyond his control. Television, it seems to me, is a kind of colour supplement to a balanced news diet. It races by, full of sound and fury, leaving very little solid information behind. Radio is more efficient at conveying the basic facts with speed and economy. Only print has the space and permanence to allow considered appraisal. It cannot be denied that television packs a breathtaking punch at times of disaster, but it is like turning everything into grand opera when all one may need is a little straightforward prose. The sheer cost of it, and of the armies of middlemen needed for everything, is, I suspect, inherently sinful. Can it possibly be worth all that money to show us Princess Di having her hand kissed by a man in Melbourne two hours ago?

In those early 1960s we had not yet arrived at the satellite nor even at videotape, though both were trembling on the brink and colour, too, was in the offing along with the 625-line picture which was to banish the venetian-blind effect of the old 405-line system. The BBC's engineers produced a monstrous video-recorder named VERA which took up the equivalent of a bed-sitting room, while Pat Smithers devised an apparatus which cabled film – alternate frame by alternate frame – very slowly across the Atlantic. Both these latter-day British miracles were swept aside by the Americans, and before long Ampex, the satellites and the Eurovision network were ruling the day. I was brought up on a TV technology that was staggering into its grave.

Our news film at Alexandra Palace was black-and-white, often on the cumbersome 35mm stock beloved of old cinema hands. We normally worked with it in negative, to save time, reversing it electronically on transmission. Thus one became accustomed to seeing the world's white statesmen as black men and the black leaders as white – very confusing when one met them face-to-face.

A large proportion of the film also arrived silent, the sound effects being added from gramophone records or a collection of sonorous junk in our own dubbing theatre. The records were limited. They included a banquet, a riot, a battlefield (alleged to be the Somme) and footsteps in the British Museum Reading Room, as well as a hardy perennial called 'Prov-town' (which was supposed to convey the atmosphere of a small town anywhere in the Western world) and 'Chinky Prov-town' (which was a small town anywhere East of Suez). The sound of a space rocket being launched was achieved by playing the stock disk of Niagara Falls very slowly backwards. I tried to enlarge the repertoire by donating some genuine recordings I had made in India, but most of these were dismissed as unconvincing. One from the middle of Old Delhi turned out to include the voice of a prostitute advertising her wares, which brought in complaints from Urdu-speaking listeners.

Into this unreal, alchemistical world it was my duty to initiate such foreign correspondents as came home on leave, teaching them to shot-list their film and write their commentaries to match. A few of them took to it with gusto. Anthony Lawrence, our enthusiast in Southeast Asia, got the idea of writing his commentary first and then forcing the local inhabitants to live up to it. I watched reel after reel of a minor epic in which he made an entire Vietnamese village retire to bed, get up and drive their oxen into the fields over and over again until every movement coincided with what he said.

Other correspondents folded their arms and said they were dogs too old to learn such new tricks. One or two treated it as a kind of party game. Ian McDougall contemptuously mastered the art of commentary in an afternoon, recorded a single masterpiece and refused to waste his time upon it ever again. Christopher Serpell was asked to do a story about the political situation in the Sudan for which we could find no pictures except some very old library footage of wild birds and fertility dancing on the banks of the Nile. To a montage of flapping wings, dusky nipples and tribal drums Christopher recorded a suave piece of analysis subliminally tacked to the pictures with phrases like *flights of fancy*, *points being thrust forward* and *throbbing with discontent*. It launched a whole school of subtly allusive soundtracks which flourished until Michael Peacock complained they sounded like *The Times* crossword puzzle. The last straw came when he heard four puns in a single story, two of which had to be explained to him.

The fact was there was a good deal of frustrated talent in Alexandra Palace, though it was being deliberately stockpiled against the opening of BBC 2. The cry had gone up for 'news in depth' and in preparation for this we began experimenting with the kind of half-hour programme which is now pretty standard; together with a departure from the old announcer-newsreader who just read what was put in front of him by somebody else, and the enthronement of the journalist-newsreader who wrote as much as possible of his own script and functioned as an editor and reporter as well. We told ourselves it was to be a reporters' programme. We entitled it News Extra.

The team included John Timpson, John Tidmarsh, Donald Milner, Peter Woods, Peter Woon and myself, most of us experienced in radio but all of us eager to break new ground in the medium before us. The question was, how were we to be truly televisual for half an hour on end instead of the usual ten or fifteen minutes?

Part of the answer, which was my concern, was to persuade the correspondents overseas to devote more of their time to shooting film, even though most of them were reluctant to desert radio, the medium they knew and respected and which they could hear playing their dispatches back to them over the BBC World Service. If they shot film it might be years before they came home and saw the result of their efforts. Ultimately this was only to be resolved by appointing extra correspondents to specialise in television. If a story is worth doing at all, it is as much as one man can do to handle it in one medium. In those days I almost had to bribe some of the old stagers to hire a camera crew and get on the road with it.

My successor in Beirut, Paddy Flinn, was lucky enough to find himself in Baghdad with a crew when a coup d'état broke out. As Paddy stood on the roof of his hotel outlining the circumstances, rebel aircraft could clearly be seen diving down to rocket the building behind him, sending up columns of smoke and flame. The trouble was, Our Man in Baghdad was keeping such a stiff upper lip that the suspicion was irresistible he was standing against a back-projection screen in some studio. In fact he was doing no such thing; but I had to cable him, 'Next time under fire flinch goddamit.'

There was no need to send messages like that to Ronald Robson, who donned his old Gurkha kit and took to the field in Northern Rhodesia against the mad prophetess Alice Lenshina. Not only did

Ronnie send back some alarming pictures of what it is like to be caught between the horns of an Impi crescent, but he treated us to some quite untransmittable closeups of corpses with their private parts stuffed in their mouths. Ronnie would have made the perfect reporter for Custer's Last Stand.

Such shipments were few and far between, even from the Congo. The Visnews film agency, which the BBC helped to found, was just getting into its stride; otherwise we were heavily dependent upon our own coverage at home and upon library film of varying relevance, some of which became all too familiar. 'Tanks *like these* have invaded the southern province . . .' we would say, showing pictures of old Russian manoeuvres. 'Over countryside *like this* the invading forces are making steady progress . . .' When you have seen one savannah, you've seen them all.

I submitted a memorandum dated April 1st proposing the recruitment of a TV news repertory company. I argued that with a couple of dozen versatile actors and a few sets, easily accommodated in Alexandra Park, we could *act* most of the day's news faster and cheaper than we could film it. The front half of an old airliner with a ramp to come down, a mockup of the United Nations rostrum and a shiny conference table would take care of the diplomatic stuff. For the rest, the steps of a presidential palace, a small assault course with a burnt-out tank, and a Chinky Prov-town beside the boating lake would handle most stories. Equity would have been pleased to co-operate but the cameramen's union might have had to be compensated for loss of expenses overseas.

Peter Woon, the most ambitious of our team, had another way of spinning out the visuals. There was a wondrous apparatus like an enormous magic lantern, used for injecting still photographs and known as the scanner. You could employ it to superimpose two or three drawings on top of one another, and with the help of the resident graphic artists elements in these drawings could be made to appear or disappear – 'animation', it was called. Exploiting the scanner to the full, Peter would hold forth as graphs rose and fell, little men queued up for work at factory gates and marched in as jobs became available and, on one occasion, a whole fleet of ships sailed onto the screen and hoisted the flags of the NATO nations. We had a tendency towards the didactic.

Donald Milner, who should have been a don at Oxford, found it particularly hard to describe any wood without adding the Latin name of every tree in it. The result was that his pieces, though well researched, were always too long by half. When told of this, his solution was to read them twice as fast. He followed me, for a time, as correspondent in India; whence he returned, in the Victorian manner, with a stately Indian bearer who became an exotic ornament to Donald's Oxfordshire village. Donald must also go down in broadcasting history for his unsuccessful attempt, as a reporter, to interview the dislikeable Krishna Menon. Amidst the hubbub at the airport could be heard the furious cry, 'Take your *hands* off me – *horrid* BBC man!'

Tidmarsh and Timpson were more relaxing company. Indeed, we used to relax pretty heavily round the BBC hospitality cabinet after the show came off the air every night. The rule was that the cabinet could only be broached if we had an outside contributor to entertain: consequently hardly an edition went out without some minor politician, don or Fleet Street pundit to provide the excuse. How some of us managed to drive home afterwards should have been a matter for prayerful thanksgiving. We usually found our wives in a crumpled heap on the hearthrug as the TV crackled and snowed unwatched.

John Timpson, of course, went on to become a fixture on the early morning Today programme on Radio 4, a role he fulfils like one called upon to play Santa Claus every day of the year. How he does it beats me – I should feel trapped in a rut and there have been times when I caught a look of desperation in his eye as yet another passing prima donna hogged his limelight. It was a just reward when they made him chairman of the Any Questions? show, but there must be something soothing in John's private life that stops him going mad. He was a fine reporter and it is a pity he gets little more to do now than read introductions and pose questions.

John Tidmarsh always had a light touch and a reputation as a good all-rounder which, perhaps, led to his being underestimated. Like many of the old reliables he is still to be heard on the World Service in the wee, small hours. My most abiding memory of him in News Extra is seated on a log in a zoo enclosure, entirely surrounded by wolves. If I remember rightly, wolves had been escaping from Whipsnade and John was there to reassure the public. He did not look entirely reassured himself.

Peter Woods, who had parachuted into Egypt during the Suez caper, had the bearing of an aristocratic mercenary and the voice James Bond should have had, had he not been Sean Connery. After a while at Alexandra Palace he ventured off to New York for a spell as the ITN correspondent, found it too much of a strain and returned to the forgiving bosom of the BBC as a regular newsreader in the old style. He knows perfectly well that he resembles a human bloodhound, but it is unkind that when anybody needs a comic newsreader in their show, they send for Woods. I once saw him on the screen dressed up as a chicken.

There were many strange features to the practice of television which made it quite unlike the cosy, rather solitary medium of radio. For a start, TV is a team game and everything you do has to be mediated through an army of editors and technicians. Instead of working in a small padded cell you find yourself seated in an empty barn, jostled along by snatches of film which begin before you are ready for them, or trying to charm the implacable lens of a camera which may have no human operator, with half your mind worrying about what is going to happen next. And when things go wrong on television, they go catastrophically wrong: you cannot just clear your throat and read it again while the pictures go careering off into the distance. You are uneasily aware that, somewhere just out of earshot, a dozen people in a darkened room are cursing your incompetence; though the only evidence of this is a headphoned floormanager grabbing messages out of thin air and miming his despair.

The old black-and-white cameras were very sensitive and needed little in the way of extra lighting. But when colour arrived, lights blazed down like the sun in the Sahara, provoking my left eye to a lecherous wink that viewers may have misunderstood. It all confirmed my love for radio, where it does not matter whether you have shaved or not, whether you are going bald, or what colour shirt you are wearing. Certain patterns will 'strobe' or flutter, and there is – or used to be – a particular shade of blue which the electronic system could not see, leaving a hole in the picture upon which playful technicians would superimpose a cavalry charge or a portrait of President Nixon, right across your chest.

Then there was the teleprompter, which enabled you to read the entire news straight into the camera without once looking down at the script. The early model we used at Alexandra Palace was essentially a large magnifying glass with a pair of electrically driven rollers behind it, between which passed a sort of toilet roll with the words typed on it. The apparatus was placed immediately under the lens of the camera and operated by a girl who peered obliquely into the works and pressed a button to keep the words in step with the reader. It was cheap and fairly reliable, though it demanded keen eyesight and tended to induce the look of a judge sentencing a prisoner to death by hanging.

ON THE BOX

The trouble was with the girls who operated these machines. They were a goodlooking bunch, and the position in which they had to crouch both emphasised their busts and gave one a clear view up their skirts. The effect was distracting and led to many a verbal fluff as the reader's eyes darted to and fro between the dreary words under the lens and the delightful prospects to one side of it. Eventually the girls petitioned for the unheard-of right to wear trousers on BBC premises and became the first in the history of the Corporation to be allowed to do so – probably the sort of thing the Official Secrets Act was meant to hush up, had I not managed to slip through its iron curtain. Nothing, I am glad to say, was done about the bosoms and at least one newsreader was provoked into marrying his prompter-girl (for a time). Nowadays the prompting is all done by mirrors and the operators sit safely out of sight in a corner of the studio.

But on the whole television was too frantic for there to be much time for dalliance, despite the inviting darkness of the viewing theatres and cutting rooms. In any case these were usually packed with cynical film editors refusing to be impressed by what they were shown, like the knitting-ladies round the guillotine. The greatest distraction for roving eyes was provided by three pretty and intelligent girls in the foreign film intake section – Caroline, Paddy and Sue – but they worked in an inaccessible loft under the dragon-like guardianship of a middle-aged Viennese named Louise, who watched over them like the Vestal Virgins. As the resident foreign expert I was allowed access to their temple and was much envied for it. Scriptwriters were constantly cooking up excuses to penetrate the loft and lean over the shoulders of the girls with anxious enquiries about overexposed negatives. Louise would blast them out of the door with orders to go through the proper channels – which was me – and I would not have dared commit the sacrilege of making a pass at her Vestals. I had a striking blonde secretary of my own, known to my lecherous colleagues as the Vanilla Ice Cream, though I think she was scared of me rather than temperamentally frigid. Anyhow, she eventually became Peter Woon's second wife and a most poised and elegant lady.

As a reward for my decorous behaviour, Louise allowed me to attend conferences of the Eurovision News Exchange, a sort of electronic swap-shop which was her special preserve. She spent long hours in a darkened room growling in many languages to Brussels or Geneva about why *their* idea of news was not *our* idea of news. In fact the North Germans in Hamburg, together with the Dutch and the Scandinavians, had standards of newsworthiness very similar to the

British. The Italians, on the other hand, did not care much what they got provided the pictures were beautiful – Lord Mayors' shows, Morris dancing and harvest festivals suited them down to the ground, while the French refused to be impressed by anything British and offered an unvarying menu of Francophone African statesmen paying their respects to de Gaulle and laying wreaths under the Arc de Triomphe.

When the Eurovision conference met in Hamburg the French refused to attend, knowing that everyone would speak English there, as indeed they did. After the day's conferring the Swiss and the Italians went to the opera while the British and Scandinavians made a bee-line for the red-light district to see women wrestling in mud – a disappointing spectacle performed by two ladies who might have been relatives of Louise, dressed in one-piece costumes and rubber bathing caps. The mud was in the orchestra-pit of the cabaret. One watched the goings-on in a larger mirror tilted over it, through a glass darkly, as it were. The exhibition (which was called something onomatopoeic like *die Frauenschlammenkampf*) consisted of the ladies tripping each other up and spattering the mirror with mud – the erotic stimulation was zero. 'Naked women in fish is more amusing,' said one of the Scandinavians as we left, 'but is expensive. And more rare. I see once on fish wharf at Trondheim.' 'Let's hold the next conference at Trondheim. The French might come.'

Meanwhile, back in Hampstead Garden Suburb, Sylvia had taken things in hand and family life was developing. The Rhodes cottage had been a godsend, but it could never have been more than a temporary billet. Once the severe first winter was past and I had recovered my composure we clearly had to find a permanent home with room for everyone to grow up in. Television news was scheduled to join the rest of BBC TV down at the White City site in West London, so we got into a car one day and drove around Richmond and Kew. They looked as foreign to us as Beirut or Damascus, so we drove back to NW 11 and resolved to stay north of the Thames.

Patricia Rhodes, never convinced that any of her children could really look after themselves (even though the youngest was now married and over thirty), was still keeping up a six-bedroom house in the Garden Suburb of which, most of the time, she was the sole resident. It suddenly struck us all that the logical thing was for her to move into the cottage and for Sylvia and me to buy the big house. It was part of a crescent named Meadway Gate, overlooking Golder's Green Crematorium and the Sephardic Jewish Cemetery – Number

Three, The Necropolis, one friend unkindly called it. A very good class of carriage passed the door on their way to funerals and the children soon discovered where the wreaths were dumped, coming home with armsful of expensive chrysanthemums and blue irises. In fact it was not as depressing as it sounds: the crematorium, the first built in Britain, was disguised as a monastery; and the Jewish graves prevented anyone building houses opposite us. The dead make quiet neighbours and the only unpleasantness occurred when some louts broke in one night and painted swastikas on the tombstones.

The Suburb has remained our base ever since. Indeed, Sylvia has the same telephone number she had when she was 15, allowing for the exchange Speedwell having become the severely numerical 455. This has helped us to maintain our roots in spite of our absences abroad; for although friends have moved around inside the Suburb, they seldom leave it. Small wonder, for it is an agreeable quarter: an Edwardian parody of a Cotswold village along the edge of Hampstead Heath, the Chiltern Hills within easy reach, and the Northern Line of the London Underground offering rapid transit to the West End, as the estate agents say.

Henrietta Barnett, the social reformer who conjured up the Suburb in the early 1900s as a challenge to the ribbon developers imagined it as an integrated community of all classes. There were cottages for the honest artisans, closes for the professional middle class and two or three avenues of mansions for the wealthy; every house provided with front and back gardens and its quota of fruit trees – *rus in urbe*. I suspect the artisans never took a fancy to it; that, from the start, it was the Mecca of Quakers, Fabians, folk-dancers and adherents of the Garden City movement; for although it has a high church, a low church, a Friends' meeting house and an adult institute, Dame Henrietta refused to allow a public house or a single shop within its boundaries. All she would countenance in the way of commerce was a tea house, which was never a success and is used now to teach English to au pair girls. Teenagers complain bitterly (as they do anywhere) that 'there is nothing to do'. Today the leafy lanes are full of media people, diplomats and politicians; while I suspect more of the inhabitants attend Golder's Green's numerous synagogues than the Lutyens churches in the central square. We are a conservation area, proof against dastardly 'developers' (though one or two have tried it on and been thwarted): you cannot even put up a potting shed unless it, too, is an approved architectural gem. The outside world considers us snobs, but we don't care a fig.

Across the Heath, below Whitestone Pond, lies Hampstead proper, jammed with ephemeral boutiques and trendy mewses, where some of the old gang from our Studio House days still survive. Less than an hour's drive to the north is Berkhamsted, so it was easy, of a Sunday, to take the family into the country for an afternoon's doting from my parents. It was a happy sunset for my father, within a couple of years of his eightieth birthday.

Frank Priestland had never been more content than he was after retiring from Cooper's, devoting himself to the parish and rural district councils, local school governorships and the bench of magistrates. It delighted him to shock his wealthy relatives by standing for election on the Labour Party ticket. But by 1961 he was drawing in his horns, resigning one by one from his various appointments as he felt that growing deafness was making him inefficient. At 78 he had little left but his dawn pottering about the vegetable garden, a lunchtime walk with the dog to the Red Lion or the Plough, and his evening snooze in front of the television where he professed to be proud of my work but was rarely awake to see it.

One summer morning he went out, played a game of bowls, drank a pint of bitter, came home and told Nelly he felt tired and was going to lie down. After a while he called out softly from the bedroom. My mother hurried to his side and found him lying dead from his first and last heart attack – a kind and lovely way to depart.

She telephoned: 'Gerry, come quickly. Daddy is very ill,' but her strangled voice told me he was more than that, and I was there within the hour. I had seen much of death in India without learning much from it; but as I looked on my father's waxen face I realised quite simply that it was not him, that the real He was somewhere else. It was not that this person had stopped and would not go again, but that Frank Priestland had got tired of his body and moved on to another life. Somehow his death was showing me that what really mattered about him was independent of his flesh, was incapable of dying, and I have never doubted that since. I wept, as most of the village did, but in truth there was nothing to regret on his behalf. He was fully clear now and complete.

On my own behalf, though, I regretted (and still do) that I had not known him better – that he had seemed to me more of a grandfather than a father, that I had not made him talk to me more about his early life, give me legends to pass on, tell me about his love affairs. How many women had he loved before my mother? How faithful a husband had he been? Was I a copy of him, or just a coward in being so monogynous myself? Above all, I regretted not having made him tell me more about the horrors he must have seen in the trenches. My mother's words as we stood at the bedside – not very logical but heartfelt – were, 'After all he went through in that dreadful war, after all he survived, and now this . . .'

If my father's life was complete, his death left my mother mentally crippled. She had no other meaning to herself but as Frank's constant attendant and there was nobody – certainly not I – to take his place. Sylvia and the children monopolised all the loving care I had in me and badly though I felt about it sometimes I could see nothing but disaster in the idea of my mother coming to live with us in London. And so she stayed on in Potten End. The dainty cooking and careful house-keeping continued, but joylessly; and a look of ineffable melancholy settled on her face as each visit to her drew to an end. There were people around who would have liked to befriend her, but her shyness was unrewarding and her increasing ill-health, basically high blood-pressure, made her withdraw more and more.

In any case, I was busy. The BBC's second television channel was about to open at last and mine was to be the first face on it, delivering a short summary of the news from a studio faked up to look like a newsroom, cluttered with typewriters and coffee cups, with me in the midst wearing a pullover.

News was the only output still coming from Alexandra Palace. Everything else for BBC 2 was to emanate from West London, from the studios at the White City and Lime Grove. At Television Centre Michael Peacock had laid on a kind of opening festival at which half of Fleet Street, the House of Commons and the officer corps of the BBC itself were to christen the new network in gin and champagne. As a symbol of his creation Peacock had selected a baby kangaroo labelled BBC-2 emerging from the pocket of a larger, maternal kangaroo labelled BBC-1: somehow they got named Hullabaloo and Custard, though I am not sure which was which. It was obvious that the opening night would be incomplete without the presence of kanga-roos in the flesh, and so enquiries were made of various zoos and circuses as to whether they could supply such a furry duo. The unanimous answer was that while one adult kangaroo might be managed the mother-and-child act could not, since the infant – far from leaning out of its pouch waving and signing autographs – would certainly hide there till taken home again, and any attempt to get it out would turn the mother into a fury of biting and kicking. So a solo kangaroo it had to be.

On the fateful night an electrical transformer at Iver, not far from my mechanical Uncle Jock, blew up precipitating the collapse of the entire power supply to West London, including the BBC studios there. Television Centre, with its tense and tipsy throng, was plunged into darkness. Producers cursed, public relations men wept, Fleet Street cheered and jeered and the kangaroo – stuck in a lift – went berserk. It was the worst disaster of its kind since Belshazzar's Feast. But up at the Palace, fed by a different power supply, everything was going swimmingly. The studio manager gave his cue, I smiled into the camera and welcomed it to this historic occasion and began chatting my way through a carefully informal account of the day's events. The man on the screen is usually the last person to realise that something has gone wrong, but I soon began to pick up clues that all was not well. There were scurryings, mutterings, unintelligible twitters in other people's headphones, until a hand appeared at the outer edge of my field of vision and pushed a strip of paper towards me. After a quick glance I found myself announcing the humiliating collapse of the said historic occasion before it had really begun. The only thing that was working on BBC 2 was me.

After appealing to my Uncle Jock to nip out and see if he could fix the Iver transformer – in vain, because Jock still only watched television with the sound turned off – I ploughed on through every scrap of unedited Reuters tape they could feed me. Small earthquakes in Chile ('Only too hideous for those involved, though the full extent of the casualty list will depend upon how thickly populated the area is . . .' I prattled); obscure foreign government crises ('perhaps not to be taken as seriously as we might here in Britain . . .'); and just occasionally a story I knew something about – everything was stretched to breaking point in the hope that Television Centre would come alive again and the show would go on. But it stayed dead, and after what seemed like an eternity of ad-libbing about Japanese fishery disputes and trains de-railed in Tunisia, I was taken off the air.

It was not the BBC's fault, nor Michael Peacock's. But Fleet Street loves to see the mighty fallen and gave them a terrible drubbing on the front page next morning. Since most of the reporters at Television Centre had been too far gone in BBC booze to write a coherent account of the fiasco a great deal was made up by the sub-editors, including two alleged interviews with me which had never happened. 'You could have knocked me down with a feather,' I was supposed to have said, 'I had never been expected to go on the air at all that night. As viewers could see, I was not even properly dressed for it. But I felt I had to step into the breach when duty called. The Director General rang me up afterwards to thank me in person and promise me promotion.'

When I telephoned to complain, Fleet Street was mildly surprised. 'Couldn't get hold of you, old man, but we reckoned it was the sort of thing you'd have said if we had done. Thought we'd save you the trouble. Can't have done you any harm.' It certainly saved the Director General trouble. He didn't ring, either. The BBC now likes to pretend that Channel 2 started the following day, when they had fixed the fuse at Iver.

Appearing regularly on television had its dubious rewards: people stopped you in the street or stared at you in the underground, while the children were fawned upon in toyshops and wished their father did something less obtrusive like collecting the garbage. But the role of presenter is a parody of true journalism and, for graded BBC staff, poorly paid by the standards of the entertainment industry. I was getting desperate to return to the front line when John Crawley, who had succeeded Tony Wigan as foreign editor, sidled up to me at the Palace bar and let drop the news that Douglas Stuart was resigning from the Washington Office. Would I like to return there as chief correspondent? The job demanded someone experienced in television as well as radio. I already knew the country. There was no other correspondent of stature who filled the bill so well.

For several days I hesitated. Sylvia, even more than I, had burned up nervous energy creating a home from scratch and settling the children into the English schools system. If we went back to America so much would have to be undone and started all over again. As for myself, I had a superstitious feeling that one should not try to repeat a success; yet paradoxically I hardly trusted myself not to assume too easily that I could. Beirut had been a catastrophe: might I not suffer an even more disastrous fall from this, the highest post that the BBC's foreign service had to offer? Most immediately, how could I break it to my lonely mother that the sole comforts of her widowhood were to fly away from her once more? Part of me longed to escape from her melancholy reproach. Yet part of me felt guiltily bound to stay near her.

Sylvia at once recognised the honour that was being done me – indeed, to both of us; for it had been made clear when we were abroad that even though the Priestlands were expensive to move around they were a remarkably trouble-free team and a net asset to the corporation. Having seen something of the world abroad there were times when

Sylvia felt that even her beloved London was a bit parochial. If I wanted to take to the road again she was ready to follow, despite the upheaval. 'But this time,' she said, 'we must keep a home here, even if we have to let it. The children must know there's a home waiting for them in the end.'

John Crawley sidled up to me once more and adapted Barry Goldwater's election slogan, 'In your heart you know he's right'. 'In your heart you know you'll go,' said John. I told him I would.

The shock to my mother was visible. She gasped as if I had punched her below the belt, and certainly wept when I left after giving her the news. I told her it was nothing to fly the Atlantic nowadays. She could visit us. We would visit her – now and then. The trouble was that while Sylvia could leave her mother with a whole squad of brothers and sisters to take up the slack, mine had nobody but me. I resented that, and felt guilty for it as well, but at the height of my powers – I was then thirty-seven – I knew that I could not decline what in my profession was the best job in the world.

The BBC wanted me to leave for Washington as soon as possible – say, immediately after Christmas 1964. The family could not move so fast but would finish the next school term and join me about Easter. Sylvia sighed: another of those single-handed removals, but she had done it before. She was mildly pleased when the BBC booked her aboard the Cunarder *Sylvania* – only mildly because she knew she would be just as seasick whatever its name.

Two days before I was due to fly off I drove out to Hertfordshire to make the farewell I dreaded. I found my mother not at Potten End but at the home of her elder sister Evie in Berkhamsted. She lay ill in bed, barely able to speak. I tried to cheer her with plans for a holiday in Washington the coming summer, but her mind was fixed on the risk of the pipes freezing in her empty bungalow. Just as she was slowly drawling out the exact location of the taps I was to turn off, she hesitated, snored, and was silent. It took me a moment to realise that what I had heard was nothing less than the death-rattle. She could have, should have, died in my arms. But all I could do was sit at the bedside and stare first in pity, then horror. She was dead. I had solved my problem, gained my freedom, killed my mother by breaking her heart.

The doctor took a more lenient view and certified her death from what amounted to a general collapse of the circulation – there was a whole string of medical phrases on the document including the ugly word 'infarction'. I took my father's old Labrador Sandy down to the vet and watched while he was gently dispatched, then walked on to the undertaker and arranged the funeral, putting off my flight to the day following. Perhaps life – a new untrammelled life – could begin at thirty-seven.

Chapter Eight

LONG HOT SUMMERS

I arrived in Washington about the middle of January 1965 feeling as if I had committed murder and fled the scene of the crime. The pursuit at my heels drew closer and the chasm before me deeper and darker. Though I had no real reason to doubt my abilities I found myself living in a continuous state of panic, running scared.

My assistant in the Washington office was the tall, dark and handsome Leonard Parkin, a most able reporter of action, especially on television. His only complaint about America was that you couldn't, in his opinion, get a decently cut suit or shirt anywhere. Unfortunately his wife could not stand the life and before long Leonard had to take her back to England – which did him no harm, for he became the durable presenter of ITN's lunchtime news. There was not a great deal Leonard could show me – probably he felt about me much as I had felt about Douglas Stuart – but his replacement, though a newcomer to the United States, was a challenge from the start. It was Charles Wheeler, who could hardly be described as my assistant or number two: in effect Washington now had two number ones, very different in temperament from one another but adding up to a formidable team. ITN sent John Whale to Washington, but with all respect for his seriousness he never became a professional threat to us. 'All they seem to want is one good anti-American story a week,' he groaned.

Charles and I took it turn and turn about, six weeks to a spell, to operate as radio man or television man. The one doing radio usually stayed in Washington voicing two or three pieces a day, while the one doing television cruised about with a camera team. That way each of us got his share of seeing America and leading a fairly normal family life; not altogether normal, since the time differential meant that London was liable to be at its most demanding around Washington's midnight.

I think it is fair to say that while Charles was by far the better television man, my speciality was the spoken word; and while he was, and remains, the superior political and diplomatic analyst, I was more concerned with trying to convey the feeling of *what America felt like*, whether it was in the context of space missions, elections, civil rights, Vietnam or just the local shopping centres at Christmas. I will not pretend we did not sometimes collide. Charles has nerves of steel, the taut discipline of the soldier and apparently no use for sleep. The camera crews, while respecting him, used to call him the Little Corporal. He is not one of those telly-personalities who naturally exude humour and warmth: there was alleged to be a bet, unpaid for years, on whether he or the stern Martin Bell would be the first to smile on camera. But put Charles into any situation and he would deliver a report that was penetrating, well-informed and utterly reliable. By contrast he must have found me disorganised, superficial and neurotic. On one occasion, in Miami, I allowed a BBC camera crew, newly arrived from Britain, to go off filming by itself in a riot area. They were stoned by angry blacks and the cameraman got a swollen ankle. London's reaction was that its cameramen were big enough to take care of themselves; but Charles thought I had been irresponsible and said so. A good officer stayed with his men and did not allow them to go swanning off into no-man's-land. He was probably right.

Not long after Charles arrived, with his Indian wife Dīp, Harold Wilson appointed a new ambassador to Washington, the former *New Statesman* editor and television inquisitor John Freeman. Freeman – though he made a fool of himself over the Gilbert-and-Sullivan-like affair of the revolt of Anguilla (which Charles not only reported but mediated on the spot) – actually had more the air of an ambassador than of a journalist. Unfortunately, from our point of view, he was now married to Charles's former wife Katie, and there were a number of embassy functions we had to attend. Wasn't it asking too much to expect Charles to shake the hand of the man who had stolen his wife and call him Your Excellency – while *she* smiled graciously at his side? Was Washington big enough for the three of them – four, including Dīp? London worried even more than I did; but in the end the stiff upper lip prevailed and there was no display of horsewhips, gauntlets or pistols at dawn in Rock Creek Park.

Charles arrived about the same time as Sylvia and the children. I had rented a pleasant frame-house (built largely of wood, that is) on 34th Street, in the inner suburb of Cleveland Park. It was within half-an-hour's walk of the office downtown, though that was a sweaty form of exercise in the humid Washington summer, and I often picked up Ross Mark of the *Daily Express* on the way. We conducted a mutually profitable trade of low Fleet Street gossip for highminded BBC analysis on the way.

The house was also convenient for the Embassy, the National Cathedral, the zoo and several schools. One of these, St Alban's, was rather too much a copy of an English public school; but another, Sidwell Friends', was a civilised Quaker version of an American high school, humane, democratic and by no means unscholarly. Jennet and Andreas, our two elder children, went to Sidwell and came to regard it with affection – quite a tribute in Andreas's case, for his operation in infancy had left him timid and lacking in confidence. Sylvia and I have always been grateful to Sidwell for what it did for him – and for Jennet – as a result of which we tend to hit back at the usual British sneers at American schooling. It may not be so literary but it made our children confident, articulate and adept at the laying out of rather solemn research papers backed up with footnotes and bibliographies.

America also taught the children practical capitalism and politics. Capitalism was introduced through that great American institution the newspaper round or 'route' (pronounced rout). The child worked its way up from a weekly free-sheet to an evening paper, eventually graduating to a morning paper with a Sunday edition like *The Washington Post*. There being no corner newsagents to take the middleman's cut, the area circulation manager for each paper dumped a bale of them on the child's doorstep and left it to him or her to deliver the copies, collect the cover price every week and (in turn) hand over the wholesale cost to the manager, keeping the difference as profit. It was illegal for the paper actually to employ child labour, but quite legitimate – indeed healthy – for the child to buy and sell papers on its own account.

The trouble was that if the child fell ill its family was expected to keep the route going. I spent a good deal of time in the winter months crossly delivering *The Star* to my neighbours. On Sundays there was a colour supplement to insert, bundles of which were dumped in the *porte cochère* of the Belgian Embassy down the road, though whether the Belgians knew about this, or that I spent those dawn hours operating a paper business from their premises, I do not know.

Some of our customers were fussy about how they took delivery and our instructions were to pander to their whims. Most of them were content with the hurl-it-at-the-front-door-from-your-bicycle method, though some always landed in the bushes. A few wanted their copies laid gently on the doormat or tucked into weather-proof holders. Squeezing the bloated editions through the average letterbox was impossible – except with an evening tabloid called *The News*, which Oliver represented in his earlier capitalist days. There was one house where the sound of footsteps up the garden path brought a frenzy of barking and scratching from within. The moment the paper was intruded into the mail-slot, as per orders, it was snatched by the beast or beasts inside and the barking was replaced by sounds of shredding and tearing. That's how they wanted it and that's how they got it. Presumably it made the dog's day.

The children's introduction to politics was similarly do-it-yourself. In an American election campaign any number can play and age is no bar. Since the candidates for the presidency do not have to come from the closed shop of Congress – almost anyone with the nerve and the money can declare himself a runner for nomination – the demand for volunteer helpers is insatiable. Andreas got a lucrative job removing the empty bottles from a Rockefeller for President office, while Jennet stuffed literature into envelopes for Senator Gene McCarthy, who lived on the next block. Oliver joined the Bobby Kennedy team and Diana, being the littlest, got stuck with Richard Nixon. But nobody told any of them to run away and leave it to the adults.

As a family we were happy on 34th Street. Old friends like the Ashers and Herens reappeared – the Heren children apprehensive that we might demand the return of Orlando the barley-sugar-coloured cat whom we had given them when we left in 1960. No need to worry: by popular demand the family imported Saki, our London Siamese, who quickly established his rule over the cats, dogs and chipmunks of Cleveland Park. Once the cat, the pictures, books and ornaments were in place, home was already half made.

Cleveland Park was a hotbed of American liberalism. The local residents got together and informed the real estate agents that they were eager to share it with any black families who wanted to move in. The agents replied scornfully that although *we* might think sixty-year-old wooden houses were picturesque and desirable, any self-respecting black with *that* sort of money to spend would be looking for something up-to-date in brick with central air-conditioning and a swimming pool. We never did get our token negroes.

The local kids were soon round to fraternise, and our own children quickly adopted American clothes, American accents, American juice and cookies and television to identify themselves with the gang. After a few months only Jennet, now in her teens and clearly following in her mother's footsteps as an artist, was capable of switching back into English ways. She even acquired an English boyfriend, Thomas, the son of a specialist attaché at the Embassy.

I think English neighbours were regarded as adding a touch of class to the block: at any rate, we got on well with everyone around us, though there was a certain tension with a blonde divorcée across the street. It should have been flattering that she fancied me and would beg me to come over and do little jobs for her, like burying her kitten when it got run over, attending the obsequies in a transparent black negligée, but her view of mankind was altogether too carnivorous for my comfort. Her brother was an international arms dealer with a warehouse across the river in Virginia, where she urged me to buy a private arsenal to fight off the rapists, communists and niggers who (she prophesied) would soon be invading the suburbs if things went on the way they were going. An attorney by trade, specialising in divorces, she got results by bugging the cars of delinquent husbands with electronic tracers. Disappointed in me, she married a militaristic Republican senator from Texas, whom she must have suited to a T.

Our blonde beast horrified the mild professor of Byzantinology who lived next to her, but was a source of fascination to another neighbour, a clinical psychiatrist, who in turn fascinated me because it emerged – during a drinking session in our garden – that he was treating someone extremely senior in the Administration and had had to delay taking up a post in the Middle West because, untreated, the man might have plunged the world into nuclear war. Exactly who it was my friend was too Hippocratic to reveal, but it plainly bothered him and me too.

There was an outburst of small furry animals all over the house. The cat mopped up the first batch of gerbils and spent hours watching the grey-and-white rats that took their place, rather as human beings will sit watching TV. I liked the rats, too, apart from their naked wormlike tails. They scampered merrily about the boys' bedroom and came when they were called. A pair of guinea-pigs provided the children with an introduction to the mysteries of copulation, birth and death, which became hardly a mystery at all thanks to their activities. The male, named Rory Calhoun, leapt constantly upon Zoë, the female, who carried on munching come what may. She was quite capable of cropping grass at one end while delivering a stream of piglets at the other. Neighbours would send their children over to absorb the facts of life from Rory and Zoë.

Down in the basement our own children conducted an illicit brewery, using a recipe for Old English ginger beer they had acquired from the BBC's Blue Peter show. When the *Washington Post* heard about it and tested the concoction it turned out to be so alcoholic that they dared not publish for fear of being prosecuted on the grounds of contributing to the delinquency of minors. Blue Peter had certainly packed a punch: a visiting American boy who refreshed himself with the beer during a rather wild game of scratch hockey with the Priestlands bicycled all the way home before he realised he had broken an arm.

My own particular pleasure at that time was eating oysters. On Saturday mornings I would drive down to the Potomac river and buy half a bushel – about forty of them – for little more than a pound from the oyster boats that came up from Chesapeake Bay. They took me a while to wash and open, but in the evening Sylvia and I would sit watching old movies on television and enjoying the rare luxury of *enough oysters*. One Christmas we even stuffed the turkey with them – a Dickensian treat I can recommend to anyone who can afford a half-bushel.

Now that all four children were going to school Sylvia, who had been able to do little more than the occasional sketch for the past ten years, was able to revive her painting; or rather, as it turned out, to pick up something that suited her talents even better. There were classes at the Corcoran Gallery in Washington and she accidentally found herself in one conducted by the printmaker Jack Perlmutter, a specialist in silkscreen and woodcut. Within weeks it became clear that these media called out instincts that had been bogged down in oil paint: an instinct for bright, flat colours in silkscreen and for tough black outlines in woodcut. The whole atmosphere of American art at that time, dominated by the huge ikons of the abstract expressionists, was something that Sylvia found intensely exciting. It liberated her from the academic inhibitions she had been brought up with and she began to create work that exhibited and sold.

Together with a group of fellow printmakers Sylvia became involved in a kind of art mission to the Washington black ghetto. Looking back on it, this was a hair-raising thing to do and only someone with her serene innocence would have taken it on – driving across the city to a ghetto school where even black teachers got mugged and stabbed in the playground and where white faces were so seldom seen that the kids stared at her as if she had come from Mars, to teach drawing and painting to the roughest of the rough. No one ever harmed her, though they would ask to feel her hair and tell her she talked 'like the Beatles'. Amazingly she found that when asked to paint pictures of 'someone you admire' they would all paint pinky-white film stars with fair hair; it was only after a year or two that the civil rights movement began to get through to them and they handed in portraits of Martin Luther King.

That, I suppose, was the biggest difference I noticed on my second coming to Washington, that blacks were at last being allowed to immigrate into the majority society, just as the Irish and Italians and Poles had done before them – even though the blacks had been in America two or three centuries longer. If you reckon that the process only really began in the 1950s, it is not surprising that it still is not complete.

The British have little to be proud of in this story, for it was our ancestors who founded the slave South and drenched it with our calvinistic theology of race relations. I found it embarrassing to visit the South and have it assumed by whites with British names that I would naturally sympathise with their point of view; more embarrassing still to hear the story of Ham and of Noah invoked yet again as justification for denying black people their rights.

Throughout the 1950s the South wheeled out all the delaying tactics it could devise, and President Eisenhower, a product of the old segregated US Army, showed little sign of urgency in fighting them. In 1957 Congress passed its first civil rights bill in eight years and within the next eight it passed three more. Those were the years of nobility and martyrdom in the civil rights cause: more than fifty people lost their lives to white supremacists like the Ku Klux Klan, and hundreds more were beaten, savaged by police dogs, shocked with electric cattle-prods, battered by fire hoses and sickened with tear-gas.

I covered many of those events as a reporter and shall not easily forget the atmosphere of terror and hatred in those backward Southern townships, nor the comradeship of the marchers, the nuns, priests and young white students from the North and West who joined hands with the local black people to defy the state troopers of Governor Wallace. In particular I remember marching from Selma to Montgomery, Alabama, with Dr King. By day we walked through swamplands festooned with Spanish moss, whose jungles sometimes concealed hit-and-run snipers, while carloads of jeering rednecks hurtled towards us, usually swerving at the last moment, and a hellish chorus of white womenfolk – their faces contorted with hatred – screamed obscenities that should have been unknown to them. By night we slept, or tried to sleep, in black churches while more cars roared by, tossing out pigs' guts and bottles of urine as they passed and the local white community kept up an all-night rumpus of bullhorns, shotgun fire and bucket-bashing. It was ill-advised to venture out of the church: I did once, and got beaten up by Sheriff Jim Clarke in person. Fortunately the marchers had regular classes in nonviolent resistance, conducted by Dr King's assistant Andy Young; so I was able to minimise the damage by falling to the ground and curling up as instructed.

By an extraordinary coincidence the BBC transmitted an interview I had with Dr King, only three hours before he was shot. It had, in fact, been filmed at his fortified headquarters in Atlanta some weeks earlier, but it concluded with a discussion of the threat of violent death and with King's moving confession that he was quite prepared for it any day of his life and was more convinced than ever of the redemptive power of suffering. Despite the obstinacy of Congress and the sinister opportunism of the Black Power extremists, he remained unshakably devoted to nonviolence.

Over the years I spent many hours with Dr King and found him intriguingly two men in one. Addressing a crowd of his own people, his voice would roll like a mighty organ in the gospel cadences of the Baptist preachers who were his forbears. Yet in private he was modest, considerate, a quiet thinker who never tried to manipulate me for propaganda purposes. He had received a highly intellectual education which might easily have cut him off from the black masses and he had hesitated before going back to them to assume the inevitably emotional role of their leader; it was only his Christian conscience that drove him to do so. Yet intellectually and spiritually he made no compromise. Questioning some of his decisions I realised that he always knew exactly what he was doing and why he must do it. Only, he confessed, there was too much to be done and too little time – even less, it turned out, than either of us would have guessed. It would be in good taste, but inaccurate, to say that all Americans grieved when he was shot. I met several, even on the day of his funeral, who thought the troublemaking nigger had got what he deserved.

There was no one capable of replacing Martin Luther King. His cross was taken up his lieutenant Ralph Abernathy, from the same clerical fold of the Southern Christian Leadershp Conference, but Abernathy was more of a Southerner at heart than King and it was no longer really the South that was the problem. Even King's influence had been limited in the ghettos of the North and Middle West, where all kinds of nihilists, nationalists, terrorists and downright criminals flourished. For as usually happens, though liberals are loth to admit it, white racism had produced an equally vicious black racism which you can trace back to the race riots of 1919 and to weird figures like Noble Drew Ali and his Moorish Science Temples, Marcus Garvey and his black Zionism, Wallace Fard who claimed to have come from Mecca and Elijah Poole – alias Elijah Muhammad – who quietly eliminated Fard and took over his Black Muslim empire.

In 1965 I attended a convention of the Black Muslims in Chicago. White reporters were minutely and intimately frisked by the body-guard of the Fruit of Islam, a colleague of mine having his stock of contraceptives confiscated. Inside the hall, Muslim sisters in nun-like robes were carefully segregated from the brothers in their smart business suits. Stalls at the back of the auditorium were selling portraits of 'The Messenger of Allah: The Honorable Elijah Muhammad', pamphlets from Cairo about President Nasser, racist comic books for kiddies and a lugubrious gramophone record entitled 'A white man's Heaven is a black man's hell', relating how 'He filled our wombs with his filthy seed and gave us half-white kids to feed.'

In the front row on the platform the boxer Cassius Clay – alias Mohammed Ali – was scowling down at the white press like a Nazi stormtrooper. The Fruit (for short) surrounded the rostrum with folded arms and the Messenger of Allah abruptly materialised at the microphone without being observed in transit. There was wild applause and everyone stood – as well they might, for Elijah was a tiny man who might easily have been overlooked but for his gaily sequinned cap. He had an apricot-coloured complexion and some-what mongolian features; his hold upon the organisation must have been based on something other than charisma.

After half an hour I found myself wondering whether this was all an elaborate exercise in black humour, for The Messenger of Allah was hallucinating in public roughly along the lines of the Book of Revelation: 'An' I see a wondrous great flyin' saucer comin' down from Heaven, made of wondrous material what you couldn't cut with no blowtorch ever made . . .' The faithful were going wild. 'Preach it like it is!' they yelled. 'Holy Apostle! Speak the Word! Make it plain!' It could have been any clinker-built chapel in the swamps of Louisiana; for of Islam, the Koran or the Arabic language there was no trace except for the ritual greeting, 'Salaam aleicum – aleicum asalaam!' Black Americans seemed to have forgotten the part that Muslim slave-traders had played in their captivity: all they could see in Islam was a successful and aggressive culture with a reputation for chopping up whites.

Of what Islam actually taught they knew little and cared less. According to Mr Muhammad, God, who was black, had produced the black race of Shabazz sixty-six trillion years ago. White folk were a perversion cooked up by a wicked scientist called Mr Yakub who had rebelled against Allah and spent six hundred years tinkering with birth control. The resulting monstrosities, white-skinned and blue-eyed, crawled away to the caves of the north to live in barbarism while the blacks developed the mighty civilisations of the Middle East. Pending the final Armageddon when the people of Shabazz will triumph, the Black Muslims must make themselves pure and self-supporting; to which end Mr Muhammad had thoughtfully created a complete retail system which the faithful were required to use exclusively. He not only sold them their robes but laundered and drycleaned them. He not only laid down their diet but served it in his food stores and restaurants. The profits were to be used to purchase a black promised land somewhere down South.

Things went along nicely until Elijah's crown prince – one Malcolm X Shabazz, a reformed vice-pedlar from Harlem – complained about the old man's unholy carryings-on with the secretarial help; only to receive the explanation that it was all in fulfilment of the prophets. The Messenger considered himself to be King David, Noah, Solomon and Lot all rolled into one and therefore entitled to every indulgence in the Old Testament. Malcolm pushed off to Harlem to found a breakaway sect which took a more restrained view of the scriptures, and a year later he was gunned down by a Black Muslim execution squad in full view of his congregation. Which was a pity, because Malcolm X was a very remarkable person. With his chilling presence and brilliance as an orator he was the only black leader who might have controlled the rioting of the late 'sixties and been able to address the white establishment with an authority it would have recognised when King was gone. In his last year he made the pilgrimage to Mecca, which profoundly altered his thinking and led him to renounce the race hatred he had once preached.

But by the long hot summer of 1967, Malcolm was dead and gone. Quite why things blew up then I am not entirely sure: there was the unemployment, bad housing and inner city deprivation that we, in Britain, have come to know. But in many ways things were getting better for black people and that, of course, is when violent revolt often breaks out – not when things are at their worst but when they are improving, but not fast enough. And typically, again, the forces of law and order over-reacted and mishandled the situation. In the United States, where every policeman carries a gun as a matter of routine and is authorised to use it on the flimsiest pretext, that meant a hail of gunfire which spared nobody in its way. The most alarming thing about covering the riots was not the mobs of looters and brick-throwers, who were fairly easy to dodge; it was lying in the gutter in some urban canyon, with the gunfire echoing and ricocheting around, wondering where it was coming from.

The trouble, as I recall it, started in Tampa, Florida, with the burning of a cigar factory – a fragrant experience. One of the local reporters taught me that with a street plan and a certain model of transistor radio you could eavesdrop the police emergency calls and probably reach the incidents before they did – 'Though not too long before,' he advised. 'They don't like to be last all the time, and it's best to hide behind them in any case. Only a fool films from behind the rioters.'

The troubles worked their way up through places like Cincinnati and Pittsburgh to Newark and the Middle West. Charles had the worst of it in Detroit; my most alarming experiences were in Newark and Chicago. In Newark I was working with the BBC's ace camera team, Bill Baglin and his soundman Eric Thirer. We arrived on the morning after the first night's burning, rented a Hertz car at Newark airport and drove into the downtown area to find it quietly smouldering and strewn with debris. The rioters had made a special point of breaking into the furniture shops and destroying their hire-purchase records, making a special target of any Jewish-owned business.

As we stopped at some traffic lights I noticed a little black kid, not more than ten years old, eyeing us thoughtfully and swinging a length of charred timber. I gave him a reassuring grin, turned my head away, and *wham* – the wood came through the window, followed by everything else the passers-by could throw. Eric, who was driving, put his foot down and hurled the car through the barrage. A couple of hundred yards further on we skidded into a group of police cars drawn up in a circle like covered waggons, guns blazing over their bonnets. Bill Baglin climbed out, mounted his camera on his belt and started to take light-readings with his meter. 'Get down!' yelled the cops. Bill remained standing and got his focus while Eric took out the gun-mike and amplifier and plugged into Bill's sound-socket. The gun-mike maddened the cops still more: 'There's a sniper in that apartment block – he'll blow you away!' I never did see any evidence of a sniper, but the police believed in him and started to blast out every window in the block with their riot guns, while I did my best to speak a heroic narrative into the camera, ending with the words, 'This is no riot – it's civil war!'

The engagement died down when the cops ran out of ammunition. Eric, Bill and I climbed back into our car, which now had no windows at all, and cruised on. Down a side-street we saw a gang of youths looting a clothing shop, and crept up behind them, filming. Suddenly they spotted us, there were yells of 'Git them honkies!' and we ran for it – your heroic reporter in the lead. There was a *clonk*, something thudded against my shoulder, and I saw spinning down the road in front of me an arm – *a white arm*. My God! They've got Bill – they've torn him limb from limb! But the next instant it became clear the arm was an artificial one, torn from the outfitter's dummy, and though his camera had a nasty dent Bill himself was still intact. The whole adventure made a nice lively piece for the BBC and Hertz hardly raised an eyebrow when we turned in what was left of their car and flew back to Washington.

Crews like Bill's and Peter Beggin's and two or three others, sent out in rotation from London, became part of our family life. Sylvia made them roast Sunday lunches, they took out our children to the movies and swimming pools and the children came to regard them as honorary uncles and said they wanted to be cameramen when they grew up. They were a joy to work with compared with the slobbish American crews I had had to hire – elderly clockwatchers who had inherited their union tickets and had as much idea of composing a picture as the garbage men. 'But that's *feature* work!' they would complain when I outlined a sequence of shots to them. 'That's at least a six-man job and you haven't allowed for coffee breaks.' Once in action a BBC crew was ready to tear up the rule book, and I often found myself working the sound gear, loading magazines or humping the tripod in a manner that made American reporters (who never touched anything bigger than a hand-held microphone) shake their heads in disbelief. It was said that ITN crews were different; that their unions insisted on them flying first class, whence they would send free drinks back to the reporter in the tourist cabin.

The relationship between a TV reporter and his crew was almost as subtle as marriage. Perhaps more so, because it was an eternal triangle. Things may be different nowadays with women in the team, but in those days a successful threesome developed a kind of family consensus which required no pulling of rank or giving of orders. You discussed the day's story at breakfast and somehow it happened. True, the reporter had to play the role of infantry officer (had the men eaten? Were their billets comfortable? Had they written home that week?) while the cameraman acted sergeant and the soundman was the driver and shipped off the film at the end of the day. But the relationship was actually more democratic than among the American teams. For one thing, the British relieved tension by constant leg-pulling throughout the day, while the Americans released it in a twice-daily explosion of rage. 'Time for the NBC crew to have its lunchtime fight,' we would tell one another. And sure enough, they would have a row which cooled them off for the next three hours.

Soundmen tend to be aspiring cameramen and therefore the most frustrated members of the crew. Two that I had used to vent their frustration through feats of randiness which they would never have dared back home. One of them had us quite literally run out of a small Virginia town, by the sheriff, for wrecking the local cat-house; while the other used to leave me a different telephone number every night, in case of emergencies, and more than once my call was answered by a drowsy female voice and a rustle of sheets before I got the perky assurance, 'Be with you in two shakes of me cock, old cock!' Camera-men, being older and more heavily married on the whole, seemed to quell their lust by retiring early to their own bedrooms to charge batteries and blow fluff out of their gates.

Not all our travelling was on riot duty. Electioneering took us from coast to coast, hopping from one candidate's plane to another when their tours crossed and snatching interviews in aeroplanes with politicians who never knew how seriously to take these British who did not actually command any votes. Spiro T. Agnew, who coined for me the immortal phrase, 'Once you've seen one slum you've seen them all', thought at first that the initials BBC stood for Baltimore Brewing Corporation, with which he was familiar since it supplied his home state of Maryland. Nixon put him on his ticket as vice president largely to appease the white bigot vote; and I once had the unpleasant experience of being caught in a hotel in Cleveland between a wave of Agnew supporters and a counter-wave of admirers of a black hero called Little Stevie Wonder, who assumed that since I was large and white I must be part of Agnew's bodyguard. Large men who go around with the famous are constantly getting mistaken for body-guards, I find. Not that Agnew – widely known as Spiro T. *Who?* – was all that well-known. He got elected on Nixon's coat-tails but soon had to resign under a cloud of scandal about his financial affairs.

Once, travelling with the Nixon campaign, the BBC crew and I festooned the aircraft with home-made banners reading 'Bring back the Monarchy – All is forgiven!' and 'Liz for Prexy – Phil for Veep!', but they were torn down angrily by the Secret Service escort. Humour is not common currency in American politics, which is why Adlai Stevenson and Eugene McCarthy never stood a chance. Indeed, it is a fairly sound rule that no candidate with a sense of wit that appeals to the English stands a hope of getting elected President of the United States.

Nixon, by that rule, was a shoo-in. He had no sense of humour whatever, being always far too busy figuring out how the person he was talking to might be trying to do him down. He was a darkly suspicious man who slammed the shutters of his inner self the moment you tried to get below the surface. We noticed that every time he received the customary ovation at some local whistle-stop he would turn and say something to the dignitary on his right which was always received with a look of fascinated incomprehension. By moving in very close with the microphone we discovered why that was: instead of saying, 'Really, this is too flattering – too kind . . .' Nixon was moving his lips but saying nothing at all. On film he looked modest and grateful, but in fact he was silent. It was very curious. We made a short feature about his campaign mannerisms which won the cameraman an award and greatly annoyed the American Embassy in London.

More tragically we were in the hotel in Los Angeles when Bobby Kennedy was shot – or rather, the crew was there, for I was a mile away in another hotel writing a script for radio and keeping one eye on the television. Within a minute I was through to London by telephone, ad-libbing an account off the screen, and there I stayed for hours. For a second Kennedy to fall to an assassin's bullet – all in a row with the shots at Martin Luther King, George Wallace, Gerald Ford and Ronald Reagan – still tempts me to renounce my affection for America. I could hardly get through my broadcasts without weeping, for it seemed that nothing would persuade this people to disarm themselves or that the constitutional 'right to bear arms' was not a gesture of virility but in the interests of raising an eighteenth-century militia. Nothing would silence the chant of the gun lobby that 'Guns do not kill people – only people do', to which the proper retort is, 'Yes – people with guns.' I could see that there must be a sickness in the heart of the killer – in most instances an obsessive desire by somebody unimportant and rejected to make the world realise how powerful and important he or she really is. But that violence might somehow be in me, too, was something I brushed aside.

With Bobby Kennedy dead it was pretty clear that the 1968 Democratic Party nomination had to go to Lyndon Johnson's vice president Hubert Horatio Humphrey. A garrulous but agreeable man, sincere, energetic and brave, Humphrey had made his early reputation as a crusading radical. But that had been years ago. Now he was the establishment's man, and at the Democratic Convention in Chicago he had to grin and bear it as the infamous Mayor Daly packed the hall with municipal employees and railroaded Hubert into the nomination. Outside thousands of young liberal Americans had gathered to protest against the betrayal of their ideals; but the Mayor's police charged them, beat them up and tear-gassed them, making it very clear that Middle America had no sympathy with long-haired peaceniks and pot-smokers.

The BBC, as was its wont at conventions, had hired a luxury suite in the main hotel in which to entertain the swarm of its own visiting firemen plus the occasional underemployed American politician. The suite looked out over the park where most of the rioting took place, its windows opening just above tear-gas level. From them Charles and I were able to keep up a running commentary on the action, glass in hand. From time to time, progressive-minded friends would stagger into the suite to wash their streaming eyes, be interviewed and take a slug of BBC Scotch before returning to the field, until the police started chasing them into the lobby and we – fearing that the doctrine of hot pursuit might wreck our boudoir – had to ask them to go elsewhere for first aid. The convention ended in a shambles with the Democrats totally discredited. Staggering out of the hall with a souvenir placard reading 'We Love Mayor Daly', I waved it feebly at one of the Chicago cops. 'Ye're learning,' he said grimly and prodded me on my way with his night-stick.

In a sense it was Lyndon Johnson's fault for getting America bogged down in Vietnam just as its youth was in the mood for love and peace. I have written elsewhere about this* and of how the Vietnam involvement went back to Kennedy, Eisenhower and even earlier; for just as Britain had felt the call of a mission to India, America had (and in some ways still has) a mission to China which was thwarted by the communist takeover. Secretary of State Dean Rusk had actually been born in China and saw his duty in terms of resisting Maoism as if it

* *America: The Changing Nation,* Eyre & Spottiswoode, 1968.

were Nazism, under no circumstances to be appeased. But whatever the crimes of the Viet Cong and North Vietnam it was crazy to attribute them to the Chinese – or the Russians. They were extensions of a private Indochinese feud which had been going on for generations, and it was simply no business of the United States what form Southeast Asian nationalism took. Nor, as events proved, had the Americans the faintest hope of winning the sort of war which had already proved too much for the better-prepared French.

But urged on by an obsessed State Department, a CIA which was out of its depth and a Pentagon which was eager to exercise and develop its forces (soldiers, like athletes, have to keep in practice somehow), Lyndon Johnson was determined not to go down as the first American president to lead his nation to defeat. A few thousand more men, and a few thousand more, and when that did not do the trick, let the bombers loose over Hanoi: month by month he waded deeper into the jungle. When Harold Wilson flew helpfully off to Moscow to see if he could mediate, Johnson drawled to me, 'If a blind *hawg* can find an acorn in a *derng* heap, good *lerk* to him Ah say!'

Having stopped the North Koreans from seizing South Korea, the Americans could not believe that Vietnam would be very different – though the fact was that Korea had been fought across an old-fashioned front-line. The early setbacks in Vietnam did not matter very much because the casualties were mostly borne by poor whites and blacks from the Southern states who made up the bulk of the professional Army. But as the demand for men escalated, conscripts had to be drafted from all over America. Middle-class educations and careers were dislocated, draft-dodging became fashionable, as the coffins were flown home to New England, California and the Middle West.

Most damaging of all in that media-conscious society, hard-working American reporters who could not constitutionally be censored got tired of taking the handouts from headquarters and began going out into the field and telling it like it unpleasantly was. By 1967 it had become all too clear that no amount of expensive hardware, advanced technology or computer-assisted analysis was going to locate the enemy, let alone destroy him. Lyndon Johnson, endlessly frustrated, deluded and diverted from the domestic politics he really understood, rounded on the White House press and told us, in effect, 'You bastards – you've done for me. I'm quitting when my term is up and I hope you're proud of yourselves.' We declined to feel guilty, but I think most of us were sorry for him. LBJ was a lovable rogue who got the wrong questions to answer. But for Vietnam he might even have been accounted a very good president; for his folksiness, vulgarity and wheeler-dealing went along with a genuine compassion for the poor and a concern to get things done for them. True, he picked beagles up by their ears, but only because it was Texas folk wisdom this was good for them (his own ears were so elongated that it looked as if *he* had been picked up by them). It occurred to me that Johnson would have made a natural Australian: I know that he greatly admired Australia and thought that if only its people would work a bit harder it might become an even bigger version of Texas in the South Pacific. After all, the Australians had answered his call for troops in Vietnam, whereas the shifty British refused him even the token contingent he craved from the Black Watch. 'Those bagpipes', he said, mistily, 'would scare the *shit* out of the Veet Cong . . .'

When in a fix domestically, the President would announce he was off to the Pacific to confer with somebody about Vietnam. Three times I found myself scrambling aboard the press plane at twenty-four hours' notice for some diversionary conclave he had dreamed up overnight, though it took all one's ingenuity to make a story out of what actually happened when we got there. The first time we went winging off to Hawaii to meet Ky and Thieu, the two-man junta, and took over the Royal Hawaiian Hotel on Waikiki Beach to accommodate our roadshow. The wealthy tourists who had been evicted to make room for us lined the hotel driveway, booing lustily as we drove in. Once installed there, half the cabinet of the United States sat on the verandah wondering why they had come, while the beach itself, cordoned off by the Secret Service, was populated only by network correspondents rehearsing their 'standuppers' to the waves. I bought a succession of mai-tai cocktails for Robert McNamara, the Defense Secretary, but he refused to discuss anything but English poetry. Threatened with severe mai-tai poisoning the press corps turned to the jugs of free pineapple juice with which the Hawaiian PR girls plied us, only to find that after three or four glasses our gums began to rot.

The next LBJ outing was to visit 'our boys' at Camranh Bay in Vietnam itself. This was supposed to be kept secret until it had happened, and the White House tried to dump me in the Philippines on the way out, as an undesirable alien. But I smelt a rat, smuggled myself back onto the aircraft while it was refuelling and threatened to tell the world what was going on if they did not take me with them. Thus I got to witness the President exhorting his troops to 'bring that coonskin home and nail it on the door', which they never did.

The third and final dash was to meet General Westmoreland on the island of Guam, most of which was solid runway and wall-to-wall B-36 bombers. We spent most of our time shopping in the Air Force PX store. The most exciting event was when the correspondent of the Associated Press got bitten in his bunk by a Polynesian polecat and was then so intensively cared for by the medical staff that he almost died.

Incidentally, it was a tradition of the White House press plane that every landing should be greeted with enthusiastic applause from the cabin, the custom going back to some far-off occasion when the pilot had had to abort his touchdown a couple of times before making it. Subsequent pilots who had not been warned about this were often disconcerted or offended, but I find myself doing it to this day, even on the British Airways shuttle to Belfast. If you ever sit next to a passenger who applauds every landing, the chances are he is an ex-White House reporter, although I gather the habit has spread to American scheduled flights.

Three times I went to Vietnam on my own for a few weeks, relieving the BBC's regular correspondent while he went off on R & R (or Rest and Recreation) among the fleshpots of Hong Kong. Saigon I found to be no Pearl of the East but a sordid, cynical place where you could hardly breathe for scooter fumes and where everything and everybody – especially every body – was for sale. The street bazaars were full of American military stores, and though the Vietnamese police occasionally raided them, made bonfires of the less desirable items and shot one or two Chinese dealers who were behind with their protection money, there was more black market than white in the city. Drastic penalties were also threatened for unofficial currency dealings but everyone (including me) changed their dollars at the Indian Bookshop, which handed over bricks of South Vietnamese piastres in exchange for hundred-dollar notes.

I felt no temptation to spend the profits on the whores of all ages and sexes who teemed and twittered in the hotel lobbies; they seemed more like birds than people. Outside the main American camps were avenues of tin shacks advertising 'Truck Wash & Cold Beer – $5' or 'Special Wash – $10' which meant the GI could screw the proprietor's niece while his vehicle was hosed down. Most dreadful of all was the aptly named 'Venus Snackbar' where the American tunnel rats – men who specialised in crawling after the Viet Cong through their underground bunkers – sprawled beer-can in hand while Vietnamese girls nuzzled into their flies. By night Saigon lacked the dignity of Dante's Hell.

American correspondents stayed at the Caravel Hotel because it was air-conditioned, though from time to time they got bombed for the privilege. The British used the Continental Palace, across the square, because although there was no air-conditioning the owner paid his subscription to the Viet Cong and one could sit on the open terrace in perfect safety; indeed, it was the most rewarding place to be in Saigon, the resort of tipsters, spies, heroes, frauds and soldiers of fortune. I once encountered a couple of British Royal Marines who, through some sort of old grunts' network, were spending a few months fighting in the US Marines, 'just to see how they're doing it'. Quite how official this was I could not make out. There was also a young British Quaker who was the only entirely reliable informant I ever met in Saigon, for the simple reason that he lived among the Vietnamese and spoke their language. At the root of the United States failure in Vietnam lay the fact that almost no Americans spoke Vietnamese and very few even spoke French, the language of the educated. The Vietnamese knew they were despised – and despised by barbarians. So the two races fought their different wars for their different reasons, each trying to exploit the other, each failing to understand what the other was about. Not that I felt particularly sorry for the Vietnamese. It became fashionable to grieve for what the brutal Americans were doing to them, but it scarcely compared with what the Vietnamese did to each other – and had been doing for a very long time.

The BBC maintained a permanent room at the Continental – like all rooms at the Continental it was alleged to have been stayed in by Monsieur Graham Greene – a room crowded with beds, boots, wickerwork chairs, broken tape recorders, empty bottles and piles of old communiqués. It looked like a bunkhouse in Dawson City during the gold rush.

My first morning alone in Saigon there was a loud explosion in the street outside. I remembered what the resting-and-recreationing correspondent Peter Stewart had taught me: 'Always wait for the *second* bang – the first is just to gather a crowd.' Sure enough, the second followed. But then a third and fourth – half a dozen in all. For the first time the Viet Cong had sneaked a mortar close enough to bombard Saigon, making a bloody mess in the flower market and a hole in the cathedral roof. If they had had slightly better fire control they might have laid a stick of bombs across the grandstand from which Ky and

Thieu were to inspect a military parade that morning. Only there was something wrong with the VC's timing as well: they fired an hour too early, the parade had not begun.

That was my introduction to the messier side of war, and there was a lot worse to come: not so much the rip of passing bullets and the slam of the exploding grenade but the obscene festoons of entrails, the god-awful smell of human sewage, the gobbets of clothed flesh and the speechless shock on the faces of the badly wounded, as if they didn't want to know it and now couldn't believe it. Once I ran into the marketplace of a town in the delta just after a bicycle bomb had gone off. A group of peasant women was still sitting cross-legged beside their piles of vegetables: only they had no heads. The worst thing is, you can get used to it, tell yourself how tough you are: I remember one of my colleagues rubbing his hands while his cameraman set up, chortling, 'Oh goody – I love blood!'

The Americans issued their correspondents with uniforms and gave them passes entitling them to officers' messing and any ride they could hitch on military aircraft. I always refused to wear the uniform – most of the network correspondents had themselves smart 'TV suits' made by Saigon tailors – but I availed myself fully of the hitch-hiking. My lack of uniform made the military assume I was some connection of the CIA, which operated its own airline called Air America. This was always easy to get onto because it specialised in supplying various irregular units of native mercenaries with their favourite sauce made of rotting fish; the aircraft which distributed this smelled so vile that few people wanted to ride in them. Even so they were less terrifying than the helicopters which flew about with their doors open and seemed to be trying to shake themselves to pieces – as often they did, for the crash rate from mechanical failure was three times that due to enemy action. I went up in one helicopter which had been equipped with an experimental people-sniffer, devised to meet the perpetual problem of where the Viet Cong actually were. In this case the proposed solution was to pick up the aroma of their urine – even the VC had to piss, it was argued – but it rapidly became clear that the chemicals in the apparatus only worked at a height which made us sitting ducks for the invisible guerrillas. In the end it was we who pissed off.

The BBC carried its noncombatant status to the defiant length of painting its transport white and decorating it with a union jack and the words *Bao Chi Anh Quoc*, which was said to mean *British press* or, alternatively, *Don't shoot this one – it's not our war*. The vehicle in question was a ludicrous mini-moke, a kind of motorised tea-tray without a roof which Peter Stewart entrusted to me with all the misgivings of a father lending his son the Jaguar for the evening. 'Now take care of it – it's the only one of its kind in the whole of Vietnam.'

After a day in it, I wasn't surprised. Quite apart from the terror of being stabbed in the back by a passing scootist, or having a grenade dumped in the rear seat, the moke was so close to the ground that the drivers of army trucks could hardly see it. Parked outside the hotel it rapidly became a public bench with a shoeshine boy operating in the front seat and a pair of male prostitutes on display in the back. I had to hire a one-legged ex-soldier to guard it and he rapidly sub-let to a black-market moneychanger.

There was a scare about mines in the Saigon River, so I arranged with the US Navy to go on a minesweeping patrol from their base at Kanh Tho. They would send an escort to take me there, they said, and what they sent was Journalist Second-Class Applebaum, a diminutive figure with an enormous .45-calibre pistol on his hip who normally pushed handouts from his desk at JUSPAO (the much-mocked Joint United States Public Affairs Office). I loaded Applebaum into the moke, which he regarded with justifiable alarm, and drove out into the countryside towards the delta. There was a *click*, and looking round I saw that Applebaum had drawn his pistol and was menacing the passing peasantry with it: 'These people have got the wrong sort of smile,' he muttered tensely. 'Keep going as fast as you can.' 'These things *can't* go very fast,' I told him, 'and if you can tell the right sort of Vietnamese smile from the wrong sort of Vietnamese smile you deserve to be something better than a second-class journalist.' But Applebaum had no humour and spent the rest of the trip moving his gun restlessly from side to side.

We reached Kanh Tho, boarded the minesweeper and spent the day trawling up and down and catching nothing. The banks of the river had been chemically defoliated some months earlier, but the effect was wearing off and the sinister jungle was creeping back to the water's edge. I had little confidence in the ability of my armoured jacket to stop a well-aimed sniper's bullet. Eventually bad light stopped play and we returned to base for the night, a joyless occasion since the naval quarters were sealed up like a prison and Applebaum developed an upset stomach.

Next morning, as soon as the gates were open, we climbed into the moke and bounded back towards Saigon, pistol at the ready once more as my escort monitored the smiles. Suddenly we hit a small hump-backed bridge over a canal, leapt into the air and came down on the other side with a colossal explosion. My God! Viet Cong! But it wasn't. It was Applebaum's pistol going off – powerful things, those .45s – and punching a big hole in the steel floor of the moke all too close to my foot.

'Right on! Right on!' yelled Applebaum, brandishing his still-smoking weapon. 'Give me that bloody pistol!' I said, jamming on the brakes. 'I'm not driving another inch with *your* finger on the trigger. And if you don't give me that gun I'll see to it the entire English-speaking world hears about your incompetence.' With Applebaum disarmed we drove back sedately into Saigon. I gave him back his gun, I still told the world, but I have at least altered his name.

The next day the moke was partially run over by a municipal garbage truck jumping a red light. Peter Stewart was bitter. 'Leave you with a perfectly good moke and what do you do? Get it shot by a second-class journalist and crushed by the dustman. The only one of its kind in the whole of Vietnam – ruined.' 'But it still goes.' 'People will laugh at it.' 'They always did.' 'You don't understand,' said Peter, 'It's the only thing flying the British flag in this whole lousy country: and you've disgraced it.'

Visits to Vietnam left me feeling very strange. In journalistic terms it was the biggest story of the day, it was the ultimate reality, what the whole of America was arguing about. And yet on the spot it was something totally different: it was not actually *about* anything, certainly not about saving the freedom of the Vietnamese. It was a way of life, a self-contained system, an economy in which people cultivated their own interests for many different reasons none of which had much to do with democracy or freedom, words which hardly made sense in a Vietnamese context. But how to go back to the United States and tell people they were pouring their blood and money down the drain? Some of them already knew it, but it was not a thing a foreigner could go about Washington shouting.

I had come to love America deeply, to respect its relentless self-criticism, its positive energy, its determination to put things right that were wrong and to achieve the impossible. When Kennedy vowed they would put a man on the moon by 1970, they did it; and I found the technology of the lunar landing programme enthralling and often very beautiful. And yet, like Vietnam, it turned out to be a wrong turning, a dead end. Today one wonders why they bothered to do it, what good was it, was it only a grandiose gesture of national pride? But I took any such doubts in my stride and in that first book of mine – *America: The Changing Nation* – I came to the conclusion that all was set fair for the American future and that Britain would do far better to become part of the United States than to take the plunge into Europe. No one was more appalled than my American friends, but it seemed to me a good idea at the time.

I wrote the book in a few weeks begged off from the BBC. The intense effort of writing it, learning to expand my thoughts for print rather than to compress them for broadcasting, nearly drove me out of my mind. I had already been working harder and harder in an effort to fend off the criticism – which nobody ever made – that I was not earning my keep. Once again the Beirut syndrome of short temper, panic over punctuality and a restless churning of the mind reappeared. For some reason it was always at its worst on Sunday mornings when we all attended service at the Congregational church next door: I would rush in at the last minute and stand swaying at the back of the gallery, terrified of falling over the edge and oppressed by the liturgy of sin and unworthiness. It was clear to me that if I did not soon give up my job, I should be exposed as a fraud.

And yet so far as the BBC was concerned, I could have stayed in Washington indefinitely. There was another reason for going. The children were growing up, Jennet was ready for art school, and if we did not get them back to England soon they would have no alternative but to qualify for American colleges and, inevitably, become Americans. Neither Sylvia nor I wanted to force that on them, nor were we inclined to send them home as boarders; so I gave London a year's notice that once again the Priestlands would be returning and that I hoped to continue serving the news department there. The problem was, as what?

Charles and I had moved our office from the cramped and unelectronic National Press building to the top floor of CBS News in downtown Washington, next to a lowish bar called the Pink Elephant, notorious for its king-size martinis. Besides space of our own, CBS gave us access to its studios, cameras and tie-lines to various hearings and press conferences, but above all it lent us intimacy with some of the best correspondents in Washington – Roger Mudd on Capitol Hill, Bob Pierpoint at the White House, Marvin Kalb at the State Department, Daniel Schorr, George Herman and above all, Eric Sevareid.

Eric, a former assistant to Ed Murrow, had the face of a Lutheran pastor and the voice of an Old Testament prophet. He also liked king-size martinis, over which he confided to me that he was constantly having to fight off invitations to stand for the United States Senate – in which, I may say, he would have been not an ornament but a monument. Instead he preferred to exert a far wider influence over the nation by delivering, daily, a short commentary as part of the CBS evening news anchored by Walter Cronkite.

If Walter was the father-figure of American television, Eric was its grandfather. Drawing on a lifetime's experience of Washington and the world he would speak an editorial of such authority that few dared contest it even when he was wrong. It was something unthinkable for the BBC, which is forbidden to have an editorial opinion, but Americans saw no harm in it provided it did not pretend to be straight reporting and they gave Eric the respect he deserved. It was he, in the Pink Elephant, who suggested I might try a similar spot on the BBC. When I explained about the ban on opinion he said it was not a matter of opinion but of analysis: 'Take the situation apart, show how it works or doesn't work – that's not opinion, it's analysis. And if somebody doesn't do some thinking on this box of tricks, there'll be nothing but pretty pictures and politicians. It sounds to me as if British politicians want to keep it all to themselves.'

And so I sketched out a proposal to the BBC, and Desmond Taylor who was then editing television news liked it and bought it. In the late summer of 1969 we packed again – including Saki the cat – and took the train for New York and the SS *United States*. The BBC's glossy New York office, high up in the Rockefeller Center, threw a farewell party for us at which Alistair Cooke was present: 'Haven't seen a lot of you,' he said. 'I'm not in your league, *cher maître*.' 'I think you might have been,' he said, patting my elbow, 'if you'd stuck it. Say another thirty years.'

The kind folk in the New York office presented me with one of those document cases that has a combination lock set to your birthday – then the latest thing in America and quite unknown in London. I mention this because it subsequently came to a dramatic end at the hands of the metropolitan police, and if you will make yourself comfortable for a moment or two longer I will tell you how.

Back in the 1950s I had written a fairy tale called *The Magic Jumper* for our daughter Jennet. Came the 'seventies and Jennet herself wondered if it might not get published? John Parker, who had been the publisher's editor for *America* (and had made me take out all the feeble jokes) had become my agent. He hawked my *Jumper* hopefully around but no one fancied it so I collected the typescript from him at his office in Chancery Lane (he now lives much more grandly in Fitzroy Street) and locked it in my transatlantic case. Then, in the way one easily might, I popped into Gamages to buy a collapsible bicycle, which seemed like a useful thing to have. I staggered back to Broadcasting House and put the still-disassembled bike in the boot of my car before I realised that I had left the fairy tale, in the document case, in Gamages' collapsible bicycle department.

A frantic race back to Holborn, only to find that the bomb squad had got there before me. 'Very worried, they were,' said the manager. 'Never seen one like that, they said. Fitted with a special timing dial, apparently. Four pounds of explosive at least.'

I traced the infernal machine to Theobalds Road Station. 'And what might have been in the case, sir?' asked the sergeant at the desk. 'A fairy tale,' I mumbled, 'a much despised and rejected fairy tale.' He went away and came back a few minutes later with the remains of the case and a plastic bag full of mutilated pages. 'Very sorry, sir. It's what they are pleased to call a controlled explosion. Not all that controlled, I'm afraid, but with an IRA campaign going on . . .'

'Never mind,' I said, 'nobody liked it. At least it ended with a bang.'

Chapter Nine

CHURCH BELLS BEYOND THE STARS

'They've seen the Empire State building and Disneyland, Niagara Falls and the Grand Canyon, Cape Canaveral, New Orleans and even that place in Mexico that sounded like a sneeze . . .'

'Xihuatanejo . . .'

'. . . Where there were cows on the runway, pigs on the beach and a coatimundi in the garden,' said Jennet.

'. . . But', continued Sylvia, 'they have to be European now and they've never seen Europe.'

So we quickly arranged a grand tour. We 'did' Paris, Venice, Rome and Athens and the children failed to be impressed. The boys played cards all over Rome, even standing up in buses. They thought Venice was a really neat idea but had too many pictures. In Athens they complained the statues were all broken. The bilingual guide at the Acropolis explained to us that the Parthenon marbles had been 'removed to safety by Lord Elgin'; and then confided to the French, *'stolen by the English!'*

Autumn came and the children were fitted back into school, the two boys into Haberdashers' out at Elstree, Jennet into Hornsey College of Art where Sylvia had been, and Diana (when she was old enough) into the girls' grammar school in the Garden Suburb. She and Oliver were somewhat mutinous against what they considered too much respectability, but, looking back, their fragmentary education round the world did them no harm. Oliver came home one day swinging a brace of pheasant: 'They've escaped from the farm over the road,' he said. 'It's easy. You put sandwich crumbs on the ground and hide in the bushes; and when the pheasants come you chase them into the cricket nets and wring their necks.' His next outrage was to launch an underground newspaper which campaigned against the inefficiency of the school bus service – a worthy objective in itself but vitiated when he came out with the headline FUCK THE BUSES! The headmaster complained that the smaller boys were embarrassing their parents by asking what it meant. After a prolonged war of nerves with the establishment, Oliver went off to a college of further education and got himself some distinguished A levels on his own; for unlike his elder brother, Andreas, he would always fight the system rather than conform to it if he thought it was being silly. Haberdashers' suited Andreas down to the ground – literally, for he fell in love with geography and geology there.

If the children were not interested in Europe (and they still aren't very much) we were anxious they should at least know something of the English countryside. We sniffed about Wiltshire and Dorset for a cottage, but I could feel Cornwall calling and eventually we found a breathtaking place in Zennor, a few miles from Land's End. Zennor is the very Tibet of Cornwall: there's hardly a tree standing because of the gales, and the natives once chased out D. H. Lawrence because they thought his wife Frieda was signalling to German submarines. The cottage had been the counthouse of the Carnello tin mine, the ruins of which lay tumbled down the cliff around it, with a ferocious view of the Gurnard's Head and its stormy bay. Sometimes there was a beach big enough for the whole parish to play touch rugger; sometimes there was nothing but a bank of pebbles because the giant Tregeagle, carrying out his Cornish version of the labours of Sisyphus, had swept the sand away.

Veor Cottage was half a mile off the nearest road, took its water from a mine shaft and had no gas or electric mains. When the gales reached force eight, which they often did, the roof shook, the bottled gas blew out and rain bubbled in through the windowframes. At first the children swore that life there would be impossible without television; but soon they were forced to discover the pleasures of beach-combing, blackberrying, exploring the clifftops and helping on the nearby farm, whose owner was our landlord. It was little more than a primitive smallholding, meant to provide half-a-living for someone who also fished or worked down the mine, but its handful of cows and pensioner donkey provided Diana's initiation into the world of live-stock that was to become her obsession. 'I want to be a farmer,' she announced at the age of twelve. 'But we haven't *got* a farm. There's no farming in this family and hasn't been since great-great-grandfather Priestland was steward to the Archdeacon of the Isle of Man over a hundred years ago.' 'I still want to be a farmer.' Sylvia blames me for the fact that Diana has scarcely had her hands off a Cornish cow ever since. When the time came for her to take her diploma, she came top in castration and de-horning, beating all the boys. 'Look at her,' moaned Sylvia, 'an absolutely gorgeous redhead straight out of the pre-Raphaelites, and you can't see her complexion for cowdung . . .'

Meanwhile back at the Television Centre I was experimenting with my Sevareid spot. I would attend the morning editorial conference, suggest a subject from the day's news, and spend the rest of the day researching it by telephone and interview. By the evening I had a three-minute piece of gemlike analysis which I delivered head-on to the camera without what I regarded as visual distractions. It was, frankly, a talking head; and without claiming to be one of them, some of the best things I have seen on television have been heads talking sense. But it was contrary to fashion at the time, and there were mutters around the table that it 'wasn't television – where were the visuals?' So I went out and filmed my spots in suggestive places like London Airport (if the subject was hijacking), Fleet Street (for take-overs) or a pile of rotting rubbish in Notting Hill during a dustmen's strike.

The reaction of BBC high-ups was good. On January 1st 1970, Charles Curran (then Director General) wrote to me saying, 'I take the opportunity of saying how much I enjoy your acute comments on the day's news – though I know they are not "comments"! I'm sure it's right that we should "give crisis a context" as Eugene Hallman puts it, even if it does give a problem of presentation.'

The problem was what I have already described. But what Curran did not know was that as he wrote I had already been eased off the air in a peculiarly underhand way which suggested more devious motives. Desmond Taylor, the editor, had been lent for a few months to the Fijian Broadcasting Service – a deeply conscientious man, he had been overworking and I think it was also intended as a refresher for him. But the moment he was out of the way his deputy (a not very communicative Scot) began cutting down my appearances to one or two a week and eventually none. Every time I suggested a subject for analysis I was told the time was needed for film of 'something happening'.

Fiji is about as far from London as it is possible to get, but there is a direct airmail service. I wrote to Desmond telling him what was going on, and also wrote back to Curran advising him that his praise had arrived too late. There were some angry and expensive telephone calls from Suva, but when Curran sent for me in person it was to say – with embarrassment on his part – that it seemed my spots did not fit; 'They slow it down – they stand out like a healthy thumb in a sore hand, if you like.'

I believe the reason was one of pure showbusiness. The film editors and scriptwriters were impatient to pack in a few more riots, fires or disasters where I wanted, perhaps, to discuss why one of those riots had taken place. It was the celebrated 'bias against understanding'. I was also aware there was some pressure against me from the political right: one MP had denounced me as 'a dangerous young man', which was flattering at the age of forty. But neither Curran nor Taylor had taken it seriously and it seemed improbable that Taylor's deputy would have felt obliged to give way to it. What no one ever suggested was that I did the job badly or boringly – I would have bowed to that if they had. Years later, when the experiment was discussed in one of the official (and of course confidential) BBC manuals the reason given for ending it was that it was unconvincing that anyone should pretend to know so much about so many different subjects – a reason never presented at the time and one which would disqualify *most* radio/TV pundits.

For a while I thought of resigning but dismissed that as conceited, resolving that some day I would return to the business of exploring the ideas behind the news. Only, after so many years of being able to rely absolutely on the people for whom I worked, this sneaky betrayal and lack of frankness left a nasty smell in my nose. Nothing like it ever happened to me again; for the BBC is not a malicious organisation and isn't even much good at organising conspiracies. There are times when one wonders if there is any organisation at all.

Salvation was at hand, and at the hands of a friend. After a decade of pampering television it was decided that the 'seventies would see a revival of radio. Peter Woon – who had appalled me by quitting as a reporter and going over to the editorial side – was sent across from television to overhaul radio news at Broadcasting House. Would I like to go with him and become part of his new look, or rather new listen? I had always admired Peter (if not always agreed with him). Radio was my one true love. Broadcasting House in the West End was a far pleasanter place to work than the wastelands of the White City. So I was grateful for the chance.

The role I was offered was to present an evening news programme on Radio 4 to take the place of the hallowed but ancient Radio News Reel. We proposed to make it essentially a reporters' and correspondents' show with much of the material coming in live while we were on the air: not all that different, perhaps, from William Hardcastle's

World at One and PM, but drawing on the BBC's staff journalists rather than a repertory company of politicians and trade unionists. We also aimed to take the news as it happened, rather than follow up stories from the daily papers. This demanded a technically advanced studio, an anchorman who could 'fly by the seat of his pants' and a production team he could rely on to keep the material coming. Compared with the rigidity of television, where everyone had to know in advance what was going to happen – where the news was even given a rehearsal – this was spontaneous and exciting.

We called the programme Newsdesk and made it a his and hers show, with Meryl O'Keefe – a former TV announcer with a gorgeous contralto voice (still to be heard on the World Service) – as my co-presenter. From time to time we went out and about as reporters, too, and had a say in the content. I insisted on a high proportion of foreign news and opposed the claim of so-called industrial news (which meant strikes) to the lion's share of the time.

Since I was the principal linkman and wrote all my own material, I found myself back in the business of near-editorialising: it was fun to see how close to the wind one could sail. I wasn't interested in pushing any particular political line, but in exposing folly and pomposity, sometimes evoking pity, even confessing hilarity or boredom. I reckoned that the franker I was about my personal feelings, particularly when rooted in some experience of the subject, the readier listeners would be to take them in the spirit in which they were offered: as a contribution towards understanding and not as laying down the law or pretending total objectivity. The motto, frequently announced, was: 'We hope it's the truth. We know it's not the whole truth. It'll be a miracle if it's nothing but the truth.'

It seemed to work, this 'news with a human voice'. Some listeners did not like the style, but many found it refreshing. The largest single section of our audience seemed to consist of business and professional people who worked late and heard it on their car radios, driving home. Our biggest disadvantage was that, coming after almost an hour and a half of PM and the six o'clock news some listeners had already had enough. Working in harness with us, from an office across the passage, was The World Tonight where the explosive Douglas Stuart worked out the exam questions which he pressed relentlessly upon his interview victims.

I was extremely fortunate with my colleagues, though I shall mention few names in that loyal team for fear of omitting some I should regret. Two of the women, Anne Winder and Caroline

Millington, who used to pilot our transmissions through an ocean of potential disaster, were among the best producers I have ever worked with – soothing but firm, knowing just when to murmur into my headphones, 'Watch it, Gerry, you're going over the top!' Another name that has to be mentioned is John Hosken who used to deputise for me as presenter. Why there are not more Cornish voices on the air is a mystery to me, but then it is a mystery why some voices appear to have three dimensions while others are as flat as cardboard. I suspect it is partly a matter of physics – the overtones in the voice – but partly a matter of making that extra effort to squeeze something more down the wire. On radio you have to overact a bit to make up for the absence of vision. But on TV, with its big closeups, you underact or you look absurd.

And there was Jackie Gillott who for a while replaced Meryl O'Keefe. Besides having a rich voice and a good brain Jackie was one of the most beautiful women I have ever met. She was one of the most beautiful women *most* men had ever met, and she knew it and – on occasion – took advantage of it, as she had done since womanhood first blessed her. She had a patient and understanding husband and two pleasant children; eventually they took to country life in Somerset to see if that would shake off her demons, and she wrote about her country life hilariously. But still she was engulfed in waves of depression and remorse.

I did not know she suffered like this when we were working together, though I realised we did not quite hit it off. I made no passes at her, but I was bewildered by the conflict between her sizzling sexuality and her demand to be treated as if she were a male working journalist. I suppose I treated her in the rather obsequious way I had been brought up to treat women and she, in a feminist mood, thought it patronising. It was not until a few years after she had left Newsdesk that I found an article by her in a women's magazine admitting to depression and describing how there was little she could do about it but weep when it closed down upon her and enjoy herself when it lifted. She had also, it emerged, become a believer and been baptised into the Church of England. I wrote to her saying, 'We are two of a kind – if only I had known – but then our sort can never talk about it, can we?'

I doubt if it would have done any good. I think depressives are incapable of helping one another, since they can hardly help themselves. In retrospect it was poignant and too late. A couple of times on our way down to Cornwall Sylvia and I stopped at Jackie's house in

Bruton (our dog pinched her dog's squirrel-tail and ate it to show who was boss) and we tried to cheer her up when a book of hers got bad reviews. But in September 1980 Jackie got the pills and the Scotch together, made sure nobody would call before morning, and killed herself. May she rest in peace.

As the BBC's religious affairs correspondent by that time I found myself giving the address at her memorial service and making two painful broadcasts in which I begged for understanding of her deadly disease and argued that it was not something a good Christian should be able to 'pray away'; for I had been through it all myself and knew the loneliness and self-loathing Jackie must have suffered.

The pursuing Furies had been closing in since we resettled in London. I tried to escape them whenever I could by flying off on news-gathering trips around the world, one of which took me as far afield as Ethiopia and Fiji; but when I got to Saigon and found it as deeply addicted as ever to violence, I wrote Sylvia a letter of such desolation that she, poor darling, was left as devastated as I and even more helpless. I knew that I had committed a crime for which the penalty was death, but precisely what it was I could not say. Probably it had to do with the utter fraudulence of my success, a deception that made it impossible for anyone, even Sylvia, to believe what I knew of my worthlessness. But 'They' knew and sooner or later They would appear to drag me upstairs to some bleak office where the files lay open revealing all. On my way up the stairs, I told myself, I might as well throw myself from the window.

But why wait? Why not fall in front of a train at Golder's Green station? And then I thought of the unpleasant mess and of the wretched driver – probably a Jamaican. Driving up the motorway one day I saw the end clearly: I would swerve into the supports of a bridge at speed. That way Sylvia might be able to collect the insurance. She would, of course, grieve for me for a time, but before long she would realise how much better off she was without me. Once or twice I toyed with the idea of jumping off a cliff in Cornwall, but in fact that was the only place where I found any peace. The very worst depressions hit me as we packed up for the drive back to London.

Teenage children are bound to cause some worries to their parents; though, goodness knows, ours were trivial enough compared with some of our friends. One had a child who went gay, another developed multiple sclerosis, another was feared schizophrenic, a fourth had Down's Syndrome. And having inherited my father's financial incompetence I was often in some kind of mess with the taxman and the household bills. But the trouble was far more deep-rooted than any of that. What brought it to the surface was an event that should have been an occasion for joy.

Jennet did well at Hornsey and graduated top of her diploma year. So did her boyfriend, the attaché's son from Washington, who had developed into a scientist of some brilliance. They decided to get married and we laid on an old-fashioned family wedding with the bride in her grandmother's Edwardian dress, Diana as a pre-Raphaelite bridesmaid, Paul Rhodes at the organ of the Garden Suburb Free Church and a throng of young artists and scientists and middle-aged relatives drinking champagne in the garden at Meadway Gate. Within a few years the marriage had broken down; certain aspects of the groom's behaviour make me reach for my horsewhip, but I think the truth was that both of them were working too hard at their separate careers to have enough time for one another. In any case that was hidden in the future and could have played no part in the sadness that descended over me as bride and groom drove away on their honeymoon. I was only dimly aware, prompted I suppose by Jennet's resemblance to her, that the spirit of my mother was present, wringing her hands.

A few days later one of the remaining children let a basin overflow upstairs, water came pouring through the ceiling and it was more than I could stand. I ran howling into the street – like a huge abandoned hound – thought for an instant of throwing myself under a car, then sank down sobbing on the doorstep.

Gently Sylvia drew me back inside and telephoned the doctor who, as it happened, was the brother of an old friend from New College days and had become much more than a writer of prescriptions to us. He listened patiently as I moaned on about 'trying my best to get things right, but nobody seems to care'. Perhaps, he suggested, I was being too conscientious, too perfectionist. Maybe I should allow the child in me to come out and play more. We had a dark side as well as a light and we had to accept both as parts of ourselves. He did know someone – to be frank, yes, a psychiatrist – who had been helpful to some of his patients. In the meantime, until I could get an appointment with the man, here were some pills to calm me down.

The pills, tryptozol, seemed to put the brakes on any emotional reaction to anything. They dried up my mouth, which made broadcasting difficult, and pushed all sensations into the distance as if I was feeling, seeing and hearing the world through layers of cotton-wool. I was suspended in a cloud of uncaring, leaving some sort of automatic pilot to fly me through the day's work on Newsdesk. But at least I could sleep again instead of waking at two or three in the morning and it seemed pointless to worry about a world that was so far away.

It took about a month to get an appointment with Dr G. He had his consulting room in one of the redbrick mansions in Fitzjohn's Avenue, Hampstead, five minutes' walk from the corner where Camden Council has hidden its statue of Freud like a guilty secret. I told Dr G. that the trouble was I had been brought up to work so hard and to such unattainably high standards that I simply dared not relax. I had been repressing the urge to enjoy life – it was a matter of liberating my unconscious and learning to become more spontaneous. I appealed to him to cure me of my inhibitions.

Dr G. responded with the equivalent of a slap in the face and a warning that *he* wasn't going to be my father-figure. 'I see you know all the jargon,' he said sharply, 'so I wonder you look to *me* for a cure. In any case, if I do take you it's *you* who will have to do all the work. Tell me, why are you punishing yourself like this? What punishment do you think you deserve?'

Annoyed by his lack of sympathy I retorted defiantly that I could kill myself if need be. It seemed to be the answer he was waiting for. 'Then you had better come and see me for one hour at ten o'clock next Thursday.' And he named his fee. 'How long will it take to sort me out?' I asked. 'I have no idea. It is up to you. *You* will tell *me* when you have had enough, not the other way round.'

I went back largely to make this unfeeling creature sorry for me. But all he did was to lie me on a classic analyst's couch, take up position in an armchair behind my back and work his way through a box of matches trying to light his pipe. There was nothing else to do but talk to him, if only to stop him asking any unpleasant questions, so for about half an hour I babbled on about my upbringing, my schooldays and my career until I dried up. Whereupon Dr G. put down his pipe and in a theatrically Viennese accent began: 'What I think you are trying to tell me is . . .' And he was unerringly right.

When the session was over I drove home and repeated it all to Sylvia, who was simply curious to know what went on in this modern version of witchcraft. My breakdown had come as a terrible shock to her, most of all because she was hurt that I had not been able to confide in her about my sufferings. But it is characteristic of the depressive that he *knows* he will not be believed, and sooner than hear his sufferings dismissed as imaginary or exaggerated he will keep them to himself. To be told that his rottenness is unreal is to be told that his very self is unreal, and it is the only self he knows, his belief in it amounts to an almost religious experience.

So, to begin with, these recitals first to Dr G. and then to Sylvia, were an ordeal for me. Yet I think this double-trenching of the ground made them more than doubly effective. Within a month I realised that the clouds were lifting, that there was a future for me, that I was not doomed.

Besides my psychiatrist and my wife a third healer was at work on me. The illness had made it impossible for me to go on attending my local church, even though I yearned for spiritual comfort. I could not bear those accusing references to sin and unworthiness, about which I knew all too much at first hand. So, at the suggestion of Jennet and Andreas (who still remembered their Friends' school in Washington) and at the invitation of Gerard Hoffnung's widow Annetta, I began to attend the Suburb's Quaker Meeting. It was a small congregation – seldom more than forty at one time – but literally a society of friends. As in most Meetings the room was bare and unadorned and the worship mostly in silence, but at least I was not confronted with that tortured figure on the crucifix telling me that I had helped to nail it there, nor was I damned with the pronouncement that there was no health in me. Now, as I listened to the Quaker message that there was that of God in everyone, which could speak directly to each if only we would shut up and give it a chance to be heard, I realised that what I was hearing on the psychiatrist's couch and what I was hearing in the Friends' Meetinghouse were the same: the assurance of repentance, forgiveness and grace (which is nothing other than the love of God received and responded to).

I suppose this seems a pious cliché, too hackneyed to carry any conviction with the sceptic. But having come by it the hard way – 'experimentally' as the Quaker George Fox put it, meaning from experience within – I cannot let it go. As a nominal Christian it had always been available to me and seemingly should have healed me, but a sick mind can only frame a sick faith. It was not until my Damascus Road experience, mediated to me by a Jewish psychiatrist in Fitzjohn's Avenue, that it had any meaning at all. Now it is clear to me that if only we will acknowledge our need of forgiveness, our need to forgive ourselves as well as to be forgiven, if only we will realise that forgiveness is constantly poured out and waiting for us, if only we will accept it, then the love within and the love without can respond to one another and circulate and we shall be saved. Jesus I see as the sign and guarantee of this, which will not be enough for some Christians, but I have written elsewhere about that – I do not want to turn this book into piece of amateur theologising.

What, then, *had* I been learning on the couch? Again, it is liable to sound hackneyed and unconvincing as well as embarrassing and I dare say my subconscious has even altered some of it, but the gist was this: I had probably been taken from the breast far too early – Dr G. saw little point in digging back into my cradle and showed no interest whatever in my sex-life – at all events, I clearly longed for much more of my parents' direct affection than I got. One reason for my nostalgia about Cornwall was that only there, on those golden holidays, did I enjoy their undivided attention.

Being sent away to boarding school before I was eight had seemed to me nothing else but punishment for some incomprehensible crime, and I hated my parents for it. But if that was how it must be I would beat their bloody school at its own game, I would reject their blandishments when I came home, and I would even punish *them* by staying away as long as possible by volunteering for holiday labour camps. The violence of my hatred, especially for my shy and lonely mother, appalled me and I did everything to deny it and conceal it. My hard work and perfectionism emerged as a way of satisfying authority so that it never need investigate me or ask questions about my real motives. So long as I scored high and avoided black marks, no one need discover what a Bad Boy I really was, a boy who hated his mother.

All of which must sound absurd from a grown man, though the truth is that part of us never grows up. I had perpetuated the pattern by marrying and leaving home as soon as I could, choosing to work abroad, and crowning it all by the return to Washington which broke my mother's heart: 'Remember how you sent me away when I needed you? Well, now you need me and I'm going!'

'How do children punish their parents?' asked Dr G.

'They leave home,' I said.

'Is it so surprising, then, that you broke down when your daughter got married and drove away?'

Obsessed by the violence I had witnessed in Vietnam and the United States I had been trying to write a book on the subject* when my collapse occurred. I could only resolve and complete it after my recovery. The coincidence came as no surprise to Dr G.

'There is violence in everyone, as those wars and riots and assassina-

---

* *The Future of Violence*, Hamish Hamilton, 1974.

tions were telling you. There is violence in yourself – such violence that you see yourself as having murdered your mother – but you could not admit that. Once you do admit it you can understand yourself and forgive yourself and even love yourself.'

He conducted me through a long and sometimes tearful pilgrimage of understanding and forgiving from which all the characters, including myself, at last emerged as having done their best by the light they had, misunderstanding and misunderstood, but all to be loved in the end for what they were. The great secret was that unless one could see oneself as loving, one was unlovable. The need to give love was, if anything, even more desperate than the need to receive it. So long as I believed that I was the boy who hated his parents, of course I was rotten and worthless and guilty of willing their death. But in fact I had shown plenty of evidence that I had been a *good* son and had brought them pride and pleasure, especially in my happy marriage and their grandchildren.

The rigmarole becomes tedious. One morning I found that I had at last forgiven myself and felt a great wave of love for everyone around me. I wrote to Dr G. thanking him and saying I should not be coming again: he wrote back wishing me luck and enclosing his final account. The treatment had lasted under six months and there has been only one minor setback – treated with something called doxypin – in more than ten years. I believe it is unusual for Depression to yield so decisively to this kind of talking therapy, but then I doubt if any two cases are the same, some seeming more chemical, others more emotional – and goodness knows where the two connect. I have known cases relieved by drugs, by lithium, by electro-convulsive therapy (which nobody need fear, even though we still don't know how it works) and sometimes by a change of diet. It seems to me there is greater hope now for depressives than for sufferers from back-pain – and infinitely greater hope than for sufferers from the dreadful scourge of schizophrenia into which, alas, depression sometimes merges. That is another circle of Hell altogether, which needs to be harrowed with all the resources we can bring to bear upon it.

I suppose that, like an alcoholic, I should claim remission rather than cure. There are certain 'trigger situations' I try to avoid, like rushing to keep appointments at the last minute; certain places, like my old schools; even certain people, particularly other depressives. The latter present a difficulty because since I began talking and writing openly about the subject I get many letters from them asking for help and many invitations to address medical schools, Samaritans and self-help groups. I respond as best I can without getting too closely involved, struggling hard to get people into qualified hands and not to set up an amateur practice of my own. One type of sufferer especially concerns me: the religious person who assumes that their faith should be able to make them whole and who is full of guilt because it does not. I do not think it can; and I have only heard from one victim among hundreds who claimed that it had.

I roared up Fitzjohn's Avenue, overflowing with love and joy, and applied for membership of the Society of Friends – to the surprise of many Quakers who assumed I already was one, as I suppose I was at heart. I had the sensation many converts have of coming home, of finding oneself 'in the place just right'. Friends have an optimism about human nature, a lack of interest in the tiresome subject of sin, which can make them rather gullible. On the other hand, they are less easily discouraged than most people. This optimism seems to be characteristic of recovered depressives; the Society is full of them and I am quite sure, from his writings, that George Fox the founder was one. So I went bouncing round the Society, talking my head off and urging Friends to pep up their theology and decide what they really believed in. I joined a ginger group known as the Open Letter Movement, who bombarded each other with pamphlets and manifestos, held prayerful seminars and visited one another up and down the country. There was Gerald Richards in Shropshire, Richard Allen in Surrey and a powerful prophetess named Lorna Marsden in York. Today, when I have calmed down theologically and have accepted Quakers for the quiet contemplatives most of them are, I am still grateful to that circle for the stimulus and nourishment they gave me.

Most of all, though, I am grateful to the late George Gorman, then the major figure in a Society which does not exactly encourage anyone to regard himself as a major figure. George, an avuncular, pipe-smoking Friend who did not think it unQuakerly to take a glass of beer in a pub, used to conduct sample weekends for 'enquirers' at the Society's retreat house in Oxfordshire, Charney Manor, where he dispensed exactly the kind of religious philosophy I was waiting to hear:

'I spend a lot of my time de-guilting people who have been torn and smashed by their sense of sin,' he told us. 'Quakers are around witnessing to the goodness of life, starting from the opposite end to original sin. No matter how rotten it looks, we believe that life is good, valuable and loving. As you answer that of God in every one, you will find that is true. It is possible to pursue it and make it happen.

'We Quakers build up a body of experience which we will not lightly cast aside; but it is not to be thought of as dogma. Friends have always felt that what matters is how you follow Jesus, not the theories about Him and His divinity. There is much scepticism among us about things we cannot *know*. Creeds are devices to keep heretics out rather than draw people in.

'There is no such thing as religious experience – just experience. Love makes sense and purpose of life, but you must trust yourself to it – trust rather than faith is the word I use.

'In loving and accepting other people you are beginning to love yourself. For the truth about life is love; and the truth about love is that it is God.'

Those are some of the notes I took at the time – May 1974 – and although my beliefs have become more complex since then there is nothing in them that has proved false to me.

Professionally I felt it was time to move on. Newsdesk had been running four years which was about as long as I had done any job and I felt the way to avoid getting stale was to try my hand at something else. The prestige programme of radio talks and documentaries department was Analysis, then anchored by Ian McIntyre. He was about to devote himself exclusively to a series about the Jews – would I be interested in taking over for a year?

I leapt at the chance of extending my range into longer programmes than I had been asked to do before. Analysis included documentaries made abroad as well as those more economically assembled from interviews in the London studio. The one drawback was the department's head, a large brooding man, one of the BBC's 'Hungarian mafia' notorious for assassinating other people's programmes, who hovered over one's shoulder like a thunder cloud complaining about 'self-indulgence' and 'insufficient rigour' and reducing female producers to tears. But my born-again optimism proved impermeable to such discouragement and I had the support of an old friend, Greville Havenhand, as my personal producer. Greville had been through the mill: he had started his career slamming doors and imitating horses' hooves for the Goon Show, and he knew me well enough to know when he was needed and when he wasn't, so that we did not waste time in two men trying to share one man's work. I was only a little offended to receive, from my new administrative officer, a note saying, 'In this department producers travel first class: everyone else goes second.' I got my own back on him by returning from a trip to Germany with all my meals receipted on a stack of beer mats.

Greville and I made some good programmes together and some not so good. A long interview with Mrs Thatcher was a failure because she refused to listen to my questions and simply played the political gramophone records she had brought with her – I hadn't the nerve to bully her. I never regarded myself as a good interviewer in the adversarial style. It seems to me that few forms of broadcasting are more futile than the encounter between the professional interviewer and the equally professional interviewee – who probably congratulate each other afterwards on 'a jolly good punchup'. When British politicians want to say something important they usually say it to the House of Commons. Anything else is a kind of tennis played with used balls, only indulged in to keep the politician's name in the public ear.

Greville and I made the inevitable After Franco – Who? in Spain, After the Colonels – Who? in Greece, and After Tito – Who? in Yugoslavia. Each had its memorable moments. In Madrid I had a weird interview with a nephew of Franco who had mildly suggested it might be time for the Caudillo to retire, and found the nephew's office richly decorated with drawings, paintings, prints and sculpture of rhinoceroses; on top of which he told us the current story of how somebody had sent his uncle a baby elephant as a gift. Franco had sent it back with regrets, saying he could not bear the thought of watching it grow old and die. All the same, die he did very shortly, clutching the left arm of St Theresa of Avila, and I think one has to be narrow-minded to deny him his credit for Spain's readjustment to democracy. It is a country I admire, more especially when I am in Barcelona.

Greece seemed altogether shiftier. It was impossible not to enjoy the political cabaret songs of Mikis Theodorakis (whatever they might mean), but I was not impressed by the smart-aleckry of Andreas Papandreou. Still, there was Melina Mercouri mixing the arts of the filmstar and the politician. When I was interviewing her for television the cameraman asked, 'Miss Mercouri – just for focus – would you look into Mr Priestland's eyes, please?' At which she leant forward and gave me a look which drew me into bed, between the sheets, into her arms and . . . 'Miss Mercouri – stop it!' I begged.

No such luck in Belgrade where everyone complained that the British Labour Party would not speak to them 'when we have so much in common'. Everybody lectured me about the wonders of the unique Yugoslav self-management system, under which every factory – and every department in the factory – holds workers' meetings to manage itself. Close questioning in two factories I visited revealed that the workers were thoroughly sick of meetings and had thought up something newer and better: they hired somebody called a manager and let him do it. Some of the interviewing I did in Zagreb; though all I remember now of Zagreb was the asparagus incident which I relate in case any of my readers wishes to cause a little harmless discomfort to an enemy for a modest outlay.

In the marketplace at Zagreb, finding bundles of asparagus on sale at a very low price, I purchased some against my return to London in a couple of days' time and stored it under my hotel bed. The room was warm, and in less than twenty-four hours the asparagus was rotting and filled the room with an odour so disgusting I could hardly get across it to open the window. It was as if a tomcat had been choked to death with garlic and been left to explode.

Getting rid of it was the problem; much the same problem as that faced by the man in Jerome K. Jerome who tried to dispose of a corrupt cheese; only nobody – but nobody – was going to mistake this for 'a faint odour of melons'. Muffling the asparagus in a plastic bag I hustled it out of the hotel and tried to leave it on a bench in the public park opposite: only a kindly citizen ran after me to restore it. I tramped for miles with that bag feeling, and probably looking, more and more like a terrorist with a bomb to plant. They threw me out of the Croatian Art Museum, where I had hoped to abandon the bag in the cloaks, because the attendant refused to check it in. Finally (God forgive me!) I abandoned it in a lofty church during a funeral service. It just occurs to me that a bunch of decaying asparagus, well placed, could do more than rotten eggs or stinking fish to say 'I hate you'.

And we did a Far East trip, taking in Thailand and Vietnam. Greville had been to my father's old school which specialised in educating the sons of the Siamese nobility, so that he could boast a useful range of old school Thais as contacts. We stayed at the Oriental Hotel where (as in Saigon) one always gets Mr Graham Greene's old room, looking out onto the river with its fringe of the old palatial Bangkok. But once you stray from its banks the city becomes one of the most poisonous and continuous traffic-jams in the world. We enjoyed Thai food, midway between Indian and Chinese, and gnawed at Thai politics: generals came and generals went, it seemed, with as little violence as possible, but the King went on for ever revered by all. Thais grew the best rice in the world, more than enough to feed themselves, and had the sensible habit of spending a few months in a Buddhist monastery whenever they felt like dropping out of the rat-race for a while. One proud father told us he would not dream of letting his daughter marry a man who had not spent at least a year with his saffron robe and his begging bowl.

I returned to Saigon with apprehension, but the black abyss had vanished and if anything I was all too complacent about the future. Two years after the signing of the Paris Agreement the Americans had gone, leaving the city to revert to its cosy ex-colonial ways and a lower standard of living. Retiring to bed under force of the curfew, to a familiar background of distant thumps and crashes, it was like 1965 all over again. *Plus ça change, plus c'est la même guerre.* But it was not, really.

The Vietnamese had seen 'the mandate of Heaven' fade from round the heads of Ky and Thieu, and while millions of them had already voted against the communists with their feet by becoming refugees from the North, they were not going to make any last ditch stand if and when the dam burst. The Americans had not helped by re-creating the South Vietnamese Army in their own image – greedy for ammunition and accustomed to calling in massive artillery and air support whenever it ran into trouble. Congress in Washington was no longer interested in shovelling in hundreds of millions of dollars, and the helicopter gunships stood in rows at Saigon airport, unflyable for lack of maintenance.

The Paris Agreement had been advertised by Henry Kissinger as peace with honour. Now both Vietnams were insisting so rigidly upon their honour that there was no peace. The agreement had provided for a complete ceasefire, the release of all prisoners, free elections, reunification, the neutrality of Laos and Cambodia, American reparations to the North and every peaceful advantage, but not one of its nine chapters had been respected. It was hard to dispute the average South Vietnamese view of the agreement as a device to satisfy the honour only of America and to bring peace only to the United States. One Saigon official told me, 'The agreement has been a disaster. On the one hand the Americans, being great gentlemen, have insisted we should not react to communist moves. On the other, the communists have been allowed to do whatever they want. And we don't have the aircraft, ammunition or fuel to stop them.'

Saigon had been betrayed. But it was a betrayal made inevitable by the original rash commitment to save it.

Not that the communists were endearing. At the weekly press conference which they were allowed to give in their beleaguered mission next to the airport they served glasses of the world's nastiest beer, airlifted from Hanoi, and hammered us with the relentless theme that they were only making war in order to enforce peace. The interpreter barked it out in precisely the accent a Hollywood bit-part player would have used for a communist interpreter. Afterwards he proudly assured me he had picked it up from the BBC's English by Radio. Everyone seemed to listen to the BBC in Vietnam. No one took any notice when Hanoi, Saigon or the American Forces Network said a town was in danger; but if I or my BBC colleagues said it was, the entire population of the place would get up and go, brushing us aside as they fled. I remember standing in the main square in Saigon one morning, waiting for President Thieu to address his people from the rostrum, and hearing my own voice intoning from several hundred portable transistors tuned in to the BBC Singapore station.

Ah, those were the days, the years of pilgrimage in the 1970s! Maddest of all was the time (I think it must have been 1971) when I set out to visit a selection of meritorious nutrition projects and found myself staggering home weeks later as a war correspondent.

My first stop was Calcutta, from where I managed to visit Bill Rhodes in his theology school at tumbledown Serampore. He was not far from the border with what was still East Pakistan, and by strolling through the nearby camp at Barrackpore it was perfectly plain to see that the Indian Army was training and equipping guerrillas for the overthrow of the Pakistan authorities. However, I had to move on.

My second stop was Fiji, where they were doing something with tapioca – teaching people to cook and eat the leaves as well as the roots, I believe. I didn't care for either and became much more interested in a local beverage called *yanggona*, a rather disgusting sludge made from pounded pepper roots which Fijians insist makes you fighting drunk but which did nothing for me but anaesthetise my lips. Anyhow, I spent a blissfully lost weekend in a little place called Levuka on the island of Ovalau – straight out of R. L. Stevenson – where they were holding a beauty contest for 'Andi Lomai Viti' (Queen of Central Fiji). The more you fancied your candidate, the more votes you *bought* for her, the proceeds going towards the school building fund, which seemed to me an admirable way of putting your money where your lips would be. All of Central Fiji had sent boatloads of eager voters equipped with money, guitars and lashings of yanggona, and we lay out under the stars on the football pitch bidding up the votes, applauding the boxing matches, and singing Handel's *Messiah* in Fijian followed by a general outburst of folksongs. Fijians are natural harmonisers with a driving sense of rhythm. 'What's *that* one about?' I asked one yanggona-crazed group. 'It tells how we came here from

Tanganyika,' they told me; and looking at the black skin and fuzzy hair of the Fijians I wouldn't be surprised. Though in other ways, with their rugger and boxing and hymn-singing they are the Welshmen of the Pacific.

Next stop was Kenya, where the Masai seemed to thrive on a diet of curdled milk with warm cows' blood. The dominant Kikuyu I found rather dour, unless you enjoyed their tendency to wax lyrical about the glories of female circumcision ('When are *you* getting done?' they kept asking the American nutritionist who was taking me round). The most engaging people I met were all Luo, and I doubt if any other tribe in Kenya would have put on a charity soccer match in which the women played the men and the women won. It was the first time I had ever been to Africa south of Egypt, and I gasped at its spaciousness, its fresh air and its golden light. As an independent country Kenya seemed to be working; maybe after the style of Mayor Daly's Chicago, but at least a great deal better than Obote's or Amin's Uganda.

Ethiopia, before the fall of Haile Selassie, was something else. Ethiopians are something else anyway, living on a diet of crêpe rubber and violent curry known as *injeera* and *waat*, heaving stones at any foreigner who passes and convinced that all other Africans are barbarians. The development project I was interested in was no more than a scheme to save a proportion of the grain harvest from the rats by storing it in raised granaries on legs instead of dumping it on the ground. Almost everyone else in Africa did it, which was probably why the Ethiopians refused to. But there was another reason. As the despairing English development worker told me, 'What's the point? Whatever they grow, the royal family pinches a third and the Church pinches a third, so why save more for that lot to grab? This place *needs* a revolution.' And it got one and now, I dare say, the Party takes everything.

Addis Ababa is neither old nor particularly interesting. I had to learn some shocking words in Amharic to blast the pimps, touts and fake-antique pedlars out of my way, and I wasn't sorry when a cable arrived from London commanding, 'War broke out India Pakistan proceed urgentest Delhiwards'.

I was back in Nairobi within hours, but it took two days more to get across the Indian Ocean because of a rumour that the Pakistanis had been bombing Bombay. What had actually happened was that the Indian anti-aircraft batteries had opened fire on a false alarm and the falling shrapnel had killed several citizens who then had to be blamed on the enemy. By the time I had reached Bombay and bribed my way to Delhi BBC correspondents from Moscow to Hong Kong had been sucked in and dispatched again to battle fronts in Kashmir, the Punjab and Bengal. 'Nothing left for you I'm afraid,' said the organiser, 'unless you'd like Rajasthan.' 'I'll take it,' I said and rushed off to the bazaar to buy myself some blankets.

This could be a very long story, but the short of it is that I reached the front in a luxury limousine hired from the Indian tourist board (the driver insisted on camouflaging it with a coating of cow-dung), in the company of a charming Sikh journalist called Iqqy Singh and with a crate of rum in the boot. Rajasthan is fairytale country and we trundled from princely palace to princely palace asking where the war was and usually receiving the answer that 'Raj Mata doing Puja' (the Queen Mother is within saying her prayers). After three or four days palace-crawling we arrived at the desert stronghold of Jaisalmer and, several miles on from that, at a place called Longiwalah on the border, the scene of a considerable battle which had only just finished.

A regiment of Chinese-built tanks had come rolling along the road from Sindh, had run into an outpost manned by a company of Sikhs and, according to textbook, fanned out to envelop it. Whereupon they got bogged down in the sand. The Sikhs had spent a jolly night keeping the crews inside their tanks and, came the dawn, the Indian Air Force had flown over in its Hunter jets and put a rocket neatly into each one. A single vehicle had survived and the Sikhs were amusing themselves driving it round in circles. Iqqy got out the rum to celebrate with his co-religionists, I interviewed the jubilant commander and we congratulated ourselves on the scoop of the war. Just as we were leaving an Indian Army captain drove up and insisted on giving a long interview on the importance of adequate supplies of bathwater for the troops: 'British troops I know do not care if they wash or not, but Indian troops are miserable without bath. Without bath this victory would not have been possible. *My* responsibility.'

Two days later I staggered into the BBC Delhi office waving my tapes and crying, 'Clear the line to London!' 'Forget it,' they said. 'The war ended yesterday. Go home.' I barely made it back in time for Christmas and as a final gesture of contempt the caviar shop at Teheran was closed for lunch.

I was now getting the hang of how to write books. My agent, John Parker secured me a commission to write a book about the fish and chips trade – a subject that appealed to me because it was not too arduous and gave me the excuse to rediscover my native land, not to mention outposts of its favourite dish as far afield as California and the Arabian Gulf. For a whole year I did little else in my spare time but eat, read and talk fish and chips, learning of its historic struggles as a trade to escape from untouchability to respectability, its regional fads and fancies, its current battle with the Chinese takeaways. Fortunately there were two trade journals with cellars of dusty files to draw upon, and I evolved a romantic picture of the dish, beginning at the time of Oliver Twist and saving the British working class from malnutrition during the most grinding years of the Industrial Revolution. *Frying Tonight* – which Bryan Gentry published from his flat in Belsize Park just before he died – was full of engravings of early Victorian frying ranges, woodcuts of fish by Sylvia, photographs of guzzling gourmets by Jennet, and it remains by far the best book on the subject because the *only* book on the subject.

Sylvia herself had taken up photography as part of her print-making. It took her months to master the mechanics and chemistry of the process but when she had done so her artist's instinct for textures and composition produced some beautiful pictures of the Zennor landscape. For more than thirty years I had been fascinated by the legends of the area and had pondered their possible basis in fact, so we put the legends and the photographs together to show, for example, how the tales of giants were always associated with hilltops where stood the ruins of Iron Age castles. The giants were almost certainly the memories of Celtic robber barons.

West of Hayle River, published in 1980 with a hundred of Sylvia's pictures and my text, is still the book of which I am most proud. Broadcasting is an ephemeral thing: it may hold an audience of millions for half an hour but it blows away in the wind. A book, however little it sells, might just survive its author. At least he can look at it on his shelves and think: I made that. And *Hayle River* preserves for me the spirit of a place where all of us, myself, my parents, my wife and children were happy together.

From time to time we have toyed with the idea of giving the same treatment to the Isle of Man, land of my ancestors' Babylonian captivity, and we have done some reconnaissance for it and found the Priestland burials in Kirk Andreas churchyard. There are Manx legends, certainly, and a feudal history which continues to this day with a county council trying to run an independent state and sliding over some pretty thin ice in the process. There is even a Manx underground resistance, pledged to the annoyance of English settlers without actually hurting them. But Man is even harder to reach than

Cornwall and frankly I did not feel the same call to it. Sylvia and I traced the ruins of the farm where the alleged spirit of a talking mongoose enthralled Fleet Street in the 1930s and got the BBC into a libel action. Coming away from the place we even stumbled on the wind-dried corpse of what might have been a mongoose, but more probably was a weasel.

On my own, I had several assignments to Northern Ireland – that albatross which has been rotting round the English neck for well over four hundred years, a martyr to its own history. It happens that I love Ireland and the Irish; sentimentally, perhaps, and doped by nostalgia for the poetry of W. B. Yeats and the old legends of Cuchulainn and Deirdre of the Sorrows; but I have met as much sheer wickedness and hypocrisy there as anywhere on earth – violence became hereditary, murder a lucrative profession, all so deep-rooted in tribalism that one despairs of finding any rational cure. I would as gladly see Ireland united as Iceland or Australia, but she suffers the strategic curse of outflanking England, and the English (the Americans too, now) could never afford to let her fall into the wrong hands: that is the heart of the matter.

I have many friends there, both north and south of the border, especially among the Roman Catholic priesthood and the clergy of the Anglican Church, and I have made a point, over several years, of doing some service there annually, usually speaking at some ecumenical gathering like Corrymeela; but even the Ulster Quakers have made little headway in the cause of peace.

I am sure that religious division is the badge and banner of Ireland's trouble rather than its cause – the cowboys just happen to be protestants and the Indians catholics – but that gives the churches little to be proud of. More than once I encountered the Reverend Ian Paisley and attended services at his affluent Belfast church ('Last Sunday's collection was £651, praise the Lord!'). As a big man myself I was at least able to stand up to his bullying. 'A Quaker, are ye?' he boomed. 'They tell me the Devil's a Quaker!' 'Indeed?' I said, 'I heard he was one of your Free Presbyterians.' 'How's that?' roared the Doctor (of Bob Jones University, North Carolina). 'I came to your service last Sunday. Great singing. And they do say the Devil has all the best tunes.'

Belfast was hideous and the strain of serving there upon the British troops was almost intolerable, particularly when they had to deal with Catholic women and children pushed at them by the IRA. It was a popular wheeze for Catholic women to bait the youngest member of a patrol until he rounded on them and lashed out or shouted an obscenity; whereupon the women would be off to his unit's head-quarters with a priest in tow to complain of the affront to their chastity. An infantry officer I met hit upon the solution: he ordered his men to keep their personal two-way radios switched on, and when the priest arrived he was treated to a tape recording of *both* sides of the exchange.

The annual party conferences were more relaxing, usually at Brighton or Blackpool. Boozy affairs, they were, with distinguished politicians groping along the corridors of hotels early in the morning, looking for rooms that were not always their own. Once, at the Labour Conference, I was accosted by Richard Crossman: 'Ah! The celebrated Gerald Priestland! And how do *you* vote, I'd like to know?' 'In secret, Mr Crossman.' 'Just as I thought – a Liberal!' And he was not far wrong.

Chapter Ten

YOURS FAITHFULLY

With our comings and goings it was a wonder we kept any friends at all; but we did, and the older the closer. My Old Carthusian mafia kept loyally in touch – particularly George Engle and Anthony Ray. Sylvia's six brothers and sisters had not only survived but remained agreeably on speaking terms. Artist and journalist colleagues seldom seemed to let go. Louis Heron suffered the tragic loss of his gentle wife Pat, but battled sturdily on at *The Times* until the Dirty Digger (Rupert Murdoch) heaved him out to make way for smaller men. Roger Toulmin appeared and reappeared, sometimes booming, sometimes despondent, often suspicious that we were trying to marry him off to some lady guest at our dinner table (in which, if we did try, we failed). Audrey Stevenson, an Englishwoman we had met in America working on *The Washington Post* and who had appointed herself honorary aunt to the children, popped up in London on *Good Housekeeping* and obligingly resumed her duties. From Ireland, Bob Elegant and his wife Moira arrived with their Tibetan terriers to carry on his epic novel writing business. From time to time other American friends flew in, asking the way to the Cotswolds.

There were new friends, too, like redheaded Robert Fox and his Dutch wife Marianne Ockinga, another print-maker who came to Meadway Gate to borrow Sylvia's massive 1897 Albion Press. Robert, I always reckoned, should have made it to the top foreign correspondents' jobs – maybe he rubbed someone up the wrong way – but he covered himself with glory in the Falklands to which he got assigned accidentally, drilled himself into becoming a para, and was decorated for negotiating the surrender of a large Argentine garrison in fluent Italian.

My own time with Analysis ran out, Mary Goldring took it over superbly, and I found myself one day discussing my future with Howard Newby, the novelist, who held some senior post in the radio hierarchy. 'I don't want to go abroad again,' I told him, 'it's getting too dangerous and I can't stand the pace any more. What I'm increasingly interested in is religion. But dear Douglas Brown has got the correspondent's job there and he'll last for ever – made of oak.'

Newby must have pulled some strings because within a week I had a call from the head of religious broadcasting to say that Douglas would be retiring in just over a year and if I would like to come and sample the subject, I might be able to succeed him. In fact, I discovered, there was a movement among the news people to abolish the post and divert the funds to something trendier like community relations. The Church lobby hoped that if someone with my reputation were available, the correspondency might be saved. The Roman Catholics were rumoured to have their own candidate and the evangelicals wanted someone with a Bible in his belt – Mrs Mary Whitehouse being quoted in the corridors as expressing alarm at the notion of a Quaker. But as one radio reverend put it gleefully, 'Saying you've got Gerald Priestland is a bit like announcing that Menuhin is prepared to join the Palm Court orchestra.'

Religious broadcasting was actually more talented than that – John Lang had been transforming it from a team of clergy who were interested in broadcasting into one of broadcasters who were interested in religion: it was flattering to know he wanted me, though Sylvia was not the only one who saw the job as a backwater at first. I told her that not only did I feel the hand of Providence in it – I could see the opportunities to travel when I wanted and poke my nose into almost any subject that took my fancy. If there was any sense to be made of the pleasures and horrors I had experienced in the past twenty-seven years, this was where to attempt it. When the appointment was 'promulgated' (as they say in the BBC) half my friends backed away as if I had confessed to a sex-change operation, while the other half started telling me things they had always wanted to tell somebody. Round the corner in the George, John Hosken, Chris Underwood and Dominick Harrod still made room for me in their drinking circle, while old comrades like Louis Heren, Bob Elegant and Robert Fox seemed positively to approve. No halo had appeared overnight; I was still a working journalist.

The trial year with religious broadcasting was fun; for a start, because I shared an office with two colleagues who generated so much laughter it was a wonder we got any work done at all. One was Ronald Farrow who looked like a rather mature choirboy, had one of the best voices in broadcasting and was said to be the most reliable high-church master of ceremonies south of the Thames. The other was Monica Furlong, adored by the churchgoing public as a spiritual writer and whose physical attractions seemed to stir the hearts and desires of half the senior clergy in England, from rabbis and canons to renegade Jesuits (plus a handful of Jungian lay psychotherapists). While keeping these at bay Monica had little enough to laugh about, for at the time her marriage was breaking up painfully. Still, with the help of a few bottles in the top drawer of the filing cabinet, Ronald and I managed to cheer her up and turn our days into one long dormitory feast.

We even contrived to make some worthwhile programmes as we went along. I took my tape-recorder back to America and made a series for the Bicentennial called In God We Trust. Americans are suckers for God and keep seeing themselves as doing the Promised Land story all over again. But as the natural state of any American church is one of schism and shocking prosperity, it is hard to persuade the far less religious British (who have been disillusioned about the Church since the days of Piers Plowman) to take them seriously.

Then I spent most of the summer driving up and down England recording the woes of parish organists and weaving them into a tapestry we called Seated One Day. It was a tragi-comic montage of marriages wrecked by too much choir practice, the havoc wrought by drought to rickety mechanisms, running repairs with knicker elastic during the sermon, the tyranny of vicars, and off-key colonels who could only be brought to heel by firm use of the tuba stop. I got a lot of help with this from Barry Rose, who spent his day whizzing up and down the Central Line between the BBC Daily Service and the choir of St Paul's. He was a first-class choirmaster and his boys loved him; but when he made a hit record of Paul Phoenix, his solo treble, singing a rather kitsch version of 'I did it my way', the cathedral chapter put the skids under him. I am glad to say that Barry came to rest at King's School, Canterbury and arranged the music for two of my most successful series.

I made something of a breakthrough by getting a programme about death on the air – a subject I could hardly overlook with the cemetery and the crematorium on my doorstep. Indeed, the entire cast of doctors, clergy, undertakers and mourners came from within a half-mile radius of our house. I had a difficult time with the manager of the crematorium who didn't want to use the word oven (because of Auschwitz) but there were no inhibitions with my favourite undertaker – seven generations in the business – who wanted to be quite sure my listeners appreciated the need for embalming. 'Believe me,' he said earnestly, 'I can remember the days when the Smell of Death wasn't just a journalistic cliché, Mr Priestland; the days when you could come into a house and find *fluids* running down the stairs, and what awaited you in the bedroom was *not* a pretty sight . . .' There were a few complaints but not many. I doubt if there are any taboo subjects left.

One reason I made the documentary about death was that death had given me a nudge only a few months before. My chest was no longer a problem once I had stopped smoking and put on weight, but the American trip had been strenuous and one morning after my return I found that I had hardly the strength to walk down the passage to the bathroom. 'I'm afraid it's your heart,' said the doctor, 'phoning for an ambulance, 'Not a heart attack as such, but it's racing out of control. We call it atrial fibrillation.' Within twenty minutes I was in the coronary care unit of the Royal Free Hospital, wired up, plugged in and watching my own heartbeat skipping wildly across the monitor screen. Lying there drowsily I thought, 'If this is what it is like to be dying, it isn't too bad. Bits of you shut down one by one. Nothing to complain about.' I forget what they did to me – I was certainly aware that people were praying for me, and that helped – but within thirty-six hours the beat was back to normal and after a few lazy weeks on the clifftop in Zennor I was back at work.

A couple of years later something more dramatic happened. I was pursuing Pope John Paul II around Mexico when an earthquake occurred: nothing abnormal by the standards of Mexico City, only 6.3 on the Richter scale, but my animal instincts panicked – there is nothing you can do about an earthquake, it is too late even to run away. There I was, eight floors up in a skyscraper being interviewed by a presenter over the line from London when the whole building started to rock and a hand grenade exploded in my chest.

The interviewer prattled merrily on, unimpressed by my strangled explanations of what was happening at my end; until I had to pull out the plugs and stagger into the corridor where I collapsed into the arms of the BBC's local stringer. The last thing *he* needed was a dying correspondent as well as a peripatetic pope.

Rushed to the Anglo-American hospital I was diagnosed as having coronary spasm – known to old wives as the Devil's Grip, which describes it well – and was treated with cylinders of oxygen and an enormous syringe of heroin. By the time Sylvia got through to my bedside by telephone I was floating euphorically. 'Don' worry 'bout me, everythingz bootiful,' I told her. 'Don't move,' said Sylvia firmly, 'I'm coming to get you.' And with the speed of a trained foreign correspondent's wife, she did. Meanwhile the hospital laboratory analysed everything it could extract from me and found that I was not badly damaged but also had food poisoning and – unaccountably – the antibodies to brucellosis. 'You work with cattle, Senor Priestland?' they asked suspiciously. 'Never mind, we fix!' And they gave me so many drugs that they precipitated gout and I could hardly walk. The malady, inherited, I guess, from my Indian Army grandfather, still comes back to visit me at unpredictable moments. I got it in Rome when the Falklands War broke out.

Sylvia's immediate task was to buy me out of hospital with several kilos of pesos, in cash. We flew home by way of Bermuda, but being February it might as well have been Ramsay, Isle of Man as far as I was concerned. Never my cup of tea, the Caribbean.

Then it was Sylvia's turn to take ill. She flew out to the United States to visit Jennet who was working for a design firm in Boston, and to call on various other friends in New York and Washington. But when I met her off the plane at Heathrow she presented an alarming spectacle: pale and shocked, with tingling pains running down one side of her body, indeed all the symptoms of a heart attack except the test results that would have confirmed it. Bafflingly the pains, the panic and the racing pulse intruded whenever she exerted herself. It took some weeks to diagnose the trouble correctly: that she had picked up a rare virus known as Coxsackie-B which produces Bornholm disease, an affliction which burns itself out in its own bad time and contrives to mimic a heart attack without actually threatening its victim's life. It is not dangerous, but for everyone concerned it is no less alarming.

The only reason I relate these tiresome adventures is to get at the effect they had on us. For by the time we had been through them and had had to face the possibility of losing and the experience of regaining one another we realised what it was that really mattered about our marriage – the loyalty through shared experience, the solidarity of the family, that it had been a rich and creative relationship and that it was time to stop trying to reform one another and accept each other for what we had become. There has been a fundamental peace and gratitude between us ever since; but I do not think we should have learnt it had we not been confronted with these simulated threats of death.

When Douglas Brown retired I stepped into his shoes and began what was to prove the most rewarding part of my career, from January 1977 to June 1982. I came to it theologically naive apart from my Quakerism – and I suppose some might call that a naivety in itself. I was influenced from the start by the publication of the English version of Hans Küng's *On Being a Christian* (still my first book of reference) and of the collection of essays by Dennis Nineham, John Hick, Frances Young and others which became notorious as *The Myth of God Incarnate* – not actually a very revolutionary book by world standards, but liberal enough to shock the insular theology of the average Anglican.

The job of the religious affairs correspondent involved the supply of reports and interviews about goings-on in the various churches to the news and current affairs programmes; and this in turn meant attending synods and conferences at home and abroad and trailing in the wake of sundry popes and archbishops as they did their pastoral thing. One little exercise which I invented was a nightly report on the Church of England's parliament called Today in Synod. It was not that the General Synod was particularly brilliant or even relevant to the welfare of the nation, but it was stimulating to sit in the gallery, making and editing my own recordings, dashing back to Broadcasting House with maybe an hour to spare and putting the best bits together into an entertaining little fireworks display. Part of the fun was playing on Synod's nerves – scolding it, flattering it, sending it up according to its deserts and seeing how members took it next morning. On the whole they liked it – the Church would always rather be teased than ignored – and it was a pity when the philistines had it cut down to once a week. I always had to be watchful for attempts by some of the more eloquent speakers – the Reverends Michael Saward, Brian Brindley and Paul Oestreicher, for example – to hog the air with carefully designed purple passages.

On the Catholic side my principal stars were Archbishops Worlock and Hume, for both of whom I developed considerable respect though of two different natures. Not for nothing was Derek Worlock known as the Ayatollah of Merseyside, and I am afraid I offended him by hinting that he stagemanaged the Catholic Pastoral Congress at Liverpool in 1980 so as to prevent too much democracy breaking out. (I shall not forget the Duke of Norfolk sitting amongst the laity, egging on the young to say what they really felt about birth control.) In the end, nothing did go forth from Liverpool that might have offended the Vatican, and the Catholic Church in England still has far too clerical a view of itself. But I have nothing but admiration for the way Archbishop Worlock stands shoulder to shoulder for Liverpool with his Anglican colleague David Sheppard.

It was clever of Rome to choose Basil Hume – Father Basil as he prefers to be called – rather than Worlock to be Cardinal Archbishop of Westminster and head of the Roman Church in England; for Hume remains at heart a Benedictine monk and although he has grown in stature among his European fellow bishops, it is his humility and spiritual intensity, forming an almost tangible envelope around him, that have impressed everyone, regardless of denomination. His honesty, too. Once, when I was recording a discussion on Church unity with Hume, Archbishop Runcie, Lord Soper of the Methodists and Bishop Newbigin of the United Reformed, relations became so warm that I could not resist turning to Hume and asking him whether he did not accept his brother Robert as a valid priest in spite of his Anglican orders?

There was a long pause and then the Cardinal replied that although the Vatican took a contrary view and although Anglican orders were probably incomplete and would need confirming, nevertheless he personally recognised them and believed their validity could be established.

To anyone but a microtheologian this was as near dammit yes to my question – and about time, too. But when Hume had finished, the other three rushed at me begging me not to broadcast the passage. I had put the cardinal on the spot, presumed upon his honesty, put him in an intolerably embarrassing situation and risked setting back years of patient negotiation . . . So I agreed not to broadcast it. But I have to say that it was not Father Basil who begged me to leave it out.

My relations with Robert Runcie became very close and there was a time when he cherished the hope that I might eventually come and work for him at Lambeth Palace. Quakers, in my view, should be ready to serve wherever they are needed; but I do not think it would have done Runcie much good if it had leaked out that I was drafting speeches and sermons for him. I helped him *ad hoc* on one or two scripts, but as a regular member of his staff I would have felt inhibited from saying many of the things I was able to say on my own account. The Archbishop's talent is diplomacy rather than prophecy, and I am afraid that either I should have got him into hot water or else I should have been obliged to resign over some of the issues he has had to face. On the whole I am grateful that the Society of Friends does not have to bother about Rome, the ordination of women, schism, disestablishment and liturgical and theological reform. Nevertheless it grieves me that the Church of England – like one of Monsieur Jean Tinguely's self-destructive machines – should be lashing itself to pieces over such issues to the neglect of the real challenge before it, the Church's failure and the triumph of apathetic atheism.

My first Archbishop of Canterbury had been Donald Coggan, a moderate evangelical who was clearly a bit nervous about my appointment. He invited me to tea at Lambeth and confided that he simply could not understand how Quakers could ignore Our Lord's injunction to celebrate the eucharist. I sipped my cup, nibbled my biscuit and asked what he thought we were doing at that moment? Coggan regarded his petit beurre with new respect, and from then on we managed pretty well, despite his headmasterly tone and my occasional *faux pas* like calling the Church of England *Protestant* and suggesting there wasn't a lot of difference between the words of consecration and a magic spell.

Within a few weeks we set off in a small party to visit Istanbul, Rome and Geneva, touching base, as it were, with the Orthodox, Catholic and Reformed churches.

Istanbul – Byzantium, Constantinople, it needs more than one name – always excites me, even when it is teeming with Turks. The treasures of the Grand Bazaar, the maritime bustle of the Bosphorus, the sublime peace of the great mosques (excepting Santa Sophia, which is grim and smelling of blood) fill me with joy. My idea of a treat is to take the ferry from the Galata Bridge, where businessmen stop to fish on their way home from the office, up the Golden Horn to Eyüp to sit for an hour in the mosque there and then climb the hill through the Ottoman cemetery to Pierre Loti's café and drink coffee.

However, *Mrs* Coggan disapproved of the great mosques so we spent no time in them on this occasion. We called on the Ecumenical Patriarch, a Greek besieged in this Turkish city and forbidden to wear ecclesiastical dress in public, then drove off to the British Consulate-General for evensong. The Consulate-General was once Her Majesty's Legation to the Sublime Porte (Queen Victoria presented a grandfather clock to the ladies of the harem) and the mission still occupies a scaled-down version of Buckingham Palace, standing in walled gardens which include an Anglican parish church by way of a chapel.

The British community and its hangers-on rallied round, and the familiar public school hymns were rolling forth when my reporter's ear caught the equally familiar but more exciting note of police sirens outside. I snatched up my tape recorder and got to the gates just as the Gurkha guards were barricading them shut. I managed to squeeze past, leaving the gentleman from *The Times* to gnash his teeth within, and followed the sirens into the main square where a Turkish version of a Brueghel massacre was being enacted.

The Turkish trades union movement had decided to hold a big demonstration that day and the square was crowded with upwards of fifty thousand people listening to speeches. Somebody – quite likely an *agent provocateur* for the government – then livened things up by throwing a couple of hand grenades. Instantly a surprising number of people produced pistols and began firing them, the gendarmerie who had been guarding the entrance to the Sheraton Hotel opened up with their sub-machineguns, and the crowd thereupon assaulted the hotel to get its revenge. The gendarmes retreated into the lobby and up the escalator to the reception area, where they entrenched themselves behind the check-in desk and picked off the rioters as the moving staircase delivered them. By the time I arrived people were fleeing in all directions, the escalator was slippery with blood and there were a dozen bodies stacked neatly in the left luggage room. It was hardly a Religious Affair but I was still enough of a foreign correspondent to see in it a much better story than the sermon through which Dr Coggan was still wending his way back at the Anglican church.

I ran back to my hotel – the dear, seedy old Park, from which nothing in the line of Hiltons and Intercontinentals will ever drag me – and scrawled the telephone number of BBC Foreign Traffic on a sheet of paper within which I folded a Turkish ten-pound note. Seeking out the hotel operator I begged her to get me the number. 'Impossible!' she pronounced. 'Never yet has an intelligible call gone through from Istanbul to London!' 'I think', I said, 'that if you look very carefully you will find you are about to create a record . . .' And she did and I had a bloody little scoop. (I also had trouble; for when, some time later, I broadcast this anecdote as an example of sinning for the greater good, listeners roundly condemned me for corrupting the morals of Turkish telephone operators and demanded my dismissal by the Director General.)

Anyhow, two hours later, when the Gurkhas sounded the all clear, the rest of the Coggan party emerged from its sanctuary to find the Istanbul fire brigade hosing down the square and making bonfires of abandoned shoes: for some reason Muslims in a panic always leave their shoes behind. The gentleman from *The Times* – not the admirable Clifford Longley, whom I revere, but a deplorable Marxist stand-in who had made the great mistake on such a trip of bringing his wife along – was beside himself with frustration and not at all sure that the briefing I was generously prepared to give on what he had missed was a leg-pull or not. The moral of this, for what it is worth, is that one has to be ruthless about dropping the worthy but routine story for a better one, that one should always keep a rapid escape route in mind, and that one should never travel with more than one can shift singlehanded in a hurry. I am afraid that includes wives.

The Archbishop's chaplain, David Paynter, who was running the trip with all the efficiency of a Swan's courier, was delighted. 'Stick with us, Gerald, and see the action!' he cried. But after Istanbul, Rome and Geneva were anticlimactic. There was a touching service of reconciliation between Archbishop Coggan and Pope Paul VI in the Sistine Chapel, with the young ordinands of the Venerable English College bawling out Newman's 'Praise to the Holiest'; but Coggan ruffled Vatican feathers by publicly declaring that we had all better get on with sharing communion, if only because back in England Anglicans and Romans were already doing it on the quiet. Once again there were cries of 'How tactless!' but I only hope Lord Coggan knows, in his retirement, that this practice – so simple, so central, so stupid to resist – has gathered strength ever since. I, along with many other non-Catholics, have gladly received communion at the hands of Catholic priests when they gladly offered it.

Geneva meant the World Council of Churches, then dominated by the black Caribbean Methodist Philip Potter. It did not particularly worry me that Dr Potter leant over backwards to appease the East Europeans and the anticolonialists of the Third World – I had learnt to live with that sort of rhetoric at the United Nations – but it was a pity he felt he could abuse the West with impunity whenever he felt like it, for it made it very difficult for me to get the World Council taken seriously at home, and Dr Potter made matters worse by cultivating a personal vendetta against the BBC. Hitting back was not difficult. The World Council made itself an easy target with its bureaucracy, its ecumenical gobbledigook and its repertory company of professional ecumenists most of whom counted for very little in their homelands. I once dined with a magnificently robed and bearded figure who declared himself to be the Patriarch of Antioch and All the East. '*All* the East?' I enquired, wonderingly. 'Yes, *All* the East,' replied the Patriarch with as much modesty as he could muster while tucking into the generous helpings provided by the World Council canteen.

The Council also boasted a retinue of ecumenical groupies who served as stewards and messengers and followed it round the world. I once attended an expensive conference on Religion and Science, held at the Massachussetts Institute of Technology near Boston, at which the groupies not only turned up but insisted upon joining in and voting. Young and goodlooking they may have been – some of them disturbingly so – but if anything they were even less representative than the bishops and theologians they were trying to brush aside. John Habgood, then Bishop of Durham and himself a trained scientist, was one of the few delegates who dared to protest at their intrusion and eventually deployed the mighty weapon of Anglican procedure to quash them. Afterwards I took him away to the revolving lounge on top of the Hyatt Hotel and restored him with exotic cocktails. 'They'll never believe me when I say I've been buying banana daiquiris for the Bishop of Durham going round and round over Boston,' I mused. 'They'll never believe me when I tell them about this conference,' said Habgood gloomily.

The gathering was so wordy that to this day nobody can recall what conclusions it reached, if any. The only other thing that stands out in my memory is that after a procession of Western speakers confessing the error of their ways in polluting the earth with industry and nuclear energy and vowing to give it all up, there came a procession of Third World speakers saying that was just a hypocritical plot to deprive Asia, Africa and Latin America of their fair shares of nuclear energy and industrialisation. Let nobody try to fob them off with fairy tales about appropriate technology and power from windmills. As usual at World Council conferences the Europeans and Americans crept home feeling they couldn't win, which I think was the intention.

More agreeable was the Year of the Three Popes – 1978 – when pontiffs were dropping like overripe pears and I spent week after week in the pleasant location of Rome, watching the roof of the Sistine Chapel for black smoke or white. Once, tinted by the setting sun, it was maddeningly pink. I had a running feud with a coxcomb of a BBC TV reporter who would keep talking over the Pope's voice on the grounds that his viewers couldn't understand Latin anyway. The fact was, neither could he – but I could. At long last the Latin absorbed with so much agony in my schooldays had come into its own, and got me halfway into Italian as well.

An even greater help was David Willey, Our Man in Rome and for my money one of the three or four best correspondents still in the BBC's service. David lived in part of a palazzo which had been nationalised by the communist city council; it was in Trastevere, near the Queen of Heaven Jail, a vantage point which gave him a head's start on the story of the robber gang which used to get let out of prison for the night to commit its burglaries, thus ensuring an almost watertight alibi. David's wife did her shopping locally and kept him up-to-date with all the market gossip. Every time a pope died she brought him back the street version of what had really happened: 'Poor Pope – in bed with this nun, he was – and at his age of course it was too much for him . . .' or, 'Naturally it was the Curia – they heard he wanted to reform them so they poisoned his nightcap . . . Or it was the Freemasons . . . the Mafia . . . the CIA . . . the Bulgarians . . .'

When Paul VI died in his summer palace at Castel Gandolfo there was a frantic search for somebody to embalm him. It was hot and all the undertakers of any repute were away at the seaside. I arrived about midnight, in one of those jet-propelled operations at which BBC news is rather good, bought up the only telephone in the square before any rivals appeared and joined the ruthless rugger-scrum of sharp-elbowed nuns waiting to view the remains.

At dawn they opened the palace gates and by the time I had fought my way into the papal bedchamber His Holiness was looking none too healthy. And by the time they got him to St Peter's for the prolonged lying-in-state, he was hardly fit to be seen and running repairs had to be made every few hours. The lobby to have him immediately canonised refused to be put off. 'Imagine – when they raised the lid of the coffin an overwhelming odour of violets filled the basilica! Incorruptible! A sure sign of sainthood!'

I cannot claim to have tipped Karol Wojtyla for Pope, or even the right stable. One of the most gratifying aspects of his election was the complete rout of the journalist speculators, including the wishful Hume-for-Pope movement. I say that not because Father Basil would have made a bad pope (though he was needed too much at home) but because I think journalists need frequent lessons in taking the news as it comes and not trying to 'preview' or induce it. Whatever the secrets of the conclave may have been, and clearly it was no walkover for the Pole, I do not think any of us in the *Sala Stampa* – the press room to the Vatican – judged the mood aright. The brief papacy of John Paul I gave the cardinals a second chance to do what the Holy Spirit had intended all along, to break with the Italian ascendancy. Yet everyone amongst the press had ruled out the East Europeans altogether and I myself was convinced it would have to be an Italian yet again. Now I think they are gone for ever, for John Paul II seems to have infused his entire church with the international spirit.

I will not pretend to be an admirer of John Paul's reactionary theology, but at least he knows how to project it – God's leading man –

so that the world's creeping atheism has at last met its match. If John Paul II did have any idea of putting the clock back to pre-Vatican-Two (not that the Council was any festival of liberalism), he seems to have thought better of it. I am reminded of what Cardinal Kroll of Philadelphia once told me (Kroll the Pole as they call him): 'I am one hundred per cent for Vatican Two – but I will not tolerate a hundred and one per cent!'

I should dearly like to know what the Pope makes of our own dear Church of England. One of the most stunning experiences of my life was when, perched with a microphone on the organ screen of Canterbury cathedral, I saw the West door swing open, John Paul and Robert Runcie enter together, the trumpets and trombones blazing out and the huge glittering congregation roaring out the Old Hundredth. As the Pope's eyes darted from side to side I fancied I could read the thoughts: 'But this really *is* a church – and they do these things even better than we do!' As they really did, that day. BBC TV lent a helping hand, and whoever devised the tableau of Pope and Archbishop kneeling in prayer at the martyrdom spot of Thomas-à-Becket has become one of the iconmakers of our time.

It was during the papal elections in 1978 that I came closer to losing my life than ever before or since. To be frank, I and a BBC pal of Scottish origins had been punishing a bottle of his national nectar in the BBC Rome office one evening and were tottering dinnerwards through the alleys near the Pantheon when a car crept up behind us and tooted to get past. We felt in no mood to give way and as we emerged into a square, allowing the impatient vehicle to pull ahead, I gave it a thump or two on its departing rear.

At once it squealed to a halt on the cobbles, four men leapt out drawing pistols, and we were rammed into the nearest doorway. They were, it transpired, a mobile anti-terrorist squad on the prowl for subversives, and feeling sensitive about their dignity as policemen even if they were supposed to be incognito.

The man threatening me brandished a small automatic in one hand and his police identity card in the other, screaming, 'Papers! Your papers! And no funny tricks!' Very gingerly indeed I drew out my passport and offered it to him. Whereupon, having both hands already full and being in a considerable frenzy, *the man passed me his gun to hold.* Simultaneously *I* declined it, *he* realised what he was doing and became even more frenzied, while his mates – thinking I was trying to disarm their colleague – levelled their guns for the kill. It concentrated my Italian marvellously. 'Don't shoot!' I begged, 'I am only a poor drunken English journalist, the religious affairs correspondent of the BBC!' This was greeted with loud cheers from two or three neighbourhood drunks who had gathered to watch the fun, and the mood changed. The anti-terrorists passed through a fleeting moment of looking foolish, then wagged their fingers at us paternally, accepted our most craven apologies and let us go. But our digestions were no longer up to the dinner we had been planning.

The job was not all popes and riot squads. Unexpectedly, what made my name in it was a four-and-a-half minute talk which took the place of Radio 4's Thought for the Day each Saturday morning and which Douglas Brown had entitled Outlook. This seemed to me a poor, inappropriate title and anyway too closely identified with Douglas for me to usurp. Douglas had been very much the straight ecclesiastical reporter – though he has since developed into a formidable columnist for the *Church Times* – whereas I was looking for yet another chance to analyse, assess and frankly comment. The bare facts of church activity commanded a very limited audience, but I felt that the values behind them would appeal to a much larger public if only one could address it in a language it could understand. Many people were put off religion because it had become a minority hobby conducted in a special code language. It seemed to me there was no reason why one should not apply to it the same journalistic motto of *Clarify, clarify, clarify* (which is not the same as *oversimplify*) that one applied to economics or diplomacy. There was 'out there' a great anonymous Church of the Unchurched, of the would–believers if they could believe, who often shared a deep apprehension of the spiritual in their lives but found nothing relevant to it in the traditional churches. Being one of them myself, I tried to address them; and had more response than I ever dreamed likely.

I renamed the Saturday talks Yours Faithfully, subtitled, A note from our Religious Affairs correspondent. Half the time they were still straight reports on conferences, pilgrimages, church appointments and religious books, but the other half I devoted to commenting on current events and theological controversies from a Christian but nondogmatic point of view. It has never made sense to me that 'the Church ought to keep out of politics'. It never used to do in the past and I do not see why it should desist now, provided it makes clear that there are theological grounds for its intervention. Not that I believe there must be one authentic Christian policy on everything. I believe that Christians should be rather unreliable as members of any party. What I tried to do was to state both sides as fairly as I could but never to be afraid of drawing the conclusion that, in the Christian light as I saw it, one was more convincing than the other.

After a while I found that you could say almost anything on the air if you knew how to say it: that is, courteously, modestly, with good humour and taking care not to wound or insult people (as I did once by saying that the blood of Christ was 'not really my cup of tea') but telling them gently things they *ought* to hear but did not necessarily *want* to hear. Constantly I told my listeners that it was not obligatory for them to agree with me and that I respected their ability to see through me just as I hoped they would respect my efforts to discern the truth.

My masters in the religious broadcasting department never once altered my scripts; indeed, apart from the usual cutting and 'spiking' for lack of space or interest, I cannot recall a single piece of mine in more than thirty years which was censored by the BBC. The response to Yours Faithfully was overwhelming. As a foreign correspondent I had been lucky to get half a dozen listeners' letters a year; now at once I began to get half a dozen a day and the flow built up until it was taking me two days in the week simply to answer the mail provoked by that five minutes' talk. The majority were always letters of thanks from people who wrote that they had long felt as I did but had not dared to say so. That, I think, is the best any allegedly opinion-forming broadcaster can do: he cannot force his views down unwilling throats, but he can articulate with professional skill what listeners have already begun to think for themselves but have not got round to putting on paper.

Even the twenty-five per cent of correspondents who wrote in accusing me of undermining the simple faith of millions invariably added that of course I hadn't fooled *them* – it was other more gullible souls they were worried about. These listeners were usually adherents of one or another of the fundamentalist, Bible-based evangelical sects who kept scolding, 'Your job is to preach the simple Gospel like it is!' But which gospel? It had never seemed to me in the least simple, any more than the supposedly simple faith which millions are supposed to cherish. Once you start talking to them ordinary people turn out to have some most extraordinary beliefs, ranging from reincarnation and spiritualism to Manichaeanism and life after death for budgerigars – though they seldom tell their vicars.

That left about forty letters a week requiring close personal attention. Some were from the clergy, pointing out errors, arguing for or against my views and – all too often – inviting me to come and preach from their pulpits. Not a few ministers seemed to use my Saturday talks as the basis for their own Sunday sermons, though I hope I never featured in their intercessions to the extent of having intoned (as I once heard), 'O Lord, as Monica Furlong has written . . .' By and large the clergy were most kind to me, especially bishops and including Roman Catholics who seemed very little disturbed by my Quakerly lack of use for high ritual and priesthood. I think Catholics appreciate better than most the appeal of mysticism and silent contemplation which, paradoxically, lay at the heart of what I was trying to say so wordily.

Once, in an attempt to satirise the fundamentalists, I did an April Fools' day talk about an invented cult known as the Footites, whose theology I based on the many references in the concordance to *feet*. The Footites made much of Our Lord's emphatic but neglected commandment to wash one another's feet and, inevitably, they suffered schism between those who went barefoot and those who held that sandals were permissible (John i v.27). I included several winks and nudges in the script, but four listeners wrote in confessing that they had long been secret Footites and where could they join? On the other hand there were loud protests when I did talks about Islam or Judaism or some pagan creation myths I had come across.

The most burdensome of my correspondents were those with problems; the normal tragedies of the human condition, the abnormal tragedies of mental illness, the tragedies of faith that fails. It made me gnash my teeth that people turned to me instead of to their local priest. My very success in the job was an indictment of the churches which should have been doing the work themselves. But so many people were either out of touch with the churches or had been repelled by them that they found it easier to write to me, whom they need not confront in the flesh, than to knock on the vicarage door. A few had been driven to misery by a distorted Christianity; like the poor woman who for over fifty years had believed that her unbaptised illegitimate baby was roasting in Hell – because that is what her good Catholic friends assured her. It was gratifying to find myself at last in two-way contact with my listeners and to feel I was being of some service to them; but I knew I was wholly unqualified for such a ministry and did my best to persuade my correspondents to put themselves into expert hands.

Some of them refused to do so. There was seldom a week, over five years, when I did not have some 'client' I was trying to stop from killing himself. The Welsh seemed particularly prone to this impulse. There was a man in Cardiff whose wife had just died painfully in his arms; and in her last moments he had told her he could not go on living without her: did she think God would excuse his 'taking a short cut'? The dying woman had replied that the God she knew was merciful and forgiving and she looked forward to his joining her at the earliest opportunity. 'So I've got the EXIT book,' wrote my Welshman, 'and I've got the pills and the bag and the whisky. I just wanted to check with you that I shan't be doing anything wrong.'

My temptation was to start ringing up the police and the local health clinic. But somehow I felt that would be a violation of the confessional and might actually panic him into action. So I wrote back immediately saying it most certainly would be wrong; it would cause a great deal of sorrow and inconvenience to others; his wife had been in no condition to think objectively; and since he thought highly enough of me to ask my advice, would he please not let me down? I recommended that he burn the EXIT book, flush the pills down the loo and pour himself a not-too-stiff whisky.

The exchange went on for about three weeks and then stopped. To this day I do not know whether he pulled through or pulled the plug, as it were. In at least half-a-dozen other cases people did write to me, sometimes years later, saying I had persuaded them to go on living. One man even went on to get baptised, confirmed and ultimately ordained as a priest.

This was well beyond the journalism I had been hired to do, but I got nothing but encouragement from my bosses in the department – John Lang, Michael Mayne, Colin Semper and David Winter – all of whom added to their broadcasting skills a pastoral concern for the listener which few other BBC departments showed. The fact was there was a very limited number of religious stories I could persuade the cynical news department to run and if I had not branched out as a self-made guru there would not have been much satisfaction in the job. What the newsroom liked was a good dirty-vicar story. They also approved of my phantom of the organ loft, a character who flitted for a time through the parish churches of the Chilterns, stealing the best ranks of pipes from each instrument with a view (I speculated) to building a super-organ of his own somewhere. An anonymous clair-voyant rang me up to say it was for a *Satanic* organ in Hemel Hempstead. I passed on her description of the site to the West Herts police, but I never heard they found it.

One of the best friends I made in religious broadcasting was Chris Rees, a manic producer of evangelical tendencies who had been trained as an audio engineer and had become a perfectionist in sound just as the finest tailor in Savile Row is a perfectionist in cloth. Who cares about steam-age sound in this age of satellite-beamed colour TV? After all, most people hear radio on the quacking equivalent of a box of corn-flakes and few of them bother to enhance it with stereo, digital, even the simple advantage of a proper aerial. Which is a pity, for radio is still a living, creative medium with new things to do for comparatively little cost. It is free of the photographic realism that shackles television, and it is still possible in radio for the broadcaster to convey what he or she really means without having it processed out of all recognition by a huge production crew.

Chris took sound very seriously. When he produced an interview it had to be done not only in digital and with two microphones for the stereophony, but with a third track added to give the not-quite-silent atmosphere of the room itself – perhaps a clock ticking, a fire burning in the background, birds twittering in the garden outside. By the time Chris had finished editing the conversation, hacking out all the *ums* and *ers* and leaving what we had really meant to say, the result was a seamless fabric which delighted everyone who took part. Chris could even correct people's grammar by making syllable transplants – tricks of the trade that sound dangerous but which, when he used them, drew nothing but purrs from our victims and not one complaint of misrepresentation in some 250 interviews.

Our first and most successful collaboration began when Chris Rees – tieless and perspiring as usual – threw himself into my office and put it to me that while we were churning out programmes *as if* the public were Christians, very few of them were any more. Wasn't it time we did something frankly instructive, a course in the elements of the Christian faith?

I agreed, but *which* Christianity? Was there some common ground on which we could all stand in the end? 'That's what we have to find out. We'll have you setting off on a pilgrimage through the great monuments of Christian doctrine, talking to their custodians, com-menting on what they have to say, getting the listener to think for himself about those pious catch-phrases in their hymn-books.'

I said I couldn't make head or tail of the Trinity – it wasn't even in the Bible. It seemed to me like the Victorian piano in the front parlour which nobody played any more. 'I'd get lynched for saying it, but I'm not sure the Muslims aren't right.'

We decided to do one programme about the Trinity, and one about the sacraments that Quakers don't use, and one about salvation and the Cross . . . We mapped out a scheme of twelve programmes plus a summing-up, in which I emerged, at the end of my pilgrimage, not as the heroic Mr Valiant-for-Truth but as the crippled Mr Ready-to-Halt – that is the passage from Bunyan that I want read at my funeral.

There was some opposition to the idea from other producers who wanted to make a multi-faith, multi-cultural series, but in the end we got our way and Priestland's Progress was born. It took us a whole year to make, charging up and down the country in Chris's BMW, collecting over a hundred interviews, transcribing and editing them, writing the book for the BBC (reluctantly) to publish, and finally assembling the programmes with Chris playing the electronic sorcerer at the control desk. For a sound picture of the Holy Spirit (The Ghost who came to Dinner) he used four different recordings of water, three different kinds of wind and five different fires, blended. I composed a jaunty signature tune, the sort of thing a not-too-pious pilgrim might whistle as he marched along, and Barry Rose cleverly orchestrated it. Perhaps the most enjoyable part of the operation was that day spent in the studio with the musicians, when we could stop worrying about the meaning of words and concentrate on getting a pretty thing right.

Priestland's Progress almost killed us. We had an entrancing secretary called (unbelievably) Amanda de Winter, and a researcher, Patrick Forbes, who located our interview victims and fitted them into a schedule; but we really needed twice the resources and the time. By the end of it Chris was so run down he contracted trench mouth *and* provoked our department head into threatening him with the sack; while I wrecked my back from endless typing and riding around in cars. But it was worth it.

The response was unprecedented: Amanda was swamped by more than 20,000 letters, most of which had no hope of getting an adequate reply. Angry fundamentalists bombarded the first two or three programmes, then gave up. Most of our correspondents thanked us for opening the doors and windows of faith for them and letting the fresh air blow through. The wife of one well-known telly personality wrote that she and her husband had always been furtive believers but had never dared tell anyone 'for fear of being thought neurotic or gullible. Now people are talking about it in pubs and at parties . . .' Some cross atheists accused me of doing the whole thing for money. And in fact the book – to the amazement of BBC Publications – did very well, rising to number two on *The Times* best-seller list. The series won the Church of England's Sandford St Martin Prize, which I converted into a handsome bronze statue of a toucan commissioned from Sylvia's sculptor friend Marie Gill. Sylvia, all this while, had not only been working away at her own prints but teaching art to old people in London geriatric hospitals, a labour calling for reserves of love and patience that I simply do not possess.

Did the Progress have any effect on me, personally? Indeed it did; though rather than converting me to traditional doctrines it made me all the more determined to keep travelling on. Doctrine – even that doctrine of the Trinity – I saw now as a useful set of tools to work with rather than as idols to worship. As for the mysteries of Christ's divinity and the Effects of the Crucifixion, with so many versions of which I had been beaten over the head to the accompaniment of 'you must believe this!', I found some sense of direction in the paradoxes 1) *if Jesus was not God, He is now* and 2) *in the Crucifixion God was saying, 'I am like this – indeed, I am so like this that so far as you can know I am this.'* Neither of these is very profound. I suppose they are versions of, respectively, the Myth of God Incarnate and the notion of God suffering in man and with man. Regular Christians might say they disqualified me from calling myself a Christian at all; and I have to admit that just as I found George Fox an obstacle to becoming a Quaker, I still find Jesus – or some of the doctrines that have been built around him – to be an obstacle between myself and the Loving Creator in whom I trust. I know that without Jesus, as without the Bible, I would have a pretty toothless sort of religion. But even before I compiled the Progress and received so many testimonies from people who had had private revelations of their own, I was aware that our apprehension of the divine cannot be limited to what the Church teaches and the Bible records; nor has it ever been confined to Jews and Christians alone.

This is tricky ground. One reason why I believe in the Church is that I am sure its disciplines are necessary as checks upon the eccentricities and excesses of do-it-yourself religion. But I know too many good, sane people who have had their own direct encounters with God for me to be able to dismiss them as neurotics, wishful thinkers or heretics. Few have had anything as spectacular as visions or voices. More often it is just a timeless moment of *knowing* which is almost invariably described as 'the most real thing that has ever happened to me'.

In my own humble case such experiences have taken the form of involuntary 'mottoes' which have appeared within me in the silence of Quaker Meeting and, despite determined efforts to dismiss them, have returned week after week until their meaning has become clear. The first, which took the question-and-answer form, 'O God, are you there – or am I talking to myself? O Man – both are true', seemed to be pointing out the very essence of the mystical way. The next: 'If not you – who will?' foreshadowed the call to the religious affairs job. Next came 'I've got something for you . . .' followed by a benign chuckle, which led me to the Progress commission and its toucan prize. And so it continues. Compared with other cases I know of, mine is prosaic; but it has caused me to take very seriously to work of the late Sir Alister Hardy's Religious Experience Centre at Manchester College, Oxford, with which I became associated as a patron.

The weakest point in Priestland's Progress was that it *assumed* the existence of God from the start. So when we had recovered, Chris and I followed it up with what should have preceded it: a series on the existence and nature of God which I called (with a deliberate touch of headline-grabbing) The Case Against God. Once again there was the intensive interviewing, the slogging through hours of transcripts, the agony of getting the book written first for the printers – and the pleasure of a day in the studio with Barry Rose and the musicians, getting my signature tune recorded. This time it was a stern, accusatory march based on a theme which had been in my head since Charterhouse.

The Case was never the popular success that Progress had been. We made it on a smaller scale than its predecessor but to some extent I think it was too way-out for churchpeople of a nervous disposition, some of whom dismissed the very title as blasphemy. And I think, inevitably, I was going out of fashion. There must always have been at least as many listeners who loathed me as loved me. But from my own point of view The Case was by far the more important of the two series, taking me *through* the figure of Jesus into the very nature of His Father, into the damning problems of unmerited suffering and of our very purpose in the universe. I know it is fashionable to suppose that year by year science must be diminishing the significance of mankind, but I believe that, on the contrary, the deeper science penetrates the more we are confronted with the only possible universe which could have produced us, a universe which actually requires our presence to exist at all. This is awesome.

The Case Against God featured some distinguished and articulate unbelievers, but atheists still complained that I rigged the evidence in God's favour. I am afraid that was inevitable; it would have been dishonest for me to have pretended otherwise; for authors do tend to know how their book is going to end as they start the beginning, especially if they have done as much preparation as I had; and while you cannot prove the existence of God in the way you can prove there is a cat in the garden, my interviews persuaded me it was far more likely that there was a God than not – that the God hypothesis was well worth trusting. So I add two more paradoxes: 3) *that God would not be the God that He is if we could prove that He was* (a proposition that left Sir Alfred Ayer almost speechless with incomprehension), and 4) *that the atheist option is necessary for God's existence.* It must be possible, and clearly it is, for two people to go through much the same experience of life and for one to emerge believing, the other disbelieving. God has to make belief in Himself optional or there is no human freedom and no divine love.

Anyway my 'case' against God was ambiguous. It was not just the case against there being any God at all, but the case against this God who more probably existed than not and who stood charged by His creation with cruelty and incompetence. Yet, when it came to the human encounters, there was something trivial about the complaints of the atheists and humanists, their anxiety to create substitute religions, and their silly parodies of what Christians do *not*, for the most part, believe. I for one do not believe in some Cosmic Puppetmaster who sacrifices His own Son to appease His own wrath at the mess He Himself has made inevitable.

On the other hand there was something compelling about the struggles of men and women like John and Margaret Bowker of Lancaster, John Vernon Taylor of Winchester, the poet P. J. Kavanagh, the Oxford philosopher Michael Dummett, Ann Semple of Glasgow, Ethel Snowball of Tyneside, Rabbi Alan Levine of Jerusalem and at least a dozen others, to assert their faith *not only in spite of but because of* life's suffering. If I have any single reason for trusting in God, it is the example of people like these. What is good enough for them is certainly good enough for me. The trust is central and I find it not betrayed. In particular I shall never forget P. J. Kavanagh's outburst when I suggested we deserved something better than the fate most of us got: 'I don't see what we have deserved. I cannot see why people think things should be better than they are. It seems to me we get *more* than we deserve . . .'

I made The Case soon after I had actually retired from the staff of the BBC. I had always kept alert by moving on to fresh woods every few years and now there seemed nowhere else to go but out. At fifty-five I could take an early retirement on reasonable terms, though the BBC – which had shown a curious lack of interest in my health after the Mexican episode – became suddenly anxious to make sure that I was leaving voluntarily and not because of any dispute, physical disability or 'waning powers' (as the staff regulations put it) which might involve the BBC in paying compensation. No, I assured them, no hard feelings. I simply felt that after thirty-three years in an everlasting English public school I wanted to leave and, perhaps, grow up as an independent writer.

And there were subsidiary motives. As a Quaker pacifist I had found it very difficult to keep Yours Faithfully on an even keel during the Falklands War: the whole operation seemed to me at first ludicrous, then profoundly immoral. It was an outrageous gamble which the British pulled off thanks to a mixture of luck, skill and secret American help, and I sailed as close to the wind as I dared in commenting on it, sometimes wrapping up my views in language which violated the rule of clarity and must have left many listeners bewildered as to my meaning. Others saw through it and wrote calling on me to resign; but whatever criticism may have reached my masters, they left me to follow my conscience.

Altogether, I wanted to get out from under my role as 'God's best man at the Beeb' (to quote one critic), before I collapsed under the weight of it. For a time I supported Colin Semper's scheme for a 'Church of the Air' with its own staff and premises in one of the disused City churches in London. But while I think religious broadcasters can be useful auxiliaries to the Church, I came to see the danger of their becoming substitutes for it. When one finds oneself becoming the focus of an unofficial church of one's own, for which one is neither trained nor worthy, it is time to back away, I thought. The height of absurdity was reached when the audience of the Today programme, in a wholly unscientific poll, voted me runner-up to Prince Charles as Man of the Year, beating both the Pope and Tony Benn. If only they had known of my follies, my selfishness, incompetence and fondness for strong liquor!

The BBC consulted its files and decided I had qualified for a period of grace leave – its own version of a sabbatical. Provided I brought back a handful of programmes the Corporation would subsidise a six weeks' visit to India which Sylvia, tied down in Delhi by small children, had seen little of during our posting in the 'fifties. Her brother, Bill Rhodes, was now Dean of Theology at Serampore, a crumbling formerly Danish town on the Hooghly, upstream from Calcutta; so we used his college as our base for a tour of India by train, working our way south through Orissa, Madras and Cochin, up to Bombay and Delhi, finally recovering amidst the tea-gardens of

Darjeeling. Outside the great cities things had changed very little, though perhaps standards of living had risen slightly and there seemed to be no more worry about whether the harvests were enough to go round. Things muddled along in their maddening Indian way – and then we realised what a miracle it all was, with the population so much greater than it had been twenty-five years earlier and the country so much more self-sufficient.

Sitting quietly on Bill's balcony in the early morning, watching people go down into the river for their ritual bath, one could not help respecting this culture, for all its cruelties and chaos. One had to acknowledge that God had been there on the banks of the Hooghly long before the Baptist missionaries had set up their printing press at Serampore and begun circulating the gospels. The gospels, it seemed, were still spreading like wildfire among the tribal folk in the North-east, but among caste Hindus and Muslims proselytisation was anathema, a cause for persecution and riots. The job of the college at Serampore was to Indianise the Church as rapidly as possible.

I gave listeners my *Nunc dimittis* on June 26th 1982 and handed over the job to Rosemary Hartill. She had become my assistant when the Progress made it impossible for me to cope with the routine assignments from day to day. With an attractive voice – something that either you have or you haven't and quite beyond analysis – Rosemary became a tough, hardworking and reliable reporter without the pretensions to punditry that I had acquired. I know at least three bishops who dread her cross-examinations, and one whom she regularly has to save from his own indiscretion. The job description that went up on the board stated that my successor 'must have tolerance and a sense of humour', which I suppose might be objected to as some sort of dastardly discrimination. That a woman should get the post was not, I think, part of any design but I was glad that it happened. I am sorry that Rosemary lost my secretary, Pam Martell, who used to filter the more vicious anonymous letters from my mail, and who danced professionally in West End chorus lines in her spare time. Not many people knew that the secretary to the BBC's religious affairs correspondent was also hoofing it in *The Greatest Little Whorehouse in Texas*.

When you are about to retire from the BBC you become aware of people darting from office to office trying to avoid you. What they are doing is collecting signatures and money for your farewell presentation. I got a handsome suitcase, which was welcome if symbolic, and an album of valedictions which turned out to be more affecting than I had expected. Weary old programme editors blessed me for my comradeship, several of the young tigers of the reporters' squad were kind enough to describe me as their inspiration and mentor, while half a dozen of the technicians who had twiddled knobs for me over the years thanked me for the courtesy I had shown them; and indeed I owed them a lot for their anonymous devotion, especially the foreign traffic managers who had picked up and recorded my dispatches from all over the world, passing on my anguished cries for money, soothing my hysterics and making me feel that *somebody* cared that it was hell out there, even if my account of it was bound to be trumped by the latest royal baby.

If there was any disappointment in all this farewelling it was that foreign news, to which I had devoted the greater part of my BBC career, stood aloof. Bureaucratically that was correct, for I ended up on the strength of the religious broadcasting department; but I had attended many news sendoffs for departing correspondents and would dearly have liked to raise a glass with my old colleagues and swapped some of the tales which have decorated these pages.

Perhaps the old *esprit de corps* has passed. Though I admire the industry and courage of some of my successors – Tim Llewellyn, Tim Sebastian, Kevin Ruane have done things that make my blood run cold – it does not seem to me that London cares as much as it used to about the style and diction of its men in the field, about good writing and performance, about keen experience vividly communicated. Part of the trouble is, I think, that *telephone* communication around the world has improved so dramatically everywhere that speed has become the prime consideration. The good correspondent is not the man who has witnessed the story and communicated the fulness of what it is like in a way that excites the imagination of the listener – who contributes, in short, what the agencies cannot give – but the correspondent who is always in his office when London calls him ready to re-hash the agencies in his own voice. If he is wise he will even tell the London interviewer what questions to ask him. Old dogs, I suppose, will always growl that the new pups aren't what they used to be; but too often nowadays I cannot tell one pup from the next, or hear much difference between the agency copy and the report from our own man in the field. It is just as bad in the newspapers: perhaps the only real foreign correspondent left writing in them is Robert Fisk of *The Times*. He not only 'is there' – he takes his reader with him.

And – Gad, sir! – what barbarous English they use in the BBC newsroom today! It is a wonder the newsreaders can stagger through it – sometimes they can't – what with the gimmicky headlines, speculative leads and ungainly cadences. Too many hacks out of Fleet Street, that's the trouble; not enough writers who can *hear* what they are writing. But, move over Alvar Liddell, I have almost done . . .

The fact is, I am enormously proud to have been identified with the BBC all these years and hate to see it brought down. It treated me tolerantly, if absent-mindedly, and taken all round it is still the best thing of its kind in the world. You have only to work in Asia or Africa to realise that the rest of the world respects and trusts the BBC in a way it regards little else. Politicians who try to manipulate or bully it, treat it as an optional extra one moment and as a subversive conspiracy the next, are tinkering with something more precious than they realise. That is why, when Mrs Thatcher's Home Secretary tried to ban a not very provocative programme about Northern Ireland, I came out of retirement and for the first time in my life joined the picket-lines outside Broadcasting House, Bush House and Television Centre. As I stood outside the headquarters of the World Service a passing taxi driver leant from his cab and yelled, 'Anyone for Moscow?'

In fact I only worked with one real Marxist in the BBC, who gave himself away by using Trotskyist code language and got himself sacked pretty quickly. I do not think the Corporation could ever be subverted by a leftist conspiracy, because no one could ever work out where the power really lay. A far greater danger is the contempt and jealousy of the lumpenbourgeoisie, with its dislike of cleverness and élitism. For it, the BBC is not crass enough; but government is working on that.

Like the Church of England the BBC's amiability will not, I fear, save it from the rocks ahead. Its greatest internal defect is its class-consciousness: there is little relationship between those who actually labour in the studios and the titled management who attend meetings most of the day. Poor fellows, they are victims of the system, too, and might plead that they were only freeing the broadcasters to get on with their business; but the number of occasions on which I sat and talked to a controller or director general about the world and work that I knew could be numbered on the toes of one foot. I should have learnt something in thirty years, but no one asked what.

From time to time my programmes were taken apart by that dreaded tribunal known as Programme Review Board, but I was never asked to attend. Perhaps that was my fault for sticking to my last and failing to climb the managerial ladder to some title like Ass. Head Nat. Hist. Progs. I arrived at a vision of the BBC that might be summed up in the following cartoon: The foyer of Broadcasting House is crowded with dignitaries arriving for the day's work. From each head floats a balloon saying 'The BBC is about Finance! The BBC is about Publicity . . . Engineering . . . Personnel . . .' Enter a shabby individual whose balloon ventures, 'But I thought the BBC was about broadcasting?' Whereupon all the other balloons turn upon it snarling 'Shuddup!' One of the few managers who took the trouble to groom the people who worked for her was Monica Simms, Controller of Radio 4. She would give wonderful parties for them – correspondents, announcers, comedians, and not a single administrator in sight.

That will do for bitterness. It could have been better, but it might have been a great deal worse. Instead of a clock the BBC presented me with the tall office chair I worked in and coveted so much. Attached to the back was a brass plate reading GRATIOR POPULO QUAM PONTIFEX (more popular than the Pope). It was not true but it was kind.

POSTSCRIPT

That seemed the natural place to end the story, which to me is really the story of victory over Depression and which I have told in the hope that it may help other victims. But as I do not anticipate a second volume, there are a few loose ends to tie up for the sake of the record.

After I had left the BBC, Angus Wright of TVS, Southampton, invited me to work with him on two series of filmed essays about practical ethics which we called Priestland Right and Wrong. The subject appealed to me – among other things, we persuaded the British Army to collaborate with us in a film about pacifism – but television is a difficult medium for handling ideas, and I have to say I found the business of film-making tedious compared with radio.

For the best part of a year I contributed a weekly spot called Priestland's Postbag to Terry Wogan's Radio 2 show, answering listeners' religious doubts, fears and queries. It was lively for a time, but like most agony columns the same questions kept coming round again and again until it was hard to find new ways of answering them. Why does God allow earthquakes? Do homosexuals go to Hell? How can I persuade my daughter to get married in church? How dare you say my dog hasn't got a soul?

I also did a weekly column on foreign affairs for the Catholic *Universe* – perhaps odd for a Quaker, but they also had Lionel Blue, the Rabbi, doing their cookery. This came to an end when Sylvia and I went off on a lecture tour for the Quakers of New Zealand and Australia. Australia we found savagely exciting, gaining steadily in national self-confidence. But New Zealand, though very beautiful, was rather dull and I gave offence by writing that New Zealanders mostly lived in secondhand cricket pavilions and were addicted to herbal tea.

A few months later, in the autumn of 1985, the British Council of Churches sent me on a delegation to South Africa. What struck me was less the moral and political arguments about apartheid than the awful inevitability of things and the feeling that it was simply too late to avoid disaster. The Anglo-South Africans had renounced political power for the good life – and very good it was, for them. The Afrikaners, with nowhere else to go, saw themselves as the chosen people and were prepared to go all the way to Masada in defence of their promised land. Outnumbered by pagans, they could only hold on by de-stabilising and out-terrorising the terrorists – and by systematic lying; while the African blacks, divided among themselves, could find neither the land nor the jobs to meet their rising expectations. Though I greatly admired leaders like Desmond Tutu and Alan Boesak, it seemed to me they had little hope of holding back the deluge. It was too late for liberals. Which grieved me; for Cape Town, in particular, was one of the loveliest cities I had been in.

I came home to a string of business and civil service conferences, booked to address them on religious and ethical subjects like Violence and the Media, Morality and Multinationals. What most appealed to me about these gatherings was the feedback I got from the audience, for writing is a lonely business and I am aware of the dangers of getting isolated in my study with nothing but a typewriter to talk to. My beloved Sylvia is downstairs with her silkscreens and woodblocks, busier as an artist than she has ever been. But she does get out into the world teaching her old folk in their hospital wards, and it is necessary for me, too, to gather in experience if I am to put anything out.

Around our ankles circulates a subculture of cats. Cats have always helped to fill the gaps in our family relationships, comforting the tearful, flattering the neglected, bridging the awkward silences and mopping up underemployed love. The elegant, talkative Siamese were always our favourites, but recently a petite and busy Burmese has added contrast – named Mi Nyoo because, as the BBC Burmese section advised, that is the Burmese for Little Miss Brown. Her present companion is a chocolate-point Siamese named Cadbury, *alias* Paper Bag from his appearance when wedged in an apple-tree waiting hopelessly for a bird to fly into his mouth. I could go on about cats, and about the basset hound we had for ten years and who finally expired on a visit to the Isle of Man – a jolly dog disguised as a sad one, obsessed with smells to the exclusion of all obedience – but pet stories can be trying for those who don't share the taste.

I am thankful, above all, for my family, whose ties are kept so devotedly in good repair by Sylvia. Jennet came through the ordeal of treatment for Hodgkins disease. Drastic though it was, if you are going to have cancer Hodgkins seems to be the one that gives you the best chance of survival. Andreas, handsome and confident, taught in a tough comprehensive school in Brent and then got recruited by a youth employment project; while his brother Oliver managed to combine a course at the London School of Economics with a practice repairing small French motorcars. Diana, sturdily refusing to budge from the far west of Cornwall, devoted herself to a hundred black-and-white cows, outrageously underpaid for the hours she works and the skill she has, but probably the most content of the four. What pleases their parents most is that, for all the disruptions of their upbringing, they have remained a loyal and affectionate team, seldom out of touch with us or with each other for long. They have delightful partners, too: would that at least one of them could find the time for a grandchild (but the old dog is starting to chase its own tail now and had better curl up by the fireside).

Having shed the children, Sylvia and I moved, to a smaller house just round the corner in Hampstead Garden Suburb, with an orchard up which I can look as I write. Our lease of the cliff cottage in Zennor having expired, we bought and converted – at ruinous cost – an abandoned Methodist Sunday School some two miles inland at the hamlet of Carfury, near the old Ding Dong mine. Cornwall still calls me – I have a novel or two I should like to write about it – but Sylvia warns me that the pixies will get me if I settle there for good.